G

Apostle

*My Adventures
in Life with
C. Peter Wagner*

DORIS WAGNER

DESTINY IMAGE® PUBLISHERS, INC.
P.O. Box 310, Shippensburg, PA 17257-0310
"Publishing cutting-edge prophetic resources to supernaturally empower the body of Christ"

This book and all other Destiny Image and Destiny Image Fiction books are available at Christian bookstores and distributors worldwide.

For more information on foreign distributors, call 717-532-3040.
Reach us on the Internet: www.destinyimage.com.

ISBN 13 TP: 978-0-7684-8103-7
ISBN 13 eBook: 978-0-7684-8104-4

For Worldwide Distribution, Printed in the U.S.A.
1 2 3 4 5 6 7 8 / 28 27 26 25 24

This book is lovingly dedicated to the four persons closest to me who shared life's journey with me and made my life blissfully happy, fulfilled, and adventurous:
My wonderful husband of 66 years: C. Peter Wagner
And our precious girls:
Karen Wagner Potter
Ruth Lynn Irons
Rebecca Wagner Sytsema

Introduction

My husband C. Peter Wagner's memoirs were released about six months before I began writing this. The title of his book is *Wrestling with Alligators, Prophets, and Theologians.* Because he wrote those memoirs to recount the events in his life that were notable, and because of space constraints, he had to leave out a lot of things that were very important to our three girls, Karen, Ruth and Becky. Since then, they have been bugging the daylights out of me to write my side of the story from the perspective of a wife, mother, and grandmother, and the homier aspects that Peter was unable to incorporate.

I was in Walmart recently, and I had the luxury of being able to tool around in my scooter (due to major degenerative joint disease and most recently a leg amputation, I have been wheelchair bound for many years). There was an end display that featured some very inexpensive books and among them was a 2003 paperback edition of Webster's New World Dictionary published by Pocket Books that sold for $3.97. Just for the fun of it I turned to the definition for "memoirs" and it was the best one that I had come across! Definition number one was "an autobiography," but definition number two really caught my eye and I am writing this account of our lives and times with this definition in mind. It is: "A record of events based on the writer's personal knowledge."

So here it is, Karen, Ruth, and Becky. It is to Dad and you three that I lovingly dedicate this, "...a record of events based on the writer's personal knowledge." Thank you, girls, for enriching our lives and joining in our fun adventures together. You have been a precious family and I thank God that you all grew up to be special, wonderful, talented and caring women. Daddy and I have been so proud of you three, our offspring.

A fellow missionary from Bolivia recently contacted me in need of some historical information about the Bible Institute that Peter headed up for many years. I then pulled all of the prayer letters that we ever wrote and combed through them and found what he needed. But those hours looking over old news and photos of our bygone years together brought back so many wonderful memories that I had to stop and thank God for the wonderful life I have enjoyed.

There have been many adventures with you girls and all of my memories are very happy ones. Thank you, girls, for leaving your childhoods in Bolivia, where Daddy and I left our youth and formative missionary and ministry years. Thank you for always supporting us in our work and for all of the fun vacation and family times we have had through the years together. Thank you for being our friends. Daddy and you three have been totally enjoyable to live with and I am grateful to God that we have been a family.

Doris M. Wagner

Colorado Springs, Colorado, and

Argyle, Texas

CHAPTER 1

My Roots And Early Life

My dad, Phillip Mueller, and his entire family came to America from Germany as part of the huge influx of immigrants shortly after World War I. This family consisted of Grandma and Grandpa Mueller, the eldest son, Uncle Jacob, Dad, the second born, then Uncle Billy, Uncle Louis, and Aunt Mary. There was another sister who passed away, and I am not sure if she died in the old country, or here in America. I was never shown a gravesite for her, so I am assuming she passed away back in Germany. I don't even know her name. All in all, I know very little about his family. I do know that Dad was born February 27, 1898.

I know nothing whatsoever about my ancestors on my father's side of the family beyond the ones I knew personally. I don't know if our family tree was rooted in barbarians, the elite, blue-collar workers, or peasants. There were a few aunts and uncles who came over in the same immigration and settled not very far from Little Falls, in the beautiful Mohawk Valley of upstate New York. So, there was quite an extended family with many aunts, uncles, and cousins by the time I came along. Grandma and Grandpa Mueller lived with us off and on at our farm located in St. Johnsville, about 10 miles from Little Falls. Grandpa seemed kind of grumpy to me when I was a little kid, but my mom and dad told me that he was not at all well and suffered from severe stomach problems. I was told that he had been run over by a wagon when he was an adult and was unable to work. Grandma Mueller did work in a knit goods factory and helped support the family.

The Mueller children were very good to their parents and took care of them in their old age. I believe they did wind up with us up until their deaths. Grandma Mueller was a sweet lady, and my sister and I especially enjoyed her a great deal. It was always interesting to me that when these individuals became American citizens, they chose to spell their name differently on their official papers. Some of my relatives wanted the name to sound as it did in German. Because our name was spelled Muller with an umlaut over the u, and there was no exact English pronunciation that matched it, the closest sound turned out to be Mueller. That was the last name that my daddy chose. Then there were those that spelled it dropping the umlaut, and that particular bunch chose the last name Muller. My uncle Louis, being the youngest and most progressive of the bunch, decided to Americanize his last name, so his tribe became the Millers.

There are just a couple of stories that were passed down. My older sister, Irene, and I had one letter from my Uncle Louis that told a tiny bit about their move from their home in East Germany to Cologne. By this time my father had already passed away and I was unable to get anything directly from him.

It seems as though they lived in a city called Poznan in the very eastern part of Germany. For some reason the slice of territory in which they lived later became annexed to Poland. My Uncle Louis said that they wished to maintain their German identity at the time so the whole family moved way over west to a suburb of Cologne in the northwestern part of Germany.

When my husband, Peter, and I had occasion to be in Germany in the 1990s, we visited the area, closely following the directions of Uncle Louis. Unfortunately, the American allies of World War II had apparently bombed out the lovely stone apartment house where my dad had lived for many years. In its place stood a three or four car garage and a vacant lot. All of the other homes adjacent to this garage were identical beautiful stone structures and looked very sturdy and beautifully built. These lovely homes clearly predated World War II and there would have been no reason whatsoever for tearing them down to replace two of them with the garage and vacant lot! We took photos of the houses and the street signs and sent them back to Uncle Louis, who said that, indeed, was where they used to live.

One story that was passed along our family concerned the time when Dad was drafted into the German army during World War I. He was stationed very close to his home and became extremely ill with the horrible pandemic of the Spanish flu in the days before antibiotics were invented. Many people, of course, succumbed to the Spanish influenza (some estimate as many as 100 million deaths) during the first quarter of the 20th century. Dad somehow got home during that illness, perhaps on a furlough, but was far too ill to return to his unit. His superiors came looking for him and Grandma Mueller said that when they came to the door and asked if Phillip was there, she told them to come in and look for themselves. Truthfulness has always been a very high value in our family, and she said, "I didn't lie!" The soldiers entered and searched the house. When they left, they said within earshot of my grandmother, "There's just some sick kid in bed in there." After my grandma had nursed Dad back to health, he went back to rejoin his unit, only to discover that the entire unit had been totally wiped out on the front lines! He apparently got back into another unit because he suffered a bullet wound to the calf of his leg. When we were growing up, my two brothers, my sister and I got a kick out of poking our fingers in the hole in his calf. It didn't seem to bother him!

Dad did tell us that somewhere along the line he worked in coal mines and then, I believe, in a steel mill. He used to be a great swimmer and soccer player and enjoyed singing very much. He told us that he used to swim in the Rhine River when they lived in the Cologne area. I really have no idea what my grandparents did for a living back in the "old country." My sister, Irene, had a lot more information, and she was the keeper of the memorabilia in the family. Unfortunately, Irene passed away before I began collecting information for this writing. I don't know what happened to the memorabilia.

As I mentioned above, when Dad and his family came to America, they settled in a small city, Little Falls, in the Mohawk Valley of upstate New York. I have no idea why they chose that spot but there were very likely friends or relatives involved. There was a large community of German immigrants there and most of them worked in factories along the New York Central Railroad and Erie Canal, mainly manufacturing shoes and slippers and knit goods, such as underwear and sweaters. There was also a large mill in town that manufactured utensils for the milking industry, I understand. Nearby there was a leather glove factory and Mohawk Rug factory. A Beech Nut factory was there that made chewing gum and baby foods. The whole valley was abuzz with manufacturing along the railroad line that had four tracks and was very busy. It was the main route between New York City and Chicago.

New immigrants were very devout Lutherans, and immediately they became part of the local Lutheran church that had services in both English and German. Daddy was also part of a German club in Little Falls that had many ethnic activities as well as a terrific men's glee club called the Menerchor. The German community often gathered in the social hall there for various festive occasions, usually weddings of friends or the extended family, and the beer flowed freely at those times. There were frequent dances also held in the social hall. These, of course, featured waltzes and polkas and a large band. I recall really enjoying watching this dancing when I was a child. When I became a teenager, Daddy would take me for twirl around the dance floor. One of my fondest memories was of Daddy and Mama dancing around the kitchen when their kind of good music came on the radio.

Very soon after arriving, Daddy immediately got to work on his naturalization papers to become an American citizen. He told us that he became very involved as a Boy Scout leader and was particularly adept at knots and other practical arts and crafts. He learned English very well. My father, although not a very tall man, was strikingly handsome.

English was mostly spoken in our home by the time I came along in 1932, as the fourth child. World War II broke out and I remember well the tragedy of Pearl Harbor on December 7, 1941. I also remember when we joined the allies to fight against Hitler and the Nazi regime, and Benito Mousselini of Italy, and Emperor Hirohito of Japan. We German-Americans kept a very low profile and avoided the language outside of our home. My parents would sometimes address me in German, but I would always answer them in English because I was, at that time, very ashamed to be of German heritage. However, I always adored my mother and father. I was very sorry later in life that I did not speak German fluently because I certainly could have. I could understand it quite well in my childhood but stubbornly chose not to speak it. Not speaking my native language became a real handicap when we visited Germany and Switzerland where the German language was used. By then I had been a career missionary for 16 years and was fluent in Spanish. Whenever I wanted to answer a question or speak German for some reason, all that would come out was Spanish!

I am not sure how my dad met my mother. But it was in that German community to be sure. They were married on March 1,1924.

In his later years, Daddy struggled with heart disease. He had his first heart attack when he was about 57. He suffered greatly from hardening of the arteries, and he died in his sleep at age 67 of an apparent ruptured blood vessel in his brain. Peter and I were serving as missionaries in Bolivia at the time, and I was unable to attend his funeral. He died on a Good Friday, and I did not even get word of it until Easter Sunday morning. In those days, missionary terms were of five years in duration and no one ever went home before their furlough time.

My mother, Caroline Loucks, was born of German immigrants in Little Falls as well, so she was a second-generation German. Mama was the firstborn of nine children. She was a very bright and beautiful lady and was always sorry that she had to quit school before high school in order to go to work to help support the large family. She carried a very unnecessary complex because of her lack of formal education. She was very intelligent, however. She had a beautiful soprano voice and frequently sang solos in church on Sundays. She sang both in English and in German. She was determined that her children would receive a proper high school education at least. We all eventually did. Irene later became a nurse, and I went on to Bible college.

When the Great Depression hit, starting in 1929 and lasting about five years, things got very hard for them. I am not sure how it ever came about, but they were able to swing the purchase of a dairy farm about 10 miles away from Little Falls just outside the tiny town of St. Johnsville. This would have been in late 1929 or early 1930. By then my sister Irene and my brother Richard were born, and shortly after the move to St. Johnsville, my brother Herbert was born. I came along in 1932.

Mama lived and worked on the farm until her untimely death by cancer in 1971. She battled cancer of the kidney, which later spread immediate friend. He was a great help to Dad and worked very hard around the farm. He also enjoyed socializing a great deal and was very popular in school.

Richard chose not to finish high school but stayed home to work on the farm. By then World War II was raging, and farmers were exempt from being drafted because they were producing the food for the nation. We were part of the New York City "milk shed," and our milk was hauled off daily to head in that direction. The dairy industry was very different in those days and mostly consisted of the family farm. Even though we were milking only about 40 head of milk cows it was enough to make a living. There was never money in excess, but we didn't seem to need it. Our nickname for Richard was "Buddy."

Buddy met and married a lovely lady from a couple of towns down the Mohawk River named Jeannie, and they eventually had five children. Sadly enough, Buddy had a heart attack at age 38, and was never well after that. By then he had his own large farm, and he and his wife Jeannie were very busy. It was only a couple of miles from our homestead, so we saw them very frequently. It was at this time that he became quite a prominent citizen in town, went back to night school, served as a member of the school board, and managed to graduate from high school the same year that his eldest son Dickey graduated!

In the days before artificial insemination for cattle, dairy bulls were used on the farm. Those of us who have been raised with dairy bulls really respect them, because they are enormous, mean, very unpredictable, can never be trusted, and can be killers. The dairy breed of cattle we raised were Holstein, black and white cows and bulls. The dairy bulls are not like the gentle, docile beef bulls, such as Herford and Angus. Very unfortunately around 1968, Buddy was attacked by a monstrous Holstein dairy bull, knocked down into a feeding trough face down with the bull grinding his back with his head and horns, and were it not for his wife Jeannie, he would have likely been killed by this ferocious animal. Jeannie was working in the barn sweeping up an area when she heard his cries for help. Armed with nothing but a broom, she ran toward the scene and began beating the bull's back with the broom. When the bull raised his head to attack her, Buddy was able to flip over and grab the ring in the bull's nose. This is the one thing that will render a ferocious bull helpless. And that's why rings are put in dairy bull's noses! They were able to get the bull back in a high-sided pen, a safe place. But serious damage had been done to his back and it certainly couldn't have helped his weak heart much!

In the fall of 1971, at age 42, Buddy suffered a fatal heart attack. Peter and I had just returned from Bolivia and were only home for one week when this happened. My mother was already on her deathbed in the same hospital when Buddy suffered this attack and passed away suddenly in the same hospital. Mama died of cancer of the kidney, liver and pancreas, within just a few days, at 67 years of age. Peter took part in both funerals. That was a sad, sad summer.

My third sibling was my brother, Herbert, born just before the move to the farm about 1930, and he was two years my elder. We grew up together and were very close. I believe now that Herbie was probably dyslexic. He was very brilliant and specialized in trivia. Whenever anyone in my immediate family questioned some fact, the quip invariably surfaced: "Herbie would know!" And he usually did! Because he was a very poor reader in school, he was thought of as being inferior in intelligence, but this was certainly not the case. I would say that of all of us four kids, he probably had the highest IQ by far!

Herbie tended to be very shy and quiet, but then, as the saying goes, "Still waters run deep." He lived at home on the farm all of his

I don't quite recall if our men were involved in the process of harvesting the ice or not. I do know that next to the vats that cooled the milk we had an icehouse. Large blocks of ice were stored there, insulated by a great deal of sawdust, and it remained frozen from winter to winter. The ice was harvested from lakes or ponds and as I recall the blocks of ice were about a 2-foot cube. It was sawed into those squares and delivered to the farmers. In later years my folks purchased a beautiful, aqua-colored bulk milk tank that was cooled by electricity. A large tanker truck would come and pump the milk directly from that large bulk tank and take it away to the processing plant. This happened after I left home, and I'm not quite sure how the butterfat testing and payment was handled.

A very important part of my childhood was our religious training. Mama read to us from the Bible as well as a book called Hurlbut's *Story of the Bible* every night of our lives. A few years ago, I found a copy of this book in an antique store and felt as though I had struck gold! By the way, rummaging through antique stores as we headed out on long drives in the summertime was a hobby of ours when I was still quite mobile.

It is a little humbling to find many of the items that I grew up with in these antique stores. Many people don't even know what the items are, but they were things that we used on a daily basis. I recall one time chatting with another customer in an antique shop. This individual was trying to figure out what a square metal strainer with a long handle could have been used for. I was very familiar with it — a "soap swisher." During World War II this was a common item in many households. Small pieces of soap were all carefully saved and placed inside the little metal basket. Pieces of laundry soap were recycled and swished in hot water to do dishes. Pieces of face soap, or other perfumed soap were swished in warm water until some nice suds formed, and we dealt with hand washables in this manner. We were taught to waste nothing!

To get back to our religious training. Every Sunday of our lives we went to the Lutheran church about 10 miles from our farm. The adults would attend the German service while the kids went to English-speaking Sunday school. Then the kids headed off to English-speaking church, while the adults in our household went to Grandma Loucks' house, (my mother's mom), maybe 20 blocks away from church. Mama would help Grandma prepare Sunday dinner, and after church all of us kids would walk to Grandma's when the weather was good. We would have Sunday dinner there, sit and rest a spell until mid-afternoon when we would need to head back to the farm, change our clothes and do the evening cattle feeding and milking.

We always received special pins for perfect attendance in Sunday school. Each kid in our family had a long string of these pins. As I recall, if the child were ill, he or she could bring an excuse and that Sunday would not be counted as an absence. But when we were well, we were in church without fail. We were rarely ill and stayed home.

Part of being reared in the Lutheran church involved going to confirmation class. This occurred when the child was about 12 years old. We had to memorize large portions of the Lutheran catechism and be able to recite by memory any portion that we were called upon to recite. The actual confirmation of the child took place on Palm Sunday and then the child was able to partake of Holy Communion from then on. Many youngsters in the church attended faithfully through confirmation but then dropped out. Our family was not allowed to do that! We attended church faithfully without complaining until we left home. It was just our way of life. The firm foundation in scriptural training has always stood me in good stead. I will be forever grateful to my parents for this wonderful start in life. I was taught right from wrong and punished when I headed down a wrong path. This early training placed my feet on a wonderful path and certainly kept me from a bushel of problems later on. My Aunt Louise played the organ and Mama frequently sang a solo at the services, both in English and in German during her lifetime. Mama had a beautiful voice.

My schooling as a child was quite interesting and is virtually non-existent in America today. It was the rural one-room schoolhouse. Located a short 10-minute walk from our farmhouse was the School District Number Eight one-room schoolhouse. All of us children attended this school from grades one through six. There was only one room, one teacher, and two outhouses, one for the boys and one for the girls. It was surrounded by orange tiger lily plants that bloomed prolifically most of the year. On the west side of the building there was a wind break made of beautiful lilac bushes that bloomed so beautifully in the springtime and smelled deliciously! There was also a very small playground that consisted of two swings, a set of rings, a metal slide, and two seesaws.

All six grades of children were in one room, and these were the children of all of the farmers within a couple of miles of that school. There were less than 20 children in all six grades at any one time. The success of children in a school like this depended entirely upon the skill of the teacher. We were fortunate enough to have a very good teacher, Miss Gladys Page. We all learned well. Year after year, when the class graduated from the high school in town, if any of them had passed through the one-room schoolhouse of School District Number Eight, they were academically at the top of the class and often were valedictorian or salutatorian. I remember one year when they were both! So even though the surroundings were rather humble, my academic foundation was solid in those early years. I struggled a bit with reading (but then had the luxury to be tutored in a one-on-one situation by the teacher), did all right in arithmetic, but the subject that captured me was geography. I was fascinated to read about other cultures, climates, and countries. Little did I know then that someday I would get to visit many of those faraway places!

Back to our lives on the farm. In order to adequately feed all of those animals, we had to raise many crops on our land which was about 167 acres. To review the animals, we had several pigs at any one time, a flock of chickens numbering between 40 and 60 birds, occasionally we raised some ducks, and every now and then had a few geese. However, the geese were worse than watchdogs, and they would sometimes attack children, usually flying up their backs pecking them on the head. Whenever that happened, said goose frequently wound up on the dinner table in a few days.

In my younger years we always had a team of horses. Dick and Herb were a black team, the first ones I remember. Horses can last only so long, and when they head off to the glue factory they may need to be replaced. Dick and Herb were replaced by two strawberry roan mares by the name of Polly and Molly. They were much larger than Dick and Herb and were very hard to handle. I recall that they ran away with a load of hay behind them one time and were only stopped when a telephone pole came between them at a dead run. I was never allowed to drive them.

This was an excellent excuse to buy a new tractor. We soon became rather mechanized, and I really can't recall what happened to Polly and Molly, but I didn't feel bad to see them go. They were pretty dangerous. Anyway, horses eat a lot and they had to be fed. Then there were all the little calves that were being raised up for milk cows, we always had eight-inch squares to be sewn together into blankets which were sent to England. England was being heavily bombed at the time, and extra blankets were needed for bomb shelters, hospitals, and other places. I knit dozens and dozens of these eight-inch squares as part of "the war effort." Another thing that we did on the farm was to collect all of our excess scrap metal and turn it in to a station which in turn got it to factories to become tanks and other needed war items.

We needed to conserve in many areas. Among the commodities that were very scarce were rubber tires, gasoline, sugar, shoes, mayonnaise, and many other grocery items as well as other imported items. Getting them here through submarine-infested waters was quite dangerous; the frequency of these shipments had been cut back, so they were rationed. Each person was provided with a book of ration stamps, and when you had a stamp for a pair of shoes, you could buy them. Stamps could be swapped around among family members. Some of the factories had been turned into war manufacturing units, so of necessity some of the staple items that we were familiar with were scarce. However, since we grew so much of our own food, we were not severely affected by all of the rationing. We were allowed extra gasoline because we lived in a rural area and needed it for our tractors in order to produce the crops to feed our animals. Our family was used to being conservative anyway, so it didn't hit us particularly hard.

We knew why we were fighting this war. According to Alexa (who I just asked, "How many American servicemen and women lost their lives in WW II?"), we lost about 420,000 of our best young men for a very noble cause—that of freedom. This number included some 12,000 American civilians who died during the war, as a result of the war. I am very sad to see so many of our young people in the 21st century who just don't get it! The world would be a very different place had we not gone to war and won. And how soon this is forgotten! Sometimes I feel that some poor decisions could lose it all and all of the effort of my generation in addition to 408,000 military lives lost, would have been in vain. They are just too young to remember. When I hear such stupid things as "the Holocaust never happened" it makes me cringe, since I heard about the liberation of the concentration camps firsthand from my uncle! I hope and pray this generation will not throw away everything we worked and fought so hard to achieve. This of course includes the freedom to spread the Gospel, to which Peter and I have dedicated our lives. Our freedom of religion is being threatened and this must stop! I was greatly impacted by the war and fearful of a world without freedom, so forgive my fervor. The war was part of the greatest generation and we are almost gone, but we completed the job in our generation, I am proud to say.

Now on to happier thoughts…

Some of the wonderful fragrances that I so enjoyed as a child were freshly cut hay, various wildflowers, the lilacs in bloom in the springtime, and the lilies of the valley that grew on the east side of our house. Probably the fragrance that I enjoyed the most occurred on a very warm summer morning when the sun would hit the clover and begin to dry up the dew. Finesse shampoo used to have this exact same fragrance until a few years ago when the manufacturer changed it, sad to say.

My mother raised huge beds of flowers near the buildings. I recall that alongside the south side of the barn she planted blue morning glories and they climbed up strings about 15 feet long that we affixed to the side of the barn. They bloomed for many weeks. There were large beds of gladiola, delphinium, dahlias, zinnias, marigolds, and many other flowers that were planted by seed or bulb. Then there were also the peonies that came up by themselves year after year. I'm sure I with all of the drippings poured over the rolls. Occasionally, Peter and I have found ourselves alone on Christmas day, and my treat is to make stuffed cabbage rolls! Not very ritzy, but incredibly delicious. A couple of years before my sister Irene's death, I had called to wish her a Merry Christmas. When she asked me what we were having for Christmas dinner, I told her that we were having stuffed cabbage leaves, and she squealed, "Boy, does that sound good!" I happen to enjoy them just as much as a roast prime rib of beef, maybe even a little more.

Hot German potato salad is always a winner. I served it at an office get-together last summer and one of the ladies said she had three helpings! As you have probably guessed, potatoes and bacon are very important in German cuisine. Another favorite, probably of Polish origin, was *pierogi*. These are simply a dough-filled turnover, but ours were boiled. My favorites were filled with cottage cheese (which Mama made from sour milk), with a tiny bit of sugar added, or those stuffed with an Italian prune-plum from my Grandma's backyard. Mama would remove the pit, fill the hole with sugar and encase it with the dough, pinch the open sides and boil. Brown butter was always the topping of choice over pierogi. Sometimes she would fill them with leftover sauerkraut and the spare-rib meat she cooked the original batch in. All leftover bits of dough were cut into strips and tossed in the boiling water to enjoy with the brown butter, like noodles.

German vegetables are always requested when the kids and grand-kids come to the house. The main one is German green beans. It is prepared with a small amount of firm, waxy potatoes cubed and placed in a cooking pot with some fresh, cut green beans. These are cooked until crisp-done, and the cooking liquid is reserved. Bacon is chopped and browned, and crispy parts are removed from the frying pan. A gravy is made from the bacon drippings using flour and the reserved bean cooking liquid. The bacon bits and a generous quantity of chopped fresh dill are put on top of the beans, and the gravy is poured over the vegetables, which is incredibly delicious. Spinach and turnips are also prepared the same way. I find this to be some of the most delectable comfort food and will be sure to include these recipes in the back of the book.

There are many kinds of specialty meats that we enjoyed as children. One of my favorites sounds really weird—it was a concoction of all of the soft parts of the pig's head ground up, added to the pig's blood, then mixed with barley and possibly a little more of the pork meaty scraps ground up. This was placed in canning jars and boiled for a long time in a hot water bath. It was called *Greis wurst,* or barley sausage. Most people would not even try it in this day and age, but it was some of our most delectable supper food on the farm. I recently located Mama's recipe in her own handwriting! I thought it was lost, and great was my rejoicing when I found it. Since most folks don't like the thought of eating blood, and the Bible says we should not eat blood, I won't bother with including that recipe. We also produced sausages of many varieties, and these were smoked in a smokehouse that was out by the fruit tree orchard. The sausages tasted very much like the Hillshire smoked sausages available today in the supermarket.

When the animal was butchered, the very first thing that we had for supper that night was the brains. These were mixed with scrambled eggs and served alongside of fried potatoes that we raised ourselves. We really loved these as children. I believe the mad cow disease scare has removed a lot of this type of food from the market today. In the early 70s in Pasadena, California, I was able to buy brains from the Market Basket just a couple of blocks from my house. When I was a child at home, we also enjoyed the liver and the tongue, but we never did eat the tripe. However, when we went to Bolivia, we found that tripe soup was very common, and most people ate it once a week. It was purported to help cure a hangover, so was readily available in the restaurants on Saturdays and Sundays.

Another dish that we really enjoyed as kids was kidneys in sour cream served over noodles. Very little of the animal was discarded. Hamburger was made from the less desirable cuts and small pieces of meat of the cows we butchered, and the bones were used for soup stock. All of the fat from the butchered pigs was cut into small cubes and rendered into lard in the wood-burning kitchen stove oven. This lard was used in place of shortening on many occasions. When it was very fresh, we would spread it on black pumpernickel bread, sprinkle it lightly with salt and scarf it down. We had never heard of cholesterol in those days, so we enjoyed it guilt-free! And, by the way, it wasn't until I was in junior high, and after the war, that we graduated from the wood-burning cook stove to an electric range.

One delicacy that was prepared to eat every Christmas Eve was called *ziltz*. The four pig's feet and a veal shank were boiled along with some spices and aromatics until all of the meat fell off of the bones. When cooled, the meat and other soft tissue was removed from the bones and chopped. It was added to the broth and then refrigerated. It turned into some of the stiffest gelatin imaginable, and this was cut into small squares and looked a lot like headcheese. The squares were doused with vinegar and it seemed to be the delicacy that everyone looked forward to having on Christmas Eve. All of our family, and all of my aunts and uncles and cousins went to Grandma Loucks' house for Christmas Eve and feasted, that is, of course, after the cows were milked.

A big treat for us was when we could afford it, was to buy a little gallon wooden barrel full of pickled herring. I'm not sure if it was imported or domestic. My guess was that it came from Scandinavia or northern Europe somewhere.

The pies, cakes, cookies, and pastries, along with other German baked goods, were a very important part of our lives growing up. My mother spent most of her Saturdays, especially in the wintertime when there was no fieldwork, baking up a storm. I remember being by her side helping (or hindering?) whenever possible. There was always delectable fruitcake at Christmastime, along with Christmas cookies made with anise seeds. They have since become a tradition in our house as well. One of the German pastries that won the heart of Peter when we were courting was a pastry that we called torn pants *(tzarisenahosen)*. Peter, however, nicknamed them "bow ties," because they were cut in strips, and one end of the strip was passed through a slit in the middle and laid out to look very much like a bowtie. These were made from egg yolks, flour and a little water, then fried in oil, and dusted with confectioner's sugar. They fell into the category of a "melt in your mouth" delicacy.

Mama also made tons of cake doughnuts, sometimes raised doughnuts and homemade raised jelly buns, as well as many varieties of cookies and fruit breads. I enjoyed working at her side and learned so very much from her. She was an excellent teacher and was extremely patient to explain things.

Funny thing—I don't recall any of us kids going through adolescent rebellion! Either there wasn't time, or we weren't allowed. We had a very strict code of conduct that was ingrained into us from a very early age. We were at all times to respect our elders, revere our teachers, and never, ever talk back to an adult. We were taught to *do* what you

the most important was a home where all of us children were loved, taught, disciplined, and molded into honest, law-abiding, hardworking, and responsible adults. We worked very hard and were appreciated by our parents. We frequently did things together as a family, like going on Sunday afternoon drives, picnics, and berry picking. Sometimes we would do some pretty earthy things, such as grabbing a bar of soap and heading down to the local swimming hole in the creek, where we would wash up in the evenings after a long, dirty, sweaty day working in the fields. I often think of swimming in the creek when I smell spearmint today. It grew wild in profusion on the banks of the creek.

In 1949 I graduated from high school with a major in home economics but had taken enough of the college entrance requirement subjects to pretty well choose my field for further education. I graduated third highest in my class and the person who graduated second highest beat me out by a mere 2/10 of a point.

I had always been drawn to nursing probably because I enjoy helping other people so much. I seemed to be gifted in helping others. Blood and guts never bothered me much because I was accustomed to seeing these things as I was growing up. I applied to the Ellis School of Nursing in Schenectady, New York, and was accepted for entrance in the fall of 1949. I was all set to leave when things happened that summer that altered my plans considerably.

What did I learn from these years of my life? I learned how to work long and hard and to enjoy a job well done. By then, my sister Irene had married and moved away, and my brother Buddy had married and moved just a few miles down our road to a lovely large dairy farm, so it was just Herbie and me and Mom and Dad left to do the farming. I could run the farm with my brother, Herbie, and give Mom and Dad a day off now and then, which they appreciated so very much and told us so. I loved seeing the beautiful dairy cattle on large, notable dairy farms. I adored working outdoors. I basked in the beauty around me, the fields, flowers, animals, and birds. I loved my music, gardening and farm work; the war was over and life was good.

CHAPTER 4

Knowing Jesus, Knowing Peter, And Knowing God's Will For My Life

The eventful summer of 1949 right after high school graduation was the turning point of my life. Let me explain.

During the last year of high school, I began to babysit for the neighbors over the hill. They were George and Francis Matis who had two young kids, Jeannie who was seven years old and Georgie, about four years old. I usually went over on Wednesday and Sunday evenings while they attended the local Methodist church evening services.

It turned out that a new pastor by the name of pastor George Wood was assigned to that church, and he preached a very strong gospel message. Many people got born again, among them George and Fanny. They took the kids to church on Sunday mornings but needed a babysitter for Sunday and Wednesday evenings and asked me. I babysat throughout the winter and on into the spring and summer of 1949. I became very close friends with Fanny, who liked my mother very much.

On August 7, of 1949, Fanny invited me, along with my girlfriend from a neighboring farm, Eleanor Settle, to attend a Sunday afternoon service at a Bible camp near Amsterdam, New York. It would turn out to be the most important day in my life thus far. Being the devout

Lutheran that I was, the thought appealed to me, so I accepted the invitation.

I had always read the Bible every night. When I was about 13 years old, I had run across a portion of Scripture in John 3 where Jesus said to Nicodemus, "You must be born again." This was not the kind of language that I had heard spoken in the Lutheran Church. I set about on a quest to find out the meaning of this phrase. I always wanted to please God, and if being born again would fall in that category, I certainly wanted to find out how.

When we drove up to the Bible camp, on the outside of the Quonset hut chapel was a sign that announced the topic of that afternoon's message to be delivered by a chalk artist. The title of the message was "You must be born again!" I felt as though I had struck the mother lode of gold that I had been searching for.

After the message when the speaker gave the invitation, Eleanor and I both went forward to receive Jesus as our Lord and personal savior. In the Lutheran Church salvation was not explained to me as a personal gift. It was news to me that Jesus died for *my* sins, that He loved *me* as an individual, and wanted to welcome me into His family. I already had a "leg up" with my knowledge of the Bible, and it seemed as though something so new and spiritual descended upon me at that time, that I saw the Bible with new eyes, and it made ever so much more sense to me. Everything felt new and wonderful! The stars looked brighter, the world was much more beautiful, and it felt as though a tremendous load had rolled from my being. Even though I had not been a terrible sinner, I knew there was something more that I was missing. I was so thrilled to have finally found it at 17 years of age, after having diligently searched for the four years since I was 13. Mom and Dad allowed me to spend the next week at that Bible camp, and I soaked up the teaching and all of the meetings. I was able to help out a lot in the kitchen and had a wonderful time. As a matter of fact, an invitation was given during one of the evening meetings, inviting people to give their lives to the Lord by serving on the foreign mission field. I figured that I was very strong, young, and could certainly do that, if that was what the Lord wanted me to do. So, I went forward and offered my life as a foreign missionary should God would lead in that direction.

During the week that I spent at the Bible camp, I spoke with some of the counselors concerning my future. Except for one person, they all discouraged me from going to nursing school, telling me that in the world I might lose my newfound faith. I certainly didn't want to do that! I was only 17 years old and figured there would be time for a midcourse correction in the future.

When I arrived home and talked with my mom and dad, they allowed me to make whatever decision I wanted to and felt was right. So, I did not go to nursing school, but spent my next year helping out on the farm and doing lots of makeover projects to the house that no one had time to accomplish previously. These included things like painting, wallpapering, and lots of other updating and repairs. My mother later told my sister Irene that it was one of the happiest years of her life, because she was finally able to take a few days off and go visit relatives and friends. Herbie and I were well able to take care of the daily chores once the heavy fieldwork was done in the summer. Dairy farming is a year-round job, and to take a day off is usually totally impossible unless there is someone to do the milking and care for the animals. I was well-equipped to do all of the cooking and whatever farm chores were necessary to accomplish at the time. I could drive the tractor, but driver education in high school had not yet become part of the curriculum. Even though I knew how to drive a car pretty well, I did not get my license, because there was no need at the time. But Herbie did have his license, so all was well. We could hold down the fort very adequately. I am very glad that all of my children were able to get driver education in high school and that they were equipped to drive the Los Angeles freeway system by their senior year in high school.

Getting back to George and Fanny. Fanny and I became very good friends and we, sometimes accompanied by my mother, would often attend many of the out-of-the-way churches around the Mohawk Valley that were in the process of being opened up by new preachers, or by Pastor Wood from St. Johnsville. In all of my years, I had never heard the gospel presented really clearly. There seemed to be a dearth of preaching the Word of God at the time when I was being brought up. I continued to babysit for George and Fanny in the evenings when they needed me.

Just a couple of days after my dramatic conversion on August 7, 1949, Jeannie Matis approached her mom and dad concerning her eighth birthday on August 15. She said that as a birthday gift she would like to go visit her friend, Peter Wagner, whose birthday fell on the same day. Peter would be 19 years old on August 15, 1949. Peter had worked for George and Fanny during the summers of 1947 and 1948. His Grandmother Wagner lived in my little town of St. Johnsville, and somehow heard that George Matis was looking for some help for the summer. Peter had accepted a full scholarship to Rutgers University in New Brunswick, New Jersey, and was studying dairy production. But that summer of 1949 he had accepted a summer scholarship to work for an extremely prestigious Guernsey dairy farm in Cortland, New York, very near Cornell University named McDonald Farms. It was a golden opportunity for him to learn the practical aspects of caring for, grooming, and showing dairy cattle, as well as learning from an outstanding herdsman. Their cattle were particularly well bred and beautiful and were some of the best Guernseys in all of America.

Unbeknownst to me, George thought that Peter and I would be a good match, and he and Fanny were anxious to have us meet, so they asked if I would go along for a ride to Cortland. Knowing how outstanding these cattle were, it was an offer I could not refuse. So off we went on August 15, 1949. We had to leave early in the morning, just as soon as milking was over so that we could get back in time for the late afternoon milking, and Cortland, as I recall, was well over 100 miles away. There were no interstate highways at the time, and we had to go quite slowly via two strip roads in order to arrive at our destination.

I formally met Peter just one week after my conversion. I was quite unimpressed. At the time he was caring for some of the cows and was in the barn actually hand milking a beautiful animal by the name of McDonald Farms Honeybloom. Because of the great value of these animals, they were not milked by machine but only carefully hand milked three times a day. Peter did not know we were coming, so it was a surprise to him. As we walked in the barn, I took special note of the fact that he had several days' worth of a beard growing, and because no one smoked cigarettes in a dairy barn so full of combustible material, he had opted to chew tobacco which was pretty messy! When he finished milking Honeybloom, he invited us into his little apartment and for some reason had to open his refrigerator door. I don't remember anything about the food contained therein (I don't think there was much food), but the two things that left a great impression on me were the amount of beer that he was keeping cool and the artificial insemination equipment that was stored in the refrigerator. Artificial insemination was just coming to the fore, and the bulls on this particular farm were worth a great deal of money. I recall that one of them was sold for $35,000 because the offspring from that animal were extremely high in dairy production. At that particular time, I was earning about $.60 an hour for any part-time jobs that I was able to find, so this amount of money, in my mind, was staggering.

Incidentally, Honeybloom went on to be the reserve grand champion aged dairy cow at the Waterloo, Iowa Dairy Show in 1949, which meant she was the second-most beautiful dairy cow in the U.S. in 1949. We have photos and paintings of Honeybloom hanging in several rooms in our home; however, concerning Peter, I was underwhelmed!!

Peter tells quite a different story, saying that for him it was love at first sight. The fact that I knew quite a bit about dairying and that I was a friend of George and Fanny probably had something to do with it. He decided that I was worth pursuing, and on his way back to Rutgers for the fall semester, he decided to visit George and Fanny and see if we could double-date to the Montgomery County Fair. Attending the fair, of course, was one of my greatest joys, and an offer that I could not refuse.

You might be wondering why we had not met before since he had been working on an adjoining farm for two summers. The fact of the matter is that summers on the farm were extremely busy for everyone because all of the fieldwork and harvesting to be done in the daytime between milkings, and the work was never-ending. I did learn that on one occasion, Peter came to help my brothers get some hay in the barn because a storm was brewing. They enjoyed a good slug of hard cider down in our cellar, but I was away with my mom and dad picking wild blueberries that day.

We had a lot of fun at the county fair, and then Peter had to leave to go back to college. Once I got to know him a little better, I was very impressed with his brilliant mind and thought, *The Lord could really use a mind like that.* The letters began to arrive, and I always answered them trying to be a testimony of some sort. I was also very impressed that he did not belittle or ridicule my faith, so I pressed on trying to win him for the Lord.

He then invited me down to the Rutgers campus to stay in his fraternity house for a very large dance and fraternity party that was held several times a year. The guys would all abandon the fraternity house and find some other place to stay. The girls that they invited would take over the house and were carefully chaperoned. The dance was a formal event, complete with gowns and corsages. There were parties and events, and in the fall, the event included a big football game. Nothing ever got out of hand, and in our case, it was all good clean fun. At that time, we were reveling in the midst of the "big band era" and I remember that some very prestigious orchestras of the day played at the gym. Since I enjoyed music so very much, this was a highlight for me, and I had a terrific time. This event was only a weekend situation, and at the end of it, the girls left and the guys got back to their studies. In my humble situation, I felt quite out of place with some of the debutante types from New York City and North New Jersey, but I did have some pretty decent-looking gowns left over from my brother's wedding and some high school proms, that I made do. I don't think Peter cared much what I looked like, he just wanted me there, and bit by bit I found myself caring for him more and more.

I later found out two very interesting facts about Peter. He had a bit of blue blood running in his veins because his four times great-grandfather was Alexander Hamilton. Hamilton was one of the founding fathers of this great country and quite involved in the Revolutionary War, sticking close to the side of George Washington. He is the author of the famous Federalist Papers and very influential in setting up our banking and monetary system, probably the reason why his face is on every ten-dollar piece of currency.

Another fascinating piece of information has to do with the reason his ancestors settled back in the 1700s in the Mohawk Valley of New York, my home. Peter told me that his ancestors were the Palatine Germans who came over in the 1700s and settled on a piece of land in the Mohawk Valley, then inhabited by the Mohawk tribe of Native Americans. However, his ancestors did not usurp land from the Mohawk Indians. The land was divided into patents with names. Peter's ancestors purchased the George Harrington Patent of land, a large piece of land stretching from the banks of the Mohawk River up to the foothills of the beautiful Adirondack Mountains. They paid the natives 800 beaver skins for that piece of property. They erected the sturdy stone Palatine Lutheran Church, completed in 1770. Peter was invited to preach the 200th anniversary sermon of that church in July of 1971. We had just returned from our missionary service in order for him to take up his teaching position in the School of World Mission at Fuller Theological Seminary. Meanwhile, my mother was dying of terminal cancer in Little Falls Hospital, and later on that week my brother Buddy would suffer a fatal heart attack. It was the last sermon he ever heard.

But there is more to the story of that land! When my Daddy bought his 167-acre dairy farm in the height of the Great Depression in 1929 or 1930, that dairy farm, the land I so loved and worked on all of my days from birth until the day I was married, was located on the very patent of land that Peter's ancestors bought for those 800 beaver skins!!! What a stunning coincidence! Now back to the story of our meeting.

Peter had made a few visits to the farm where he met my family, and they all liked him very much. He loved to help my dad with some projects around the farm, and I remember one time they had to repair a floor on the second story of the barn. Peter began calling my daddy "Pa" which brought a tear to my daddy's eyes. As I mentioned before, my lovely sister Irene had married a sailor by the name of Zane Wagner, who was absolutely no relative of Peter's family. It was just an odd coincidence, and my guess is that it would be quite rare for two sisters to marry someone with the identically spelled surname and not be at all related! Anyway, Zane called Daddy "Phil," and Peter really got major points by calling my daddy "Pa."

Whenever Peter came to visit, he bunked with one of my brothers and was usually the first one up in the mornings and got the milking started. My mom liked him very much and always kept busy making him pies. He was particularly fond of elderberry pies made from the elderberries that grew wild along the hedgerows of our farm. They were very plentiful, just for the taking. We also really enjoyed the pastries that she made. I cannot ever remember a time when there was any kind of dissonance between Peter and any of my family members. He just sort of seemed to belong from day one!

In January of 1950, I was able to lead him to the Lord in our farmhouse living room when he came up to visit over the Christmas break. For him it was a dramatic, sincere conversion, and his old nasty habits dropped off immediately. He had been a very heavy drinker and gambler. Actually, that was how he earned his extra spending money. His father taught him how to play poker and all about the odds, and he was quick to learn very well. His fraternity brothers couldn't quite figure out what happened to him, but they put up with him because he was such a help to them in their studies.

Our courtship continued by letter mostly. Long-distance telephone calls were extremely expensive to make at that time, so we had to make do with paper and ink.

During the early part of the summer of 1950, I went back to the Bible camp where I had first met the Lord, and, oddly enough, there was another guy there who was on his way to be a missionary to Africa. We were somewhat attracted to each other. I did tell Peter about this and promptly got a telephone call from him as soon as I got home. The call consisted of a brief three-word sentence: "I'm coming home." He soon convinced me that his feelings for me ran very deeply, and I promptly dismissed the other guy from my mind, a decision I certainly never regretted.

A few weeks later, the first week in September, Mom and Dad, Herbie and I were able to attend the New York State fair in Syracuse. Peter had accompanied the McDonald Farms string of show cattle to the fair. He was to be at the fair with those cattle for a whole week. He asked Mom and Dad if I could stay. The only accommodations at the fair for the cattle exhibitors were sleeping on hay bales in front of the cows and using the public restrooms. There were dozens of people around and there was really no fear; the people who were showing the animals were all very decent individuals, and I had Peter to watch out for me. Mom and Dad agreed, and I spent the week having a ball wearing Peter's work clothes and taking care of those gorgeous animals.

I recall one morning there was a group of individuals from the local radio station who were walking through the barns with the then-Governor Thomas E. Dewey. It was quite a thrill for me to see this gentleman whom I had admired! Our job was mainly to keep a lookout for any time a cow would raise her tail, thinking of having a bowel movement. We would immediately be there with a fork or shovel, remove the manure, and put nice clean straw all around the animal. They were to be kept in pristine condition for the public. For many of the families that came through, it would be the first time the children ever saw a live cow. I remember I almost collapsed in laughter when a little boy was watching me giving a cow a drink of water from a pail at the same time Peter was milking her. He said, "Look Mommy, they put water in one end and milk comes out the other!"

After the fair, with the cattle being safely delivered back to McDonald Farms, Peter came up to say one last goodbye before heading back to Rutgers. I was unaware, but one evening, out on our front porch, we were all sitting together enjoying one of the last balmy warm evenings we would have. Peter took me aside, slipped a beautiful diamond ring on my finger with a diamond that I could actually see. He brought me back to Dad, and asked, "Can I have her, Pa?" He, of course, agreed, and our family began to celebrate the engagement. It turned out that he had spent his entire summer's earnings on that ring! It is one of my greatest treasures.

Since he was headed off to college and it was nearing mid-September, we originally were looking at having a Christmas wedding. In order to facilitate things, because in those days in the state of New York, blood tests were required in order to get a marriage license, I suggested that we get the blood tests before he left for college. At least that much could be done. It was after having received the results of those tests that we discovered they were only good for 30 days. Either he would have had to make another trip up to the farm for another set of blood tests, or we had to get married in 30 days. Since the blood tests were not very agreeable to either one of us at the time, we decided to make an attempt at getting ready to have a wedding in 30 days! We chose Sunday, October 15, 1950 as our wedding day, but it would need to be in the evening after the milking was done so that all of our farmer friends could attend. No one had ever held a wedding on a Sunday evening in our church, so this was really breaking new ground!

My father promptly sold a cow in order to have some cash for the purchases needed. We immediately ordered our wedding invitations, and our family worked frantically in order to come up with the wedding gown, bridesmaid gowns, flowers, and all of the other details needed. One of Peter's fraternity brothers who had a spectacular baritone voice would be the soloist. My piano teacher agreed to be our organist, and the wedding party consisted of Peter's sister Margo, my sister Irene (who was my matron of honor), and my two closest girlfriends, Joan Gardner and Eleanor Settle. Peter chose my two brothers, his cousin Phil, and his closest fraternity brother, Jack Stover, who was also studying dairy production with him, to be his best man.

Somehow or other we were able to pull the whole thing off. Mom and I made the wedding cake and did all of the food for the reception, which was held in the Sunday school rooms. The ceremony was held at Christ Lutheran Church in Little Falls, New York, actually the same place where my mother and father were married. I decided to have a romantic candlelight ceremony and knew where I could borrow the standing candlesticks. I understand from my cousin, Helen, who has been the church organist there for years, that it was probably the first and last candlelight ceremony to be held in that church.

Because Peter was just a little over 20 years of age and the legal age for a man to marry was 21, his father had to sign the license giving him permission to marry me. He always let Peter make his own decisions, so he signed although in his heart it was a bit reluctantly. He was aware of the fact that Peter had become a Christian and was now

deciding to be a Christian missionary along with me and the thought
of that did not make him or his mother at all happy. I, on the other
hand, did not need to have parental consent, because I was all of 18
years of age, and, as a woman, was considered an adult in the state of
New York! Because we were both so young and were married rather
precipitously, some of my relatives were rumored to have said that we
were far too young. They speculated that maybe I was pregnant, and
that it certainly might not last. With the passage of time, however, we
proved them to be very wrong.

The ceremony was almost hilarious, so much went awry!

My sister Irene, my maid of honor, had not made an announcement, but she was pregnant with her second child and could barely
fit into her gown. I had chosen pastel colors of powder blue, pink,
and pale green for all bridesmaids' gowns, but the green one had not
arrived by the day before the wedding! It was Eleanor's dress, and fortunately her sister, Jane, was a dress designer and seamstress. She stayed
up all night long making a dress identical to the others for Eleanor! It
was perfect!!

I had always dreamed of carrying calla lilies in my wedding, so I
ordered them from the local florist. However, they were unavailable,
and the florist made a substitution without consulting me—a dozen
gigantic white "football-type chrysanthemums," that seemed to weigh
a ton!

I had been raised in the church and knew every nook and cranny
of the building. To my knowledge no one had ever dared to have a candlelight service previously. As my daddy and I were about to make our
grand entrance to march down the aisle. I noticed that there was a light
on above the pastor who was officiating at the ceremony. I happened
to know where the light switch was, so I simply flipped the switch to

turn it off. I have often wondered if there was enough light for Pastor Schultz to be able to read the ceremony!

In that particular Lutheran church, the organ was at the back of the church and in a pitch-black choir loft. Little did I know that the same switch I just had flipped also turned off the lights for the organist! The soft candlelight didn't get anywhere near up to that crow's nest! It left her in utter darkness! She had to send her sister-in-law dashing way down the street to her car to locate a flashlight. She had forgotten her music when she was halfway to the church, had to turn around and drive back about five miles, grab the music, then drive the 10 miles to the church. So, when I arrived at the church, I was met with total silence because the organ was not yet playing. I was immediately informed that she had forgotten her music, dashed home to get it and would soon be back. Within just a few minutes the organ music began, and because she was such a magnificent musician, no one knew what I had done. The flashlight arrived and unfortunately it only was able to shine one place at a time. The most important place of course was the music, but the organist could neither see her fingers, the keys, nor her feet in order to play as she really wanted to. My guess was that she was very busy barking out orders to her sister-in-law as to where the flashlight was most needed at anyone particular time! Later, in the reception line she simply said, "Do you know what you did to me?" I was aghast, but she pulled it off without a flaw! I can't remember, but I hope we increased her honorarium a little.

The groomsmen also had their problems. My brother Buddy came down with a case of food poisoning that day and was feeling quite green. Jack Stover was playing football the day before and dislocated his shoulder, so he had it in a sling. Peter's cousin Phil had somehow sprained an ankle the day before, so he was hobbling about. Still, they all made it and were standing there in a beautiful row.

Probably the worst disaster of all was that Pastor Schultz, who officiated at the ceremony, forgot to tell the audience to be seated when he began the ceremony, so everyone stood through the whole thing! Some of my poor short relatives saw absolutely nothing. But we got legally married!

The reception seemed to go okay, and we left for a magnificent honeymoon in the Adirondack Mountains in a 1938 Dodge we had bought for $400 with our wedding money. We had a spectacular Indian summer that year, and the trees were breathtakingly beautiful. After several days in a rustic cabin in the Adirondacks at beautiful Blue Mountain Lake, we drove off to Peterborough, New Hampshire, where we were hosted by the American Guernsey Cattle Club. They were attempting to somehow recruit Peter to join their ranks, and they paid for several days of our honeymoon. I am glad that did not come to fruition. I have no idea what happened to their organization, but their beautiful brick building was turned into senior citizen housing the last time we drove through Peterborough. Even the hotel where we stayed on our honeymoon had been torn down. It had been quite a historical landmark, built in 1833, and we couldn't figure out how they ever got permission to destroy it. Of course, by that time it may have been condemned! When we checked in on our honeymoon, we were told that we had a private bath, as long as we locked the door leading to the next room!

The next week we moved to our new home in New Brunswick, New Jersey. It actually was a 26-foot trailer that had been turned into housing for the GIs who were studying at Rutgers. By 1950, most of the GIs had finished their schooling, and the emergency housing was made available to married couples who were students. Peter had freshly painted the inside my favorite shade of pale green, and I loved it. It was pretty rustic, with no running water. One had to run to the outside faucet to bring it in by the pailful and run back out when it was filled with used water from the kitchen sink drain to empty in one of the many outside drains. We needed to use community showers and open laundry sinks (no washing machines), and public toilets. But we were so very much in love that the surroundings didn't matter a bit, as long as we were together.

My relatives had thrown a shower for me, and all the Lutheran Church ladies attended, many of whom I did not know because they attended the German service, but Mama sure did! (Mama did all the cooking for both the showers and the wedding reception. In order to pay for my wedding, as I previously said, Daddy sold a cow to get the cash.) That shower produced small appliances, dishes, linens, pots and pans, etc. Fanny Matis threw another one for me, attended by the farmer neighborhood men and women and my high school friends, and boy, did I ever clean up with gifts! Fanny's shower was called a "Pounding." The gang gathered at someone's farm and all drove into our front yard honking their horns to beat the band the evening after we returned from our honeymoon. The goal was for folks to supply staples for a pantry, such as a pound of shortening, a pound of sugar, etc. All of those gifts were placed in a large laundry basket and it was filled to running over with pantry items: soups, canned meats, canned vegetables, coffee, tea, cereal, sugar, flour, spaghetti, cereal, rice, toiletries, and laundry items. Each item had been individually wrapped and I was to guess what each one was before I opened it! After those two showers, I had everything I needed for my new home except a waste basket and a teakettle.

That move was quite a change for me, because I was born in the very house that I left the day I was married. I really missed my home and family a great deal. But it was to be the first of many moves, and life was very pleasant and exciting with Peter. We were so very much in love! So, we settled in, and one of his first projects was to see that I got a driver's license. I got a job at a local grocery store as a cashier. That paid very well—92 1/2 cents an hour for a 45-hour work week and that included three ten-hour days, one eight-hour day and one seven-hour day.

After getting my driver's license, it was during our first winter that we learned an extremely valuable lesson concerning tithing. The money that we earned was always just barely enough for survival. But we felt that we should do what the Bible said and tithe our incomes anyway.

One morning as I was on my way to work, I drove down the rather steep hill out of our trailer park. When I pushed the brake pedal to stop at a stop sign before entering an extremely busy highway, I got a terrible shock when my foot hit the floor and the brakes were completely gone. I almost panicked, but had the presence of mind to pull up on the emergency brake as hard as I could, and the car came to a stop just a few feet short of the busy highway. I was able to get the car over to the side of the road and somehow managed to get a hold of Peter who was in class. This was in the days before cell phones, mind you.

One of his buddies loaned Peter his car to come and get me to work and then get our car to an auto repair shop for new brakes. The mechanic said that the car would be ready by evening but that we had to pay up in full before we could pick it up, because he just did not trust the college students. Peter and I scratched together all of the money that we had and came up with $40 in cash. The bill was $90 and somehow before sunset we had to come up with another $50. I remember that this all happened on a Thursday, because my grocery store work week was Wednesday to Wednesday, and we were paid on Fridays. I went to my boss and asked if I could have my paycheck a day early because of my predicament. I had put in my full work week so had already earned it, I figured. He refused me by saying that it was against the company policy, but that he could personally loan me the money. I don't know what came over me, but I got a bit miffed and refused his generous offer.

Peter picked me up in his friend's car and we headed off to the repair shop with our $40 in hand hoping that the mechanic would allow us to pay the rest of the money later on. As Peter was driving, he said, "Oh by the way, I picked up the mail on my way here," and he handed me two letters. I opened the first letter and, lo and behold, it was a $25 belated wedding gift from a colleague of Peter's father. We had been married for almost five months! I was aghast to find the other letter contained a $25 gift from his mother. We had exactly the $50 that we were short! This all happened within a few blocks of the auto repair shop. The mechanic allowed us to endorse the checks over to him, and he was totally paid! That may have been our very first miracle as a couple. We had decided that God had taken note of the fact that we had been tithers and took care of us right on time when we had a financial need. We decided never, ever, to stop giving God His portion of our earnings. Over the years we have gradually increased our tithe as our incomes have increased and have found Him to be totally faithful.

I later had the opportunity to land a job that was far less taxing on my health, since I was becoming quite anemic by working so hard in the grocery store. I sold sandwiches for an Italian company that sent us out in vans visiting factories and construction sites. It was a great job, and I was able to make as much money working five six-hour days as

I did in a 45-hour work week as a cashier in the grocery store. I had the prices of most of the 2000 items in the store memorized. We had to enter the price of each item by hand. We had no baggers most of the week and had to bag everything ourselves as checkers, except on Saturdays, as I recall.

Peter was able to secure a wonderful part-time job working afternoons and evenings as a janitor at a local Mercury auto manufacturing plant. He was responsible to clean the infirmary area every evening. Since he was such a hard worker and so well organized, he was able to complete his eight hours of work in less than four hours and spent the rest of his time doing his homework. As long as he got the job done well there was no problem, and this was an acceptable arrangement with his employers. Peter graduated with honors from Rutgers with a B.S. in Agriculture and with the specialization in dairy production. Our parents all came to his graduation as did Peter's sister, Margo, and his lovely grandmother.

Between the two of us, we were able to save some money and take a very leisurely month-long trip across America in July of 1955. We leisurely explored the many national parks that we had hoped to see when we were children. I had traveled no farther away from my home than places in New York and had only been to New Jersey as a newlywed. We were on our way to a new home in Pasadena, California, in order for Peter to attend Fuller Theological Seminary, founded by radio-evangelist Charles E. Fuller, and I had enrolled in the Bible Institute of Los Angeles to prepare to serve God on the mission field.

We arrived in Pasadena in August of 1952. We soon obtained jobs in the seminary, and Peter put his janitorial skills to good use working at a local junior high school, and later on in the newly constructed seminary building that opened in 1953. Under a few layers of paint in one of the downstairs janitor's closets at Fuller, some archaeologist may find some day Peter's inscription on the wall, "Mop more in '54."

He and I were also houseparents overseeing two houses full of single men, who were just out of college and had decided to prepare for the ministry. These houses were right on the Fuller campus, and it was very convenient for us. Basically, my job was to keep all of the public areas, bathrooms, living rooms, kitchens, halls, stairways, porches, and sidewalks clean at all times. In exchange I was able to work off the rent for our tiny apartment in one of the houses. In the three years that we were there, we really enjoyed our time and fell in love with the men in those two houses.

I commuted daily to BIOLA College in downtown Los Angeles, about a half hour drive if there were no accidents on the Pasadena Freeway. Both of us were able to receive some tuition scholarships and work off the rest of our bills. When it came time to graduate, we left the Los Angeles area totally debt-free! Peter had chosen the regular Master of Divinity program, and I had chosen the regular three-year Bible college program, majoring in Bible. However, I was only able to complete two of the three years because I became pregnant with our first daughter, Karen.

Before I even knew I was pregnant, I became violently ill with what we thought might be an ectopic pregnancy, but instead was a large, benign tumor on an ovary. I needed emergency surgery. A few days later it was confirmed that, indeed, we had a child on the way. We had kept up our Blue Cross health insurance, so it was completely paid. A very healthy Karen was born in December of 1954. I remember that it cost us $1 when we checked out of the hospital bringing Karen home. The insurance didn't pay for her birth certificate. At that time, it was unthinkable for a mother to leave a child in order to study. I devoted my time to motherhood and my "public areas."

During our three years in Pasadena, we were put in touch with a Quaker church in the city of Bell, about a half-hour south of Pasadena. This was Bell Friends Church. They asked my Bible school for an adult Sunday School teacher. I asked the church if it was okay for Peter to fill that position and I could help in the children's department. They agreed, so Peter got his very first volunteer teaching position. His class grew quite large. The people there became our closest friends during that time. Peter and I also led the children's church. The people there soon caught on to the fact that we were starving students, and they arranged for a family in church to invite us out to dinner every Sunday afternoon after church. These were some of the finest people we ever knew, and when the time came for us to leave and head off to the mission field, they picked up the majority of our support.

Just for the fun of it, I read Ruth Bell Graham's memoirs entitled: *It's My Turn* (Fleming H. Revell, 1982) as I was preparing to pull my thoughts together for the writing of these memoirs. She tells a hilarious story (on page 42) about her being a missionary kid fresh out of boarding school in Korea, but who had grown up in China. It was her first year at Wheaton College in Wheaton, Illinois. Thanksgiving was approaching, and she was having lunch with Harold Lindsell when he asked Ruth if they had turkey for their Thanksgiving dinners in China. Ruth replied "No, we ate bastards." When he looked very startled, Ruth went on to say "Yes, we had one every Thanksgiving. They were quite good." Harold then changed the subject quite abruptly. Later on when she was recounting this experience to her sister Rosa, who had been sick and in the infirmary that day, and telling how startled he was, Rosa set the record straight. Once she stopped laughing, she exclaimed,

"Oh, you nut! They weren't bastards. They were bustards! They were wild geese called bustards." Poor missionary kids each have similar stories to tell as they try so hard to integrate into the American culture!

I tell you this because I also had an encounter with the same Harold Lindsell family. He, Mrs. Lindsell, and their four daughters lived in the house on campus right next door to our house. I became friends with Mrs. Lindsell during my pregnancy. When we brought our baby Karen home from the hospital, it was a new and strange experience for me. The babysitting that I had done was caring for toddlers or grade school children, and I don't recall ever having changed a diaper! I had no family or close friends nearby for coaching of any kind, and pretty well relied upon the instructions given by my pediatrician. Dr. Lindsell was teaching theology and a missions course at Fuller at that time. I used to babysit for the Lindsell children from time to time, so we became friends.

Since I was a new mother, Mrs. Lindsell appeared at my door to make a friendly call one afternoon only to find me in tears because I could not stop Karen's crying. Attempting to follow the feeding instructions very carefully, it was still an hour before feeding time for Karen. Mrs. Lindsell picked up Karen and said, "This kid is hungry!" I tearfully explained to her that feeding time was still an hour away. However, she persuaded me to give her a bottle right away, and Karen promptly went to sleep after having drained its contents. I have never been able to nurse any of my children due to a condition called chronic cystic mastitis. I found this quite funny because my whole life I had been involved in milk production and when it came time to produce some of my own milk for my own offspring, I was unable to do so! Mrs. Lindsell helped me work out a better feeding schedule for Karen, and in turn, Karen immediately responded by eating every three hours and sleeping from 7 PM until 7 AM by the time she was just one month old. Since she was my first child, I had no idea what a wonderful baby she was.

Near the end of Peter's last year of seminary, we applied to the South America Indian Mission and were accepted. We were looking at working in conjunction with a Christian boarding school where Peter could use his agricultural skills by working the fields and helping to grow crops for food. Peter graduated from Fuller and we began to get ready to leave for New York again to pack and say goodbye to our parents and relatives.

In early September, we spent our last day in Los Angeles attending the Los Angeles County fair. It is enormous and much larger than many state fairs. It was the first day of the fair. We had a great time, but I apparently ate some tainted food, because on our way up to San Francisco the very next day to visit some seminary friends, I became quite ill. By the time we arrived at the home of our friends, I began to run a fever. By the next day, diarrhea and an extremely high fever over 104 degrees had set in. Both Peter and Karen came down with a less violent case of diarrhea but escaped the fever. I was far too ill to care for Karen, so poor Peter took over, never having changed a diaper up to that point!

He learned quickly. And these were cloth diapers that had to be laundered! It was in the days before the invention of disposable ones. So, the task of rinsing the diapers out and laundering them fell to him. I was so violently ill I needed to have a doctor make a house call. After examining me, he declared that I had a serious case of food poisoning (botulism?) and without the new antibiotic he gave me, I might not have lived. As I recall, our hosts did not catch it, but it took me a week to mend enough for us to continue on our journey home.

We got home to the farm, spent the fall helping out there, and had our last Christmas with both sets of parents before we readied ourselves for leaving for Bolivia in February of 1956 for our first five-year stint on the mission field.

What did this period of my life teach me? Mainly that God had a wonderful plan for my life, that He provided me with the most loving, responsible, exciting husband and father on planet Earth available to me. He taught us that we didn't need to worry about lack, and that He was always going to meet our needs and bless us with marvelous friends. The dear people at Bell Friends Church would become very close lifelong friends and colleagues. One sweet lady, Irene Main, would hand-address over 300 envelopes for our quarterly prayer letters to our constituency. Another secretary would mimeograph the letters. Irene hand-folded them and licked the stamp on each letter, very lovingly, I might add. We had led her two boys to Jesus in children's church, and she and her husband Glen were so very grateful. Irene worked as head of the baked goods department in a large grocery store also, so this work was done in addition to that. When we were in California for our furloughs, Irene saw to it that we had boxes of all the bread, pastries, and other baked goods we could eat. Another church member worked in a dairy, way back when milk and dairy goods were delivered to homes. We had all the milk, butter, and variety of cheeses we could ever want. One of the members of the church was a dentist who took Peter, Karen, and me into his office on his day off and placed each one of us in one of his three dental chairs. His wife, an RN worked as his assistant. He cared for all of our dental needs as his gift to the mission-ary cause. What precious people! We were so very loved and prayed for faithfully.

God showed His faithfulness to us over and over again. He taught us from His Word and gave us a deep love for His Word and for our Christian family. He gave us the faith to launch out into the unknown to try to build His Church on another continent. He gave us the grace to leave our families and loved ones, which was a might difficult. Still, He accompanied us and gave us all we needed to head off to the mission field for terms of five years at a stretch. And He had an army of people here on the home front who were caring for all of our communication needs, praying for us, and loving us.

CHAPTER 5

Santiago And San Jose De Chiquitos

Then came January 8, 1956.

That was the fateful day when the Auca Indians murdered the five American missionaries in the Ecuadorian jungle. It got magnificent photo coverage in *Life Magazine,* among many other magazines, as well as major newspapers and other media. This sent an extremely uneasy feeling through our parents, and it made it just a little more difficult to leave, but we finally drove down to West Palm Beach, Florida, with my mom and dad, said our tearful goodbyes and departed for Bolivia on February 25, 1956. By then Karen was 14 months old and an active, very happy toddler.

I took my very first airplane ride from Palm Beach to Miami. We had a four-hour layover and then proceeded on our long journey from Miami to Lima, Peru, aboard a DC6 airplane stopping several times along the way. This was in the days before jet airplanes and the rides were considerably bumpier. We had to keep Karen on our laps because she did not have a separate ticket or seat. We overnighted in Lima and then proceeded on the next day aboard a DC3 on Pan American Grace Airways, Panagra for short. We flew from Lima south to Arica, in the northern corner of Chile.

These Panagra planes were piloted by Americans, and since we understood no Spanish at all, it was very good to know what was going on. The DC3 planes, lovingly nicknamed "Gooney birds," held 21 passengers and remained in use all of the time that we were in Bolivia, and some are probably still going on! They were incredibly durable and reliable and held up very well on the dirt landing strips of the smaller cities. Arica was on the west side of the Andes Mountains, and the pilot made an interesting announcement. He informed us that we were about to jump over the Andes to La Paz, Bolivia, and that it was the fastest, highest climb anywhere (at the time). We had one tube that we could sniff a little oxygen from between the three of us. Karen had fallen asleep, so she got a frequent sniff.

By the time we landed in La Paz, at an altitude of 13,325 feet, I had become pretty lightheaded. We were not told to deplane, as I recall, so I simply stayed on with Karen, and we proceeded on to Cochabamba and eventually Santa Cruz. Santa Cruz was a city located deep in the jungle and was extremely hot and humid with no paved streets at the time.

We spent another night in Santa Cruz and the next day headed out for the last leg of our journey. We were still on Panagra Airlines, so we boarded another DC3, flew all the way east to the Bolivian town of Puerto Suarez on the Brazilian border, and then back to our destination of Robore. Here we were met by George Haight, our senior missionary, and we got loaded up into his '48 Chevy truck, and headed toward Santiago over a dirt road and through four rivers. It was only about 14 miles, but it could take anywhere from two to six hours, depending upon whether it had recently rained or not and how swollen the four rivers were. The back of the truck was loaded with supplies and over a dozen people either coming or going who needed a ride.

We were welcomed by Mrs. Haight, Beth Earle, Alys Aldering, and Joyce Johnson, our co-workers. Mr. and Mrs. Haight established the primary school way back in 1932, the year that I was born. When we began working in Santiago de Chiquitos, there were about 135 boys and girls in the six grades. There were several national teachers, and our closest friends became Luis Bravo and Flora Balcazar, the adopted daughter of the Haights, who also was a graduate of a Bible institute in Argentina. Because Flora was bilingual, she became our Spanish teacher.

Life was very different from that to which I had been accustomed. I remember our first night in our new home, and how frightened I was, especially of the dark. The only light was from small kerosene lanterns, and it was difficult to see my surroundings. I recall that the sun rose very early in the morning because we were below the equator and it was February—summertime in the tropics. The donkeys were up and about roaming around the town square called the plaza. On our first morning there, one had wandered up on our porch and let out a mighty bray nearly frightening me to death! It was only about 5 a.m. but the sun was already way up in the sky, and he was just busily roaming around foraging for food. (I remember seeing a donkey with a shirtsleeve hanging from his mouth being chased out of the front door of a house down the street from ours one time.) However, these were extremely gentle creatures, and didn't cause harm for the most part.

Water was carried up in barrels from the river a few blocks away. For this task, a tractor pulling a high-sided wagon was used. It was the only water we had, and drinking water had to be boiled and filtered. It was in this same river that everyone bathed and washed their hair. There were women for hire who would take our laundry down to the same river and wash it with lye soap, beating the stains on the rocks, and laying the soapy white clothing in the sunshine to bleach it out a bit. Everything was then ironed with a massive charcoal iron in an attempt to kill all any remaining germs. Our toilets were outhouses, located quite a walk away from the housing areas for obvious reasons. All of the cooking was done over wood fires. Mr. Haight raised cattle for the school and an animal was butchered once a week. Since there was no refrigeration, the carcass was hung in a screened area, although it by no means escaped all of the flies, and by the end of the week maggots frequently infested what was left. The cooks would just bang the meat hard in an attempt to get as many off as possible, and the food often included lots of onions to kill the flavor.

There was quite a large vegetable garden, and I remember the main vegetables grown were squash of varying varieties, onions, and collard greens. Rice was the main starch, and yucca and corn were other staples. Bread made out of regular white wheat flour was baked daily.

And then there were bananas! I was told there were 21 varieties of bananas. We had oranges, grapefruit, and lemons in abundance. There were many mangos as well, but I was highly allergic to them, and after eating three small ones one day, I came down with a severe case of "mango poisoning." I had never had a food allergy in my whole life. The area around my eyes and mouth became very leather-like and I got an extremely serious case of hives, but fortunately my throat did not close off. I got a case of hives every afternoon for the next three months and was treated with Benadryl capsules. These made me very sleepy, and I often fell asleep in evening meetings because there was so little that I could understand at the time. Spanish is very easy to sound out and read or sing to a familiar tune, even though one does not know the meaning of the words yet.

The mission compound did own a crib, so Karen had a place to sleep that was safe. The first week we were there, I remember putting

Karen down for bed one evening and for some reason I picked up her red blanket and gave it a shake. Out dropped a very large scorpion on to the brick floor that immediately went into his stinging mode, with his tail held high above his back! Had it stung her there would've been dire consequences, if not death because she was still so small. Scorpions are quite easy to kill with the heel of a shoe or a broom because they stay so still while in their attacking stance. From then on, we checked our beds quite carefully and knocked out our shoes every morning before putting them on.

It seemed as though we always had to be extremely conscious of our surroundings because many of our new, unfamiliar bugs and plants either stung or gave you a rash. There were giant centipedes over nine inches long that stung ferociously. We never did meet up with any of these, fortunately, but we were always on the lookout to shake out our clothing. I got the fright of my life once when I took a lantern out to my kitchen area after dark and saw literally hundreds of cockroaches scurrying all over our pots and pans and walls. It's a good thing that everything that went in those pots and pans got sterilized over a fire. The outhouses were literally crawling with huge cockroaches as well, and I must confess that it was the first time in my life I had ever seen cockroaches. These were the enormous tropical variety about two inches long. Having lived in the Northeast of America, we just did not have them. There may have been some in the cities, but certainly not in a German household where things were squeaky clean. And we always had to keep a lookout for snakes, many of which were venomous. There were boa constrictors as well as anacondas and alligators in the lakes. We later learned that many of the lakes and rivers were teeming with piranha, the man-eating fish. So, we learned to become extremely observant of our surroundings.

Our first task was to learn Spanish. Because of Peter's high IQ, he rapidly bolted ahead of me, and our class of two was divided in half! We were each tutored and crept along at our own speed, but we had so much opportunity to speak Spanish that actually we picked it up pretty quickly. The Bolivian people around us were very kind, understanding, and patient.

Our first year and a half were quite difficult. We both contracted a serious case of dysentery that lasted the entire year and a half and was quite debilitating. Because Karen was a toddler, she quickly picked up a case of pinworms, and we had to give her some pretty strong medication to get rid of them. She also had a few roundworms, which are inevitable for kids, but to find one of these eight or nine-inch-long worms in the morning diaper can be quite a shock for Mama.

Looking back, we now know that within the first year, I suffered from a pretty serious case of culture shock. By the time we had been there about eight or nine months I became quite depressed. Karen was in incredibly active, cheerful child, and it seemed as though everything around us was dangerous or hostile in some way. I recall, for example, that one Sunday morning before church, I asked Peter to please take Karen for a walk so that I could have a time of devotions alone. He came back about an hour later, and the young man he had met up with who accompanied him on the walk was dragging an enormous bushmaster snake that he had killed just inches from Karen. This snake strongly resembles the big diamondbacks of Texas and the South, except that it does not have a rattle to sound a warning to things coming too close to it. So, in that sense it is more dangerous. I am certain that the angels were watching out for her!

However, the Lord showed me how to get myself out of that depression. It was by helping someone else who needed my help. For some reason my interest in nursing was put to use in Santiago, and I was doing everything from pulling teeth without anesthetic, to helping people with eye infections and delivering babies, etc. There was a toddler about a year old who had fallen into a fire and his arm was severely burned. I was able to nurse him back to health and become friends with his mother. There was another instance when a young man was literally bleeding to death from a molar that someone else had extracted but had not applied pressure to the hole. He had become extremely anemic, but I was able to get him some iron shots, and a good diet, and nurse him back to strength. By taking an interest in others around me, and by helping them, my depression lifted. Tears came to my eyes one day when I realized that I was singing in the kitchen as I was baking a pie! The dark night of my soul had passed, and the sun shone once again. I decided that was no way to live and never allowed myself to slip into that kind of a situation again. It only lasted for about two or three months, mercifully, as I recall. By this time, we were beginning to handle Spanish enough to be more comfortable with it and that helped a great deal. It took away a feeling of helplessness because of not being able to communicate.

We had a couple of close calls with Peter. Several months after we arrived, Peter was up very early in the morning, as was his habit, and he went out to build a wood fire in the kitchen stove of the school to give the employees a head start on breakfast. It was still somewhat dark, and he stepped in an ants' nest near the wood pile that had set up shop there during the night. The fire ants began swarming up his body under his pant legs and biting him ferociously multiple dozens of times before he got back to our bedroom where he quickly got out of his pants and brushed them off. However, the damage had been done, and we soon discovered that he apparently had a severe allergy to those ant bites. His body began swelling up, and his lips, ears, and face started to turn purple. I had no idea what to do! He then wrote me a note saying: "I can't breathe through my mouth." The only thing I could think to do was to quickly grab a jar of Vicks VapoRub because I knew that sometimes it opened my airways when I was severely congested. Then I prayed what was probably my first healing prayer, partly screaming it out: "Lord, open his throat!" There was no time to get him in the truck and drive the several hours to Robore, so I just prayed. After what seemed like an eternity but was probably a half hour, the crisis passed. The symptoms slowly subsided, but it took a couple of days for him to get back to normal.

He had another interesting close call a few months later when he was out working on the tractor and somehow tangled with a wasp's nest. They also swarmed about his body and stung him several times. This time his lips and ears became swollen and turned purple, but it was not quite the close call as with the fire ants. We were then extremely careful knowing that he had an allergy to bee stings.

Just as an aside, we also observed the fascinating phenomenon of army ants when we were living in Santiago. They would invade and kill every bug and cockroach in their path. There was one way that we protected ourselves while we were sleeping, and that was to place the leg of each bed in a large tin (about the size of a 3-pound coffee can), filled with water. Since ants don't swim across water, we all were safe while we were sleeping. They entered either under the cracks of the doors, or through the glassless windows. It was one of the most fascinating exhibitions that I have ever laid eyes on, to see these creatures coming out of the jungle seemingly from nowhere and marching in file, several abreast. They would then come together and form a very wide stream of ants, first a foot, then 2 feet wide, then a yard, and so on. They would then destroy every living thing in their path. Every now and then they would get into the mission kitchen and thoroughly clean it out. Dozens of them would capture an enormous cockroach and apparently sting it, rendering it helpless. They would then proceed to devour all of the soft tissue of its body but leave the brittle wings behind. This was one of the reasons why we kept so much of our food in large covered tins or barrels.

Another very interesting thing happened during our first year in Santiago. The Bolivian government had just passed a law that for the very first time in history women could vote. Many of the older women in town were illiterate but qualified to vote. Since the '40s and '50s, public and private schools proliferated and most of the young people were literate. There were several candidates running for president at the time and there was a great deal of passion surrounding the political parties represented by these candidates. Slogans were frequently painted on walls. It was decided that in order to have an accurate election, the ballots for each political candidate would be printed on a different color paper and distributed all over the country. However, a very strange thing happened in Santiago. The ballots that arrived were only of one color—yellow as I recall. Those ballots just happened to represent the party in power already. Because the women were so very anxious to vote, they had to vote for that party or not vote at all! Of course, these ballots were distributed to the men as well, so the party in power had quite a landslide in Santiago!

Our baggage did not arrive for well over a year, and we had to make do with the clothing that we have brought down in our luggage, which wasn't very much clothing at all. Actually, it was 44 pounds for Peter, 44 pounds for me, but none for Karen because she only paid a 10% fare to ride along on our laps. Peter eventually had to travel all the way to Montevideo, Uruguay, and bring it back to Bolivia by boat and train. It turned out to be a 35-day trip leaving me alone with Karen. I did ask a teenage girl to sleep in an adjoining room to ours so that I would not be alone.

One night when Peter was gone, I heard a strange sort of a splat in my bedroom, where Karen was also sleeping in her crib on the other side of a curtain. I grabbed the flashlight that we always kept by the side of the bed and investigated. I soon saw a coral snake that had apparently fallen from the ceiling, wiggling around our bedroom brick floor. These snakes are rather small, maybe only 12 to 14 inches long, and quite thin, but are extremely venomous. I called to the girl in the next room to bring the baseball bat, but I was unable to rouse her with my screams. I quickly jumped up on the bed and was able to reach a very large shoe bag that was hanging on the wall. We probably had six or eight pairs of shoes stored there, to keep them off of the floor and away from any creepy crawlies that might be on the floor. I recall that I was shaking violently, but I had about 12 rounds of ammunition in the form of shoes there on the side of the wall. However, because I was shaking so badly, I was unable to stun it with a few shoes because I kept missing it. I also think it was probably a bit dazed from the fall, and it was advancing toward the bed quite slowly. I didn't have a clear target because there were so many shoes already on the floor and the snake kept crawling in between them. Finally, I had the last shoe of Peter's left in my hand, but this time I waited for it to get into a clearing, took careful aim and hit it right on the head with the heel of Peter's shoe. When I was sure that it was dead, I got down off the bed, and found a long thick wire, picked it up, and tossed it out the back door into our patio. By then my young guest had awakened, but I told her to go back to sleep.

Then I began to think, *What if it had fallen in Karen's crib or my bed?* I found myself very wide-awake and unable to sleep, so I struck a match to the kerosene lamp that gave out probably between the equivalent of 10 to 15 watts of light, pulled the chair and the lighted lamp close to my bedside, and opened my Bible to the Book of Psalms starting with Chapter 1. I figured that if I couldn't sleep, I might just as well read some Scripture. I didn't get very far at all before I came to Psalm 4:8 which reads, "I will both lay me down in peace and sleep, for thou, Lord, watchest over me." I had read enough, blew out the lamp, and settled back down in bed. Karen had slept through the entire commotion!

The next morning, I looked out into the patio for my trophy. Alas, during the night, the flesh from the snake had been entirely eaten by ants, and there was nothing left except a pretty, wispy white skeleton! There was nothing to do but to toss it in the trash, and praise God that, indeed, He was watching over us.

When Karen was somewhere between two and three years old, we had to make a trip up to the city of Cochabamba from our new home in San Jose, a couple of hours down the railroad line from Robore. We can't remember the reason why, but we decided to take the train from San José to Santa Cruz, take care of some business in Santa Cruz, and then continue up to Cochabamba by plane.

The trip to Santa Cruz by train merits description. The train was the one that ran through our town of San Jose from the city of Santa Cruz to the Brazilian border. It was powered by wood and many people along the railroad were able to cut and sell some of the very hard wood that grew in the jungle to the train company. It was quite exciting to take a trip in the train. Whenever more wood was thrown on the fire in the boiler, a substantial shower of red-hot cinders would be emitted. These would then shower back through the open windows on to the passengers packed tightly together on the wooden benches. It was not unusual at all to smell burning clothing. The windows were kept open when it was not raining in order to let in a bit of a breeze and some fresh air to deal with the oppressive heat as well as the smells of sweaty humanity. My guess is that the train was going all of 15 to 20 miles per hour.

Since there were no restrooms at all on the train, I carried a potty for Karen. Whenever she tinkled in the potty, I would just dump it through an open window, and more often than not, the liquid would fall nearly straight down to the edge of the railroad ties. Whenever the train would stop to take on wood or water or we would arrive at a village, the passengers would quickly get off the train and head for the jungle to relieve themselves. It was quite a simple maneuver for the gentleman, who would take a few dozen steps and simply turn their backs on the crowd. However, it was quite a different story when it came to the women. We had to brave our surroundings and head off into the thick jungle where we could be somewhat hidden. The trick was to get back far enough so that no one else had gone back farther than you had. And of course, you weren't the first person there, so it was not only the creepy crawlies that you had to look out for!

The women who lived in the towns often made a livelihood out of selling food to the travelers. One of the main finger foods that was substantial was the *empanada*. It was a meat and vegetable-filled pastry that was very delicious. There were also green corn tamales in season, and some set up tables and served stew or soups, or even fried beef, rice with a fried egg on top, boiled yucca, or boiled ears of corn. These were served in low enamel soup plates. Fruit and bananas were frequently available as well, and many sold drinks made of tamarind, lemonade, or *chicha*— a slightly fermented drink made of boiled cornmeal and sugar. A very dark roasted coffee was available for breakfast along with bread, some cracker-like pastries made from corn flour and cheese or from yucca flour and cheese. We fell in love with these snacks. (To this day, I make some of the corn flour and cheese snacks with ingredients that Karen can find in the Los Angeles area in the Mexican markets.) Needless to say, when we ate or drank from these dishes that we knew were not washed in hot water, we blessed and sanctified our food and drink and God seemed to protect us very well. It was odd that the only food poisoning that I ever got was back in the United States! We did not have to pack food for these long journeys other than some simple cookies or crackers as snacks for Karen. We did however take a jug of water that was safe to drink.

The trip to Santa Cruz took three days. As I recall it was somewhere between 200 and 300 miles. The big problem was the Rio Grande that flowed between us and our destination. So, the entire first day was spent getting to a little town called El Pailon on the banks of the river. That night was spent on the train although a few people might have found a place to bunk outside somewhere. Most people stayed on the train and just laid down where their feet were during the day unless they could somehow curl up on the narrow wooden bench that was only about 4 feet long. Sometimes people were fortunate enough to find an empty boxcar. They would stretch out on the wooden floor as best they could. On one occasion I felt pretty cramped stretched out on the boxcar floor, so I told Peter to shove back a little bit. He balked somewhat, saying that it would be quite indecent for him to move any closer to the woman behind him! Waking up in the morning after having slept on a wooden floor usually meant a very aching body. I recall on one occasion when we were sleeping in the passenger car, we brought a hammock and strung it up using the slats of the overhead baggage rack, and Karen sleeping in it was probably the most comfortable of anyone in our car.

People traveling on the train were not always well. Some were on their way to see doctors in the city. The only place left for Peter one night was on the floor below a man that he thought might've been in advanced stages of tuberculosis. Mercifully, the man carried a large open tin can to use when he coughed and spit. But it was a pretty miserable night for Peter who slept with his head tucked inside his shirt, hoping for the best. We have always been amazed that we did not pick up any of these communicable diseases that we were exposed to. I remember once that Karen tested positive from having been exposed to tuberculosis, and I'm sure that's not the only thing she was exposed to. Her health has always been superb.

The next day was spent moving all of the passengers and baggage across the raging river. At that time the United States was helping Bolivia by building the Dwight D. Eisenhower railroad bridge across the Rio Grande. However, there was one major problem they encountered. The town of El Pailon was located at a major bend in the river. As the bridge advanced, every rainy season saw the swollen river move more and more as it ate out the opposite riverbank. There was a very long bridge that had no river below! During the years that we were there, an attempt was made to drive some very large wooden stakes the size of railroad ties (but about three times as long) very close together to keep the river contained in the same place.

In the meantime, we had to hire a large rowboat that held about eight to ten passengers along with their baggage. The first time I got on one of these rowboats, I dropped my only pair of sunglasses in the river as I was climbing on board. They were gone forever. There were ropes tied to the bow of the rowboat, and men would pull the boat and its load considerably upstream. When they had got to a certain point, they would let the ropes go and the oarsman would paddle like crazy as the swift current in the river quickly pulled us downstream. The object was to get across the river at the approximate location where there were oxcarts waiting on the other side to transport baggage to another waiting train. It was quite a long walk over the sandy, stony, dry riverbed, maybe about a half-mile to get to the other side. It was very common to see women with their suitcases balanced on their heads transporting them over. Since it took all day to complete this task, we spent another night on the train waiting for us on the opposite bank of the river. When all of the passengers and their baggage were ready the next morning, we took the final leg of the journey on to the city of Santa Cruz, arriving there sometime in the late afternoon.

I loved going to the many open markets there. Many imported foods were available, and I particularly enjoyed being able to buy ketchup, mustard, walnuts, olives, and even some canned fruits and vegetables from Brazil. It was not uncommon to see a few rats scurrying about, as well as dogs roaming freely among the food stalls. There were also hand-hewn wooden bowls and platters as well as large wooden spoons and other carved wooden kitchen implements that I thought were pretty cool. I brought a number of these back home to America and still use them to this day.

I can't quite remember what our business was in Santa Cruz, but once it was accomplished, we headed out to the airport to board our plane to Cochabamba. The airport was extremely busy when we were waiting for our plane, since several planes had arrived within a short time of each other and it seemed as though people were shoulder to shoulder in the rustic little terminal. Somehow Peter and I got separated, and when we finally found each other again we had a terrible fright when we realized our three-year-old Karen was with neither one of us! We began searching frantically calling her name among the crowd, but to no avail. It was particularly frightening to us because children were often stolen to become slave servants or even worse. A little blonde blue-eyed girl, which described little Karen, would bring a very high price! After being sure that we had covered every nook and cranny of the airport public areas searching for her, Peter got permission from the authorities to check around the outside areas. There were several planes on the ground at the time, and when he climbed up the steps to the plane soon to leave for Buenos Aires, Argentina, there sat little Karen all strapped in a seat ready to go on her airplane ride that she knew was coming. When she saw the airplanes on the runway from the waiting room, she had wiggled between the narrow space in the uprights of a wrought iron fence and simply gotten onto an empty plane! We once again praised God for rapidly answered frantic prayers! Business accomplished, we flew back to Robore and got on the truck and back up the bumpy road to Santiago and home.

About this time, there was some sort of an altercation between Mr. and Mrs. Haight and our mission board in the States, and we were put in charge of the Bible Institute that had recently sprung up by the board in the U.S. Although Peter had been doing quite a bit of work with the agricultural part of the mission station, our attention had to be turned to the Bible Institute. When the dust settled, Mr. and Mrs. Haight stayed with boarding school that they had started, along with Alys and Joyce. Peter, Karen and I along with Beth Earle and Luis Bravo and his family were ordered by the mission to pack up the Bible school: the students, and all of our home furnishings and the Bible school furniture and teaching materials. We were to move it all via a railroad boxcar 80 miles west to a small city of about 3,000 inhabitants along the railroad tracks a little closer to Santa Cruz, called San Jose. We had been in Santiago only about a year and a half when all this mess happened. But we were about to strike out on our own in a brand-new work and we loved the idea. We adored Beth, Luis and his family and anxiously looked forward to a new beginning.

What did I learn from my early days as a missionary in Santiago? The first, tough lesson was that missionaries are not all saints of God. We did not all get along well all the time. We got caught in the middle of a nasty mission split. We fell victim to seeing the worst in our colleagues at times. We learned how to care for ourselves in a hostile, jungle environment. We fell in love with the Bolivian people and many became our close friends. We learned how to live at the end of the road, dependent on God to care for us in a secluded environment. Because there were so few people to speak English with, we learned Spanish quickly and well. I learned never, ever, to eat mango again!! Peter learned to watch out for ants and bees and wasps. We learned to watch carefully over our very active and very happy little Karen who loved life so much no matter where she was. We fell in love with the Bolivian food and fruit drinks, and I greatly enjoyed learning to cook my newfound cuisine.

We had several close calls with Peter's life, my life, and Karen's too. But God brought us through every one of them. I learned how it felt to be depressed, which was a very new experience for me, and to have culture shock, and I could lecture new missionaries how to avoid or get delivered from the ravishes of a new culture because I had been there. When I felt depressed, my way out was to help someone else worse off than I was, and the depression lifted. It only lasted three months, and I was on top once again. I learned many new medical skills and was able to minister to very hurting people who really appreciated it.

CHAPTER 6

Our San Jose Assignment

As far as I know we were the first resident missionaries in this town. We found some property on the outskirts of town and were soon able to set up shop there. We no longer had opportunity for our agricultural training to be put to much use, but I guess in the long run, people are a little more important than corn and cows. I did have a very nice vegetable garden, and we really enjoyed that. As a missionary you learn new things and often have to let go of some old familiar things, but that comes with the territory. Peter became quite adept at making furniture and we soon had desks and chairs and were off and teaching.

I became good friends with a number of women from town while Peter joined the Lions Club and was able to meet quite a few gentlemen there, Little by little, we were welcomed by the people of San Jose. I made a deal with the ladies who became my friends: I would have classes on cooking and baking, and while we were eating the food that we had prepared, they would allow me to teach a simple Bible class. The more advanced ladies were very interested in cake decorating. We had a great time with this project and when one of them suddenly became a widow, she was able to move to the city of Santa Cruz and support herself and her family with a thriving cake decorating business. (On one of his last trips to Santa Cruz, Peter met with this lovely lady who, along with her family, has since become a Christian and is doing very well. She is as old as I am! We were thrilled!) We found several believers who had moved to San Jose in order to work with various jobs connected to the railroad line, and we had a little congregation of about 15 counting us, to start with. We turned one of the rooms of our house into a meeting room and we had plenty of space for what was needed. It looked like it had been a former garage or big workshop of some sort, but was very clean. I played the pump organ, and when we did street meetings, I played the accordion. The people are very musical, and most young men know how to play the guitar. Music is very important to the Bolivians, and I had a lot of fun with it for many years.

I continued on with the teaching, meetings, and evangelization as we were able. I also taught Karen kindergarten and first grade, using the Calvert correspondence school, as most missionaries of our time did. I really enjoyed our time in San Jose. The weather was a little hotter than Santiago, but we soon became accustomed to it.

Our living quarters, Bible school classrooms, Peter's office, storerooms, a living room to entertain guests, a water supply tank consisting of 55-gallon drums, a couple of faucets, and an old fashion chain-pull toilet surrounded a large brick-floored patio area. There was a very large drain hole that ran under some classrooms, and when it rained the drain hole that allowed water to run out from the enclosed patio would frequently flush out enormous toads, and I would guess that they weighed between two and four pounds! However, they did their job by eating many of the insects that roamed around. They were not harmful, just a little frightening to bump into in the dark. I had highwire clotheslines running across the patio where I dried clothing when necessary.

We occasionally made our own dried beef jerky. It was simply sliced very thin, rubbed with an ample amount of salt, and stretched over the clotheslines. It usually dried in the hot sun before flies could set up shop on the flesh. When roasted over hot coals, it was absolutely delicious, and it would keep for weeks if properly stored in a tin with a tight-fitting lid.

This brings to memory a rather funny, but what could've been tragic, story. One day Peter went into the little outdoor toilet room. Let me describe this toilet. It had a door that was about 6 feet high but left about a 6-inch open space at the top to let in plenty of light when the door was closed. Whoever was using the toilet at the time, would then toss out through the space at the top one of the signs used on airplane trips, but this sign was attached to a long string. The sign stated both in English and Spanish: "This seat is occupied." The bright green sign could be clearly seen from across the patio and it was very convenient to know when the toilet was being used. Our toilet paper was usually the foreign edition of Time magazine because it had nice thin paper. Our second choice was *Reader's Digest,* because that paper was just a little softer than most magazines with shiny paper. The used paper was placed in a metal wastebasket and dragged out into the center of the brick patio every couple of days to be set on fire. We did not dare jeopardize our delicate plumbing. The metal wastebasket was formerly a 5-gallon tin used to hold the "white lightning" corn liquor locally distilled and enjoyed by the hard drinkers in the area. I took a sip once just out of curiosity, and it tasted like 90% rubbing alcohol. It was awful!

The little toilet room had a cement floor with a drain hole out the back so that the floor could be easily cleaned by dumping a pail of water on it and sweeping it thoroughly with a broom. The dirty water went out the drain hole that led to a walled-off large plot of ground with a couple of fruit trees, my big vegetable garden, and Peter's carpenter shop. Because the potty room was a fair size, we stored a broom and some gardening tools in one corner.

Anyway, on this particular day, Peter proceeded to lower his trousers and take a seat. He suddenly realized that he had company in the room—a large bushmaster snake was coiled up in a corner behind him! He jumped up grasping his trousers with one hand and with the other hand grabbed a gardening hoe called a pala that resembled an ice-chopping implement. He partially pinned the snake down, which had begun to make a getaway into the drainage hole but was in a quandary as to the next step. He did not have another hand to either pull up his trousers or open the door, and he kept pinning the snake with his one arm and the straight hoe. He did not really want to lift up the hoe for fear the snake would get away. Finally, he had to let go of the hoe and the snake managed to slither out of the drain hole into the backyard. He searched for it as soon as he had his pants back on, but never could find it.

Our food horizons were greatly broadened in San Jose. A train came through a couple of times a week and from the boxcars emerged people who lived in the high valleys and were able to raise a wide variety of wonderful vegetables. We now had potatoes in abundance, and that made this German girl very happy! We were able to buy beets, carrots, onions, cabbages, peas, and many other fresh vegetables. I had a kerosene-run refrigerator and was able to keep meat, milk, and butter, and do all sorts of wonderful things because of it. Also, I was able to share ice with anyone who came to ask for it because of a sprained ankle or toothache. My mom and dad sent us a small generator, and we were able to have some light in the evenings and electricity now and then. I could even plug in my little Singer sewing machine in the evenings when the lights were on, so I was able to keep up with my mending and a few sewing projects after Karen had gone to bed. We really had some wonderful conveniences compared to Santiago.

Occasionally during the rainy season the streams would fill up and spill over, creating lagoons. There were fish of an unknown variety that would get trapped in the lagoons, and we would go fishing for them. They were rather bony but were a change on the dinner table from our steady diet of beef. One day the Bible school students, Luis Bravo, Peter, four-year-old Karen and I, were out fishing in one of these temporary lagoons. My guess is that the lagoon was about 50 feet across. The good Lord has built within me an excellent judge of measurements and distances and my guesses are usually never far off at all. Karen was walking along the edge of the lagoon directly opposite from me on the other side of the lagoon. I saw in the distance, very close to Karen, an enormous snake, my guess is it was over 10 feet long and probably a boa constrictor. It had its head raised up about a foot off the ground. I began screaming "Karen, run!!" Karen understood the panicky tone of my voice, and began to run, but directly toward the snake! It looked as though she were chasing it! I still vividly see in my mind's eye a picture of that huge snake with its head raised wiggling away from Karen as fast as it could, until it took a left turn and headed off into the tall grass, and Karen kept running around the edge of the lagoon until she got to me, safe and sound. My guess is that she scared the poor reptile half to death, and it was fleeing for its life. Or did an angel scare it off? I am a firm believer in guardian angels and have seen some at work firsthand!

Peter and Luis Bravo occasionally went alligator hunting, and the alligator tails were delicious to eat. One day when they were in the swamps, Peter discovered some landlocked clams. He brought some home, and being the adventuresome soul that he was, he decided to eat some raw ones. He gave some to me and I ate a couple. It was sort of like Adam and Eve in reverse, because both of us, within a couple of days, came down with a horrific case of yellow jaundice. We now know that it was hepatitis A, the dirty kind that is frequently contracted from improperly prepared food, or dirty hands. Karen did not become ill because she didn't eat any of the clams, nor did she catch it from us, thank God! We were both extremely ill and debilitated for several months. Peter never missed a day of his teaching, even though he could not stand for very long. He taught his classes lying in a hammock! I was very glad to have a girl working for us who could take care of things and do the cooking. When we arrived back in the United States on our first furlough, we were tested, and it was confirmed we indeed did have hepatitis A but that no liver damage had occurred to either of us. However, we could never be blood donors because of this.

The city of San Jose, where we lived, also had an airport with a dirt runway, and we got a Panagra flight complete with American pilots once a week. One time there was a close call on takeoff when the engine "swallowed a piston," but the pilots were able to bring the plane to a stop before the end of the runway. They were in for a couple of days' layover in San Jose. San Jose did not have a hotel, so we invited the pilots to stay with us. We had a great time! We fed them some alligator tail and fresh hearts of palm salad straight from the jungle. They in turn, had several boxes of emergency items that they gave to us. There were things like canned tuna and canned fruit, things that we had not seen in quite some time.

It was an exciting time when the huge DC6 plane from Lima, Peru, landed on the small grass airstrip bringing the new engine for the DC3. A great number of the people from San Jose ran out to the airport to watch the pilots change engines. When they were finished, they loaded the faulty engine back on the DC6, and barely cleared the treetops as they took off on their way back to Lima. By the way, the grass was kept mowed by letting the cattle in to graze. Sometimes when the pilots would notice animals on the airstrip they would circle low around the landing strip a couple of times to chase the cattle off. This particular pilot, staying at our home, told us of one time during the previous year when he was landing in a neighboring village and the plane came to an abrupt and sudden halt. When they deplaned, they discovered that an enormous boa constrictor had gotten tangled in the landing gear and met with his (or her) demise.

About a year after this incident, we had a terrible plane crash in our little town, killing all 21 passengers aboard. This time the plane and all of its contents totally burned, and it was very sad. Two of our Bible school students had tickets to be on that plane, but two of the local nuns were given their seats instead and our boys were bumped. We were very sad to be there when the mother superior was trying to identify the bodies of the nuns and finally settled for two charred corpses that she supposed were the right ones. All of the charred bodies were lined up in a row. But people never seem to lose their sense of humor. There had been a crate of ducks or geese aboard, and whoever did the lining up added the remains of the birds to the row. It did add some levity to a totally gruesome situation.

One of my great joys has always been baking. I had the pleasure of learning to bake in a great big brick beehive oven. Once I got the hang of it, baking was quite a pleasure. The beehive oven was also in the famous backyard near my vegetable garden and Peter's carpenter shop. I usually took one whole afternoon a week to do the baking, which frequently included bread, cookies, and other Bolivian delicacies that I learned how to master—well sort of! In my old age watching the Food Channel on TV, I see that many folks pay a fortune to get these ovens imported from Italy for making pizza. Mine was a huge beauty and came with the house. Everyone used them in eastern Bolivia.

A roaring wood fire was started in the oven and allowed to burn for about a half hour, or until the wood had burned down to hot coals. Then a sort of broom-like implement was fashioned out of a wooden pole about five feet long with a number of short but very leafy green branches, obtained from the jungle, lashed on to one end. The hot embers of the wood fire were pushed out of a hole in the back of the oven with a metal rake onto a safe, bare spot behind the oven. The floor of the oven was then swept with the improvised broom mentioned above. If it was too hot, the green branches were dunked in a bucket of water to further clean the floor and to cool down the oven. If it was still too hot, we kept dunking the broom in water and shaking the broom all around the inside, sprinkling water all over to cool it down. The glowing coals heaped on the ground at the back door of the oven were sometimes used when ironing needed to be done. The hot embers were carefully shoveled inside a charcoal iron and put to good use ironing clothing. Then the leafy part of the hand-fashioned implement was dipped in a bucket of water, and the ashes were carefully swept from the hot brick floor of the oven. It was then ready for the loaves of bread and other baked goods.

You always sort of had to guess what the temperature was. If when you stuck your arm inside and the hair got singed off, it was probably a little too hot. One could cool down the temperature rather quickly by dipping the leaves of the homemade broom in the cold water one more time and shaking them violently over the brick floor, thereby cooling it off a few degrees. When the oven was the approximate temperature needed, the back hole was covered with a bent piece of metal, usually the top of a 55-gallon drum. It was held in place by a few stones, and after the items to be baked were placed in the front of the oven, another similar cover was placed over the larger front hole, to keep the heat in.

After the baking was finished, the oven would stay warm for quite a long time. Some of the Bolivian delicacies we made were sort of like crackers, and in order for them to dry out and become nice and crisp, once the major baking was done and the oven had cooled down, they were left all night in the warm oven to become thoroughly crisp. On one occasion, we also baked an entire cow's head all night and threw a feast for our friends the next day! It is considered to be a major delicacy. The oven frequently did not entirely cool off for another full day.

I was told by a neighbor that the people who lived in that house before us awoke one morning to find a beautiful jaguar, who had wandered in from the jungle just a couple of blocks from where our house was, peacefully sleeping inside the beehive oven because it had been a chilly night. I never did find out how it was made to leave, or if it was killed, but I certainly wouldn't want a jaguar in my backyard with me or my family! I believe that these are the most beautiful big cats to roam the jungles. I have also been told that they are the one big cat that can never be fully trained or trusted.

The bed that we slept on was interesting. There were a couple of rows of sturdy wooden poles across the head and foot area, and about 4 feet of flimsy springs to support a person's torso. On top of that was placed a homemade straw mattress. It would mat down with use, so I would have another one made to go over the spring area and fill in the sagging spot.

Houses in the city of San Jose were built with adjoining walls and in our particular house there was no ceiling, just the bottom sides of the bare roof tiles were overhead. The rats used the supporting wooden structure as their superhighway by night and would run around the houses in the entire block. I frequently was able to see a group of them traveling railroad style, single file, nose to tail. There was at least a half dozen of them, sometimes many more! They knocked down dirt from the mud stucco that held the tiles in place. We finally got sick and tired of that, so Peter rigged up a wooden frame, and we stretched a large piece of plastic to form a canopy over the top of our bed. It was much more pleasant just to hear the dirt hit the plastic then to have it fall in our ears. Of course, we were thoroughly covered by a mosquito net as well.

One of the strikingly beautiful enjoyments of life there was to observe the orchids. I was not feeling well one day, and a child came to our door selling some of the wild orchids that he had harvested from the rocks and trees in the jungle. It was the height of the dry season. The little guy had harvested about 20 plants that he had pulled off of the rocks in the jungle and tied them to a stick about a meter long. Peter bought and presented me with a meter of orchids! These orchid flowers were about 5 inches across, beautiful purple cattleyas, the kind that girls would wear to a prom when I was young. These particular orchids had the most gorgeous scent of faint cinnamon and clove, and as I recall there were over 30 blossoms! That was enough to cheer up this old gal! After the blossoms had faded, the orchid plants could be lashed on to small logs and rigged up with nails and strings, rawhide laces, or wires and hung from the lower branches of fruit trees in a person's backyard. Once established, they bloomed every year and were such an elegant extravaganza to look forward to in the midst of a jungle village! Poor missionaries with not many flowers to look at except a profusion of orchids in their backyard!

When we went for walks or rides in the jungle, there were gorgeous tiny yellow fronds of orchids that hung from the trees and bloomed in great profusion. They were named "angelitos" or "little angels" by the locals. They looked like yellow angels with big wings. Their botanical name is oncidium. They often grew on stems of three or four feet of blazing yellow blossoms that had to be pushed out of the way with your arms or shoulders when you were walking! One time when we were on a hike up into the mountains behind Santiago, we saw plants of miniature purple orchids in the forms of cattleyas, with blossoms about the size of my thumb nail. There were dozens of them on each stalk growing alongside a stream. I don't suppose anyone ever got to see them, because usually there were no humans back in that part of the mountains. But there they were, just blooming their little hearts out and glorifying God all by themselves! While we were on that particular hike, we saw numerous pairs of colorful macaws, flying over the trees and screaming as they flew. Some pairs were red, and others were brilliant blue. The view across the jungle from the little short mountaintop we had reached was breathtaking and will be forever etched in my mind's eye. It was just a sea of pure, gorgeous trees of varying shades of green, some very tall, some short, but all crowded together with some palm trees here and there. It was without any trace of humanity as far as the eye could see. The air was so pure that the horizon faded to shades of blue.

It was quite common to see these macaws or other gorgeous, brilliant green parrots of many sizes in folks' backyards. They had somehow managed to tame them. There was a large green parrot that was a pet living in our mission compound in Santiago. I tried to hold it on my index finger once, but it decided it didn't like me and clamped its beak ferociously to the meat between my thumb and index finger. The only thing I could think to do was to snap my wrist and shake it off on to the ground. Then I took a broom and swept it back toward the dining room, from whence it came. It became my enemy and for days every afternoon it would come across on the adjoined tile roofs and scream at me for what seemed like hours on end. I hated that bird. I was glad to leave it behind when we moved on.

We also became enamored with the magnificent butterflies that were so beautiful. Karen collected them and made a lovely wall hanging out of about 20 different kinds. The most beautiful ones were large, actually much larger in size than our monarchs, and were an incredible iridescent cobalt blue. There were others about the same size, but mostly black with the iridescent blue wide stripes on both wings. There was another, a little smaller, and it was black with multiple brilliant green iridescent stripes and designs. There were solid smaller iridescent blue ones as well as numerous others in varying shades of yellow and white, as well as huge moths that were also lovely.

The jungle contains a beauty all of its own! But one must constantly be on guard against plants and bushes with huge thorns or those that caused rashes. To say nothing of the wild animals and reptiles that seemed to abound everywhere.

Most of our fellow missionaries worked in the small villages around the eastern part of Bolivia. However, there were two couples and one single lady who were linguists, and they were assigned to evangelize an unreached tribe of jungle nomads, the Ayore (pronounced "eye-o-ray"). Actually, this tribe was quite feared by the local villagers because in times gone by, they had killed five New Tribes missionaries and several more Bolivian nationals. The media never picked up on the story, as they did with the Auca of Ecuador. The adults of this tribe were pretty well naked, except for a few strategically placed feathers of jungle birds worn by the men, and woven fiber skirts worn by the women. All women were topless. The children and young people were totally naked.

They also had the shocking custom of burying their first child alive, and when the adults became elderly and no longer able to keep up with the travels of the tribe, they simply laid down in a hole and were buried alive as well. Peter's second book, *Defeat of the Bird God,* was written about Bill and Harriet Pencille and the evangelization of this tribe. Janet Briggs was the single lady who helped reduce their language to writing along with Bill and Harriet, and later Chuck Ramsey and his family as well as John and Phoebe Depew joined forces with them to work on the mission station. John and Phoebe Depew offered to set up a new mission station for a portion of the tribe that had a major run-in with the tribal chief and decided to settle upriver about 20 miles from the first mission station. This was absolutely isolated in the middle of the jungle, between the village of Concepcion and the Brazilian border. Phoebe and I became good friends, and she was the only white woman who had ever been that far into the jungle. When Peter and I were due a vacation one year, I decided that I would go to visit Phoebe, because she had been isolated for months on end.

So, Peter, Karen who was four years old by then, and I decided to go out to the mission station and see what the work among the tribe was like. We flew into Concepcion and were met there by Bill Pencille in his Jeep. Then we struck out to the mission station where Bill and Harriet worked. As I recall it was about a 15-mile drive through the jungle without much of a road. At one point when we were nearing the mission station, Bill had employed some of the Ayore men to help clear the land just a little more for the improvised road to improve a little for the jeep to get through. It was lunchtime and we came upon this group of about 15 men—totally bare naked! They were cooking a great big pot of stew over an open fire, and it was mainly rice and green bananas. The green bananas had turned the stew a brilliant purple color, and Karen was fascinated by it. When it was time to eat, the guys broke off bark from the tree branches and fashioned themselves scoops. Karen had no interest whatsoever in the sandwiches that we had packed but did want to try the purple stew. It is amazing how children adapt! She seemed to take no exception whatsoever to the fact that they were naked and sat down and joined the party, enjoying her purple food very much. The fact that it had just rained and had supplied each of the workers with a free shower meant they were all very clean and shiny. This was our first introduction to the Ayore people group.

Bill told us many stories about befriending and eventually evangelizing the Ayore. I'll just recount two brief ones. He brought donated clothing to the station, and whenever they went to town, Bill insisted that they be clothed. He said that one day he was ready to take some in his jeep, when out of his hut came a man, proud as a peacock, fully clothed in long johns! He thought that he was about as clothed as a person could be!

Another time, Bill had to blow his nose, and the Ayore around him looked very quizzical. They had not seen a handkerchief before, and they asked him what he was saving "that stuff" for when he carefully folded up the handkerchief and put it back in his pocket. I thought that was a hilarious story. Sometimes, indeed, fact is stranger than fiction!

When we arrived at the mission station we were put up for the night in a mud and stick hut, with giggling faces peering in the windows. We had to turn out the lights to get undressed for bed, but I must admit I didn't sleep a whole lot. The next day we struck out on horseback—Peter on one horse and Karen and I on another. We had a guide to lead us along the river to the new mission station and the Depews, somewhere between 20 and 25 miles, I believe.

It was dry season and the river had ceased to flow, but there were pools here and there in the riverbed. We had not taken canteens with us, so we simply drank the water where we found it. When we arrived,

Phoebe had prepared a wonderful duck dinner for us. There was a bit of a hole between the firebox in her small iron cook stove and the oven, so some of the smoke seeped into the oven and gave the duck a fabulous flavor! Phoebe asked where our canteens were so that she could clean them out, and we told her we didn't have any but had drunk the water from the river. Phoebe turned white and got a frightful look on her face. She told us that the Ayore had poisoned all of the water in the pools with a very toxic pod from a certain jungle tree, that would stun the fish that had collected in the pools. They would then harvest the fish and bring them home to dry on wooden racks. This was a source of meat for them. So, it turned out that we had been drinking poisoned water all day long! Strangely enough none of us became ill, nor did we even get a stomachache!

I have been told that the last half of Mark Chapter 16 isn't in the "best manuscripts" of the New Testament. However, we are testimonies of the fact that verses 17 and 18 are certainly very true: "And these signs will follow those who believe: In My name they will cast out demons; they will speak with new tongues; they will take up serpents; *and if they drink anything deadly it will by no means hurt them....*" (emphasis mine). We had a wonderful time together during the rest of our vacation.

Now, back to the family. When Karen was about 18 months old, we decided that we would try to have a sibling to keep her company. However, that was not to be, and I did not become pregnant until the year before we were ready to return back home on our first furlough in 1961. Terms back then were five years long. I had a very difficult pregnancy and I was threatening miscarriage off and on during the first five months. I actually went into labor in my fifth month. We did not have a doctor in town, but one was sent to our village of San Jose as an intern just at the time I had gone into premature labor. Peter got him to our house, and he prescribed some massive doses of vitamin E. He began reciting pages from his medical book on the subject of premature labor, and I was very grateful for his help. My labor pains subsided, and I did not deliver at that time.

By late 1960 our congregation had grown to about 40. I was feeling fine again so when Christmas rolled around, we decided that since it would be our last Christmas with these friends for a while, Peter and I would throw a Christmas Eve party for the whole church. We got lots and lots of beef in the form of steaks and ribs and made a massive fire in our backyard. A couple of the other ladies and I fixed all the trimmings, and we had a wonderful celebration. The beef ribs were roasted over the hot coals after being rubbed down with salt, pepper, garlic, and the favorite spice of many Latin Americans, cumin. They were delicious!

John and Phoebe Depew had just returned from their furlough and were staying in San Jose with us. All during the party and on up until midnight I had what I believed to be some sort of pressure pains, because they didn't feel exactly like labor pains. But about midnight I came to the realization that the baby was going to be born anyway, and it was 10 weeks before her due date in the first week in March. Almost everybody in town was still partying, except the gentleman who ran the local drugstore, who also delivered babies, and we called Phoebe in as well. Ruthie was born at about 2 a.m. on Christmas Day, weighing in at just a hair over 3 pounds. Phoebe bathed and dressed her, and Peter proceeded to bury the placenta in our famous backyard, probably between the whitewashed beehive oven and the vegetable garden.

Check it out the next time you go to buy food— most of the small chickens for sale in the supermarkets weigh over 3 pounds, and Ruth was 19 inches long. She was very, very slender, but had a fierce desire to live. I had no milk, because of my chronic cystic mastitis, but my very close Bolivian friend, Guillermina Mendoza, one of the ladies from church was nursing her one-year-old son and volunteered to devote one of her breasts exclusively for Ruth and use the other one for her Alberto. I fed her for the first few days, maybe a little over a week, with breast milk and an eye dropper until I was able to have some powdered formula sent down from the city of Cochabamba. She then graduated to baby formula and a bottle.

The first afternoon of Ruth's life, I was holding her when she suddenly began to choke. In all probability it was some mucus, but I did not have an aspirator, nor would I have known how to attack the problem. Then she stopped breathing and had turned blue. I just remember grabbing her under the arms and shaking her, screaming, "Breathe, Baby, breathe!" I must have jarred the mucus loose, because she immediately obliged by starting to breathe once again. Or, it might have been God's rapid response to my second healing prayer! We actually did not name her yet because we really liked the name of Ruth and so feared that she might not live. She responded so well that we decided that she had earned the right to her name. The amazing thing was that the first week of her life she lost some weight and got down to 2 pounds and 14 ounces.

Ruth was born in the same bed where she was conceived, and her first crib was a footlocker with a folded-up blanket covered by a pillow-case on the bottom for a mattress. The top of the footlocker was held up with a sawed-off broomstick, and a mosquito net was thrown over the whole thing. Mercifully I had one of the very old editions of Dr. Benjamin Spock's *Baby and Childcare.* In the very back of the book, there was a very short section entitled "Emergency Care for Premature Babies." I understand that portion was not in some other editions of that book. But God provided an edition that contained it for us! It set up a schedule for feeding milk and water, and it also gave instructions on keeping the child warm with hot water bottles. This proved to be a very delicate task and a few times her temperature got up over 100, and one morning it went as low as 91°. It was a question of keeping the hot water bottles filled with warm water and moving them either toward or away from her body as necessary. This went on for only a couple of weeks, but I was up feeding her every hour and a half around the clock. Soon it got to be two hours, then three, but Ruth was a full six months old before I was able to sleep six hours at a stretch. Soon after her birth, she came down with a very serious case of yellow jaundice and was so yellow that she was almost orange. I now know that I should have put her out in the sun, but Dr. Spock didn't tell me that, so she just "gutsied" it out until she got pink again. She was so very cooperative and fought for her life so hard that together we were able to overcome.

However, during those first few days of her life, we did not know if she would make it or not, but we certainly prayed hard that she would. Peter later told me that he was prepared for Plan B, just in case she didn't make it, and he had already picked out boards for her coffin that he himself would build should she die. She was so tiny that I needed to cut a Curity gauze diaper (I would guess they measured about 36" long by maybe 16" wide) into the thirds and fold it several more times to fit her wee frame. I made her a tiny dress fashioned after a dress from a doll of Karen's. One day Peter was holding her on his lap, and I was astonished to notice that her lower leg from her knee to her ankle was just the exact same length and width as Peter's index finger that was held alongside it at the time! But that wouldn't last long.

Once Ruth was over her jaundice, she began eating quite well, and by the time the first week in March rolled around, the date that she should have been born, she weighed an amazing 7 pounds and 10 ounces! I never heard of a preemie gaining weight that quickly! I must confess that occasionally I fed her a smashed banana, because in the days when Karen was a baby, solid food was begun quite early.

My sister Irene gave birth to twins in the late 1940s, a boy and a girl. The boy did not make it, but Laraine lived. She was born in a sterile hospital, immediately cared for by skilled medical personnel, and was in an incubator for a long time. She was kept in the hospital for several months—three, I believe, and was finally released not yet weighing 5 pounds. I am so amazed with Ruth's progress in those early days! She seemed to thrive in spite of the ignorance of her mother, but she certainly responded to love and good intentions and with much prayer from us and many people in the United States who were concerned for her as well.

Peter was able to use the special boards that he had picked out for a coffin for another happier project.

Her little legs seemed quite crooked and weak, and when we finally got back in the States and had her thoroughly examined, we discovered that she probably had deposits of bile left on her brain when she had the jaundice, or so we were told that by the doctor who examined her. We were also told that she might be mentally retarded, and that was quite a blow to hear. That was the best guess of the doctors. We were told that she would probably not walk until she was at least five years old, but once again, beating the odds, she did walk a few feeble steps holding on to things when she was 18 months old and finally walked when she was three, almost four years old. However, she stumbled and fell very frequently and most of the time there were Band-Aids on both her knees and both her elbows. She split her chin open multiple times as well. She spent her first few years looking very thin and, in spite of her eating very well, was not able to get chubby at all—she sort of resembled an Ethiopian child in a time of famine.

We were told to keep her going on a tricycle so that her legs would strengthen, and she greatly enjoyed this until she got bored with it and graduated to a small two-wheel bike with training wheels. However very shortly thereafter she asked to have the training wheels removed and was doing quite well on her two-wheeler. We even found her one day riding her daddy's 28-inch bike with her leg poked under the brace from the handlebars to seat and balance herself somehow. Then, by the time she was in grade school, she asked for unicycle, and mastered that in no time at all. She pretty well outgrew her condition, and people that don't know her history have no idea what she went through in her childhood. She still has to be very careful when she walks, and every now and then an ankle will give out, and she will stumble and fall.

Just as an aside, let me fast-forward to her wedding in 1985. We were members of the very large Lake Avenue Congregational Church in Pasadena, California. The aisle of the main sanctuary where her wedding ceremony was to be held was very long, and Ruth wanted to cover all of her bases, one of which was her fear of turning an ankle and falling while walking down that very long aisle with her dad. She has always been uncomfortable in high-heeled shoes and frequently felt how unstable they were with her condition. She told me that the only footwear she owned in which she was comfortable was her cowboy boots.

As I recall they were gray and would not do as an accompaniment to a white wedding gown. But they did sort of act like ankle braces and made her feel confident and strong. So, I got the bright idea to cover them with white satin. At that time, her sister Karen had a coworker in her hospital whose mother was a seamstress and was able to cover the cowboy boots with some elegant white satin. They looked beautiful, and Ruth marched down the aisle with the assurance that she would do just fine—and she did!

But back to San Jose and 1960!

It was around this time that I suffered a rather unfortunate accident. Way back when we were still in our student days in Pasadena, I was baking a chocolate cake one day, beating the batter with an electric stand mixer. I thought that one of the beaters was falling down, so with the machine still running, I stupidly tried to lift the top lip of the beater back up in place. While pulling my hand back, my right index finger went through the beaters with a click, and it severely bruised my fingernail. Since I had suffered many injuries similar to this in my youth, I didn't think much of it at the time. I did notice that it was very difficult to pull a needle through fabric with that finger and my thumb, for some time.

But one particular day, about four years later, I had a bit of a discipline problem with Karen and gave her a swat on her bottom with my right hand. To my amazement I felt the tip of my index finger break. The next time we traveled up to the city of Cochabamba, I went to see a doctor. When we both looked at the x-ray that he ordered, we saw some extremely large white cells had grown in the broken parts of the bone of my fingertip. Fearing that it might be bone cancer and that it could possibly spread, the doctor suggested that I either get the bone removed, allowing the tip of my finger to sort of flop, or that I get the end of that right index finger amputated to the first joint. I opted for the second choice and had it surgically removed.

The tip of my finger was delivered to me in formaldehyde in a small glass bottle. It was up to me to get it over to the lab for an analysis. On the way over, I recall that Peter and I were in a glass store, purchasing a piece of glass for something or other, and I left the store, inadvertently leaving the glass bottle with my fingertip behind. When I realized what I had done, we quickly return to the store and I asked the owner if he had found a finger. He looked a bit puzzled but when we retraced our footsteps, we found that I had left it in the midst of a display of some sort. After waiting a few days, we went back to the doctor to see what the results might have been. His desk was piled up with three or four huge piles of files and papers and he began looking through them for the lab report. He never did find it, but he assured me that he had read it and that the tissue was benign.

So, we went back to San Jose and I began trying to play the piano and type without an index finger. It took some real doing, but eventually I was able to compensate somewhat, and although not quite as fast and accurate as I was before the amputation, I bungled my way through the projects as best I could. However, not enough of a pad of flesh was left covering the end of the bone, and whenever I accidentally hit it, I got the sensation of a nasty electric shock in my hand. This would be corrected on our first furlough when a bit more of the bone of the second joint was removed and covered much more adequately with a pad of the surrounding flesh. Although still a bit uncomfortable to this day, a half-century later, it's nowhere near as bad as it was at first.

One other incident occurred in the early months of 1960 that was noteworthy. Our mail was a little on the unreliable side—a few things were lost, strayed or stolen over the course of our time in Bolivia. It just so happened that the entire mail system of the whole country went on strike. This particular strike lasted for an entire six months. Mind you, this was in the days before intercontinental telephone calls, e-mails, telegraphs and cell phones. We relied entirely upon the snail-mail postal system and short-wave ham radio for our communication with the outside world. In San Jose there was no newspaper. However, a couple of the missionaries in another part of Bolivia did dabble in ham radio. I don't recall all the details, but I do remember that one of the ham radio guys got the message to pass down to Peter and Doris Wagner in San Jose. The message was: "Your mother has died." The sad part of this was we did not know whose mother had died, and what might've been the circumstances surrounding her death.

It was at least three months later before the strike ended, and much to our dismay, we were told that the stacks of mail in La Paz were so huge that the postal employees simply struck a match to some of the stacks, in order to get rid of some of it. We waited and waited, and somehow got the word that sacks of mail had arrived a few hundred miles down the railroad track in the city of Santa Cruz. Peter, in his desperation, decided to strike out for Santa Cruz in an attempt to hurry the mail along to San Jose. Missionaries in that part of the world were highly trusted individuals, and when Peter inquired about the mail, they simply handed over all of the mail for San Jose that had been left after the fire in a big mailbag. Peter, somewhat resembling Santa Claus with a huge bag on his back, delivered the mailbag to the post office in San Jose. We soon found a letter from Peter's sister Margo telling us that their mother had died very suddenly after contracting pneumonia. She was only 53 years old. So, at least for the time being, after several months of anguish, we were able to grieve over the right person. By the time we arrived home on furlough the next year, Peter's father was happily remarried, and we were able to meet Phyllis, his delightful new wife, who loved him dearly and took excellent care of him until his dying day.

Toward the end of our first term in San Jose, a very frightening occurrence took place in a small city in the Beni called San Joaquin. The philanthropic organization named the Rockefeller Foundation from America decided to make an attempt at eradicating malaria in Bolivia, I am not sure if it was all of South America or not, but we were targeted. They sent teams of workers armed with DDT and sprayers to every single house in the tropics that they could locate. This three-year project was called SNEM, or something like the "national project to eradicate malaria." Our houses were sprayed once a year for three years. When we knew that the sprayers were coming, we needed to pull everything away from the walls and stack it in a heap in the middle of every room, covering it with sheets or canvases or whatever we could find. If pots, pans, tools or the like were left hanging on the wall they were simply sprayed over. The DDT was spread up and down the walls almost all the way up to the very high ceilings that each house had in order to help keep it cool. This was quite a task, but it seemed as though every house that we knew about was sprayed. The object was to target the Anopheles mosquito. The way malaria was spread was through approximately 20% of the mosquitoes infected with the malaria bacteria. The female mosquito would bite the victim, then retreat to a wall in the house, then return and bite a second time. If the mosquito became contaminated with the DDT, it would drop dead before the second bite, and the human being would be spared the disease. From our observation, many people did get malaria but in varying intensities. One of our close coworkers got cerebral malaria when he was a missionary child somewhere, and he suffered severe attacks of high fevers and chills every now and then, as he did all through his life. But very few people seemed to be that severely affected, and we personally did not know anyone who actually died from it.

A strange thing happened in the little city of San Joaquin. Shortly after the homes were sprayed, the cockroaches that seemed to be in an extremely abundant and never-ending supply, began kicking around and dying on the floors of the houses. The cats belonging to the owners of the houses, played with and eventually ate the cockroaches. Then the cats all died. Then an epidemic of hemorrhagic fever broke out. It became so serious that it totally wiped out one third of the population of the city, well over 700 men, women and children. Some of our church members there became ill, but none of them died.

Several nations sent medical personnel specializing in tropical diseases to study the situation. There was one team of doctors from Panama who arrived to help with this study, and one of the team of three also died. As I recall it took over a year for the personnel to figure out the root of the problem. It seems as though that when the cats died, a myriad of mice from the jungle infected with this hemorrhagic fever bacteria overtook the little town and invaded the homes. They fed on the supplies of rice from the recent harvest, and in so doing, urinated on the rice. Unfortunately, this particular bacterium was not killed by cooking the rice. It was the main staple food for the inhabitants. It seemed as though the only way to stop the plague was to get rid of the mice and to keep the rice in a tin container tightly covered.

The large, far-away city of Santa Cruz all pulled together and decided on a possible solution. People who had multiple cats would simply donate them. They filled up an entire DC3 airplane with hundreds, possibly thousands, of hungry cats, and when they got to the city of San Joaquin, they simply opened the door! The cats may have been killed by eating cockroaches infected with DDT but were not harmed by eating the mice that were infected with the hemorrhagic fever bacteria, and the plague was stopped. So much for upsetting the balance of nature! The hemorrhagic fever killed many more human beings than malaria would've killed in a century or two. I never did hear what happened to the SNEM project after that.

During our last few years in San Jose, it became quite apparent that we were needing to make a change in mission boards. The leadership of the South American Indian mission did not quite know what to do with Peter. I believe I am correct in saying that he was the only seminary graduate among the ranks, and his writing urge was beginning to develop. The mission would not allow him to send any of his articles directly to a magazine without their first reading, censoring, and approving the articles. At one time they had held 14 magazine articles in their possession without returning them to him. All of our prayer letters had to be read and approved before they were sent out to our constituency.

But I believe the thing that was the most difficult for us was that the government of the mission was in West Palm Beach, Florida. If we saw a need in a neighboring village and wanted to go over and help in some way, or to hold any evangelistic event, we had to secure permission from West Palm Beach before we were allowed to make the trip. We felt this was a waste of valuable time in some instances. We really enjoyed our coworkers, but felt it was time to move on to a mission with local government in Bolivia. We had traveled around Bolivia a little bit and came to know the people in the Bolivian Indian Mission, (later named the Andes Evangelical Mission) headquartered in Cochabamba. We liked what they were doing and applied for membership. We were accepted and would return to the city of Cochabamba after our furlough.

It was about March 1961, and I had been tutoring Karen through kindergarten and first grade. However, the realization came to Peter and me that Karen's English was minimal, actually, virtually non-existent! There just wasn't anyone around that she could speak English with, because all of her playmates were Bolivians. We feared the fact that she would not be able to carry on a decent conversation with her grandparents! For the next three months we spoke to her in Spanish, and then said the same thing over again in English.

Because we felt that Karen was very bright, we probably started her in school a little early. Since she was born on December 29, it is often a little difficult to know exactly when to start school for a child born that time of year. It turned out that because of her background, she was lacking in some American social skills, and the school decided that it was best to have her repeat first grade. Karen was six years old at the time and was a very happy, sanguine, people person. She was so highly fascinated by being in a classroom of 30 students that she had great difficulty concentrating with so much activity around her. She just did not want to miss out on anything that was happening! On one occasion I went to her classroom to have a parent-teacher consultation, only to find that she was seated in a corner facing the wall! The teacher informed me that this was the only way she was able to concentrate enough to finish an assignment. We always suspected that Karen had a definite sanguine personality, and this certainly confirmed our suspicion. Karen really loved life and wanted to live it to its fullest every single day. Even today, 50 years later, she is that same vivacious, pleasant person, and is usually the one in charge of the parties and potlucks for the employees in the unit at her hospital.

We left Bolivia in June of 1961. We had thoroughly enjoyed our time in San Jose, and it was with mixed feelings that we left. The work that we were doing was very fulfilling, and many of the Bolivian people in our church became very dear friends.

We arrived in West Palm Beach and went through our physical exams as was required by the mission. We passed with flying colors, and as a matter of fact, for the first time in many years I was no longer anemic, probably because my diet was mainly meat, vegetables, and grains.

When animals were butchered in Bolivia, two kinds of meat were sold: meat with bones at one price or meat without bones at another price. When we were living in San Jose, Peter and I became friends with many of the people who owned beef cattle, mainly through his contacts in the Lions Club. These gentlemen would sometimes send a messenger to our home stating that early the next morning they would be butchering an exceptionally healthy, fat animal. If I would send my meat hooks with the messenger along with a piece of paper poked on the hooks indicating which cuts of meat I wanted, they would be saved for me, and all I had to do was pick them up the next morning at my convenience. Bread, usually in the form of rolls, was baked daily at many bakeries around town, so we would often by a few dozen and store them in a tin when my homemade bread had run out. Often for supper we would have a steak sandwich fashioned from the rolls and filet mignon or boneless rib eye steaks. Peter and I sometimes joked with each other as we were dining: "Poor missionaries, nothing to eat but filet mignon!" I don't recall up to that point in time ever having been able to afford filet mignon when I was buying meat. Each of us was declared in excellent health.

As I said before, because the South America Indian Mission did not exactly know what to do with Peter, when we handed the leadership our resignation, it was accepted within a matter of hours, and probably with quite a sigh of relief.

What did I learn from our first term as missionaries? I learned that we were cut out to be missionaries and loved learning a new language and culture and dearly loved our new friends. I learned that missionaries are definitely not all saints but that we all have some flaws that need working on. I learned that God protects us even in the most hostile and dangerous surroundings and that we can fully depend on Him to provide for us and to see us through the most trying circumstances, such as when our baby Ruthie was born at the end of the road in the jungle. I learned that not everyone understood Peter and some didn't know how to handle his brilliance and felt more comfortable excusing themselves from it, but that was just our superiors. We adored our new-found Bolivian friends and the adventures of jungle living. We praise God for sparing the lives of all four of us time and time again. We are thankful for the many occasions when we saw the snakes and other scary things in time to get out of harm's way, but what I want to know when I get to heaven is how many other times there were occasions of grave danger that we never knew anything about. My guess is there were many other times when God shut the mouths of hungry jaguars or snakes while we just went our happy ways and walked right by them. Peter and I became even closer than ever before, and we continued to work together and loved it. God gave grace to lose Peter's mother without being able to say goodbye, but we learned how to take tragedy in stride and keep moving on. We learned the importance of having mission government on the field in order to move more swiftly and in a targeted manner. We learned how to make do with little and be as happy as ticks doing it. I learned how to deal with my three-month bout of depression and how to overcome it, so I could help other new missionaries get through culture shock. And I could probably write a whole other chapter of things we learned and became richer for them, but enough said.

CHAPTER 7

The Move To The Andes Evangelical Mission

How we did enjoy seeing our family again and spending the summer and working on the farm with my folks, whom we adored! After visiting friends and the extended family, we moved again and settled down in Princeton, New Jersey, where Peter attended Princeton Theological Seminary in order to earn a Master of Theology degree. Princeton, New Jersey, is a delightful city—maybe a bit snooty, but delightful! It is the home of Princeton University as well as Princeton Theological Seminary. At that time, it had quite a high rate of millionaires living there. Most of them commuted into New York City for their day jobs. Just a little over a block from our new home was a modest, white wood-framed house with a historical landmark sign in the front stating that it had been the home of Albert Einstein in his lifetime.

We secured some totally furnished housing—a lovely two-bedroom apartment right on the seminary campus that had been set aside for returning missionaries, mainly Presbyterians. We became dear friends of a Cuban Presbyterian couple, and it was the wife who taught me how to make a mean chicken and rice dish, *"arroz con pollo."* That was an enormous family treat, and we looked forward to it with great anticipation in the days before both Peter and I became diabetics and unable to eat much rice. I have had to learn how to alter rice recipes a little, so that the protein and vegetable components are greatly increased and the rice is greatly diminished.

Peter dug into his studies with great gusto. The topic of his thesis was "The Marian Theology of Thomas Aquinas." I spent the year as a housewife, caring for Karen and Ruth by day, and cooking, cleaning, shopping and running the household. It was a wonderful time of relaxation for me. The occasional visit to family and old friends was quite a treat. We made a trip back to California to visit our dear friends at Bell Friends church.

After some packing, including a gas stove complete with an oven that was a gift from some friends and an electric refrigerator, as well as an electric washing machine, and saying a final set of goodbyes, we headed back to Bolivia in early October of 1962. We dearly loved the Bolivian people and by then our Spanish had become quite acceptable. We were excited to return to our adopted land although our living conditions would be very different from that of the jungle.

For starters, our new home was perched 8400 feet high in the high valleys that were the foothills of the Andes. Our second-floor apartment overlooked the garage that belonged to the mission. Missionaries who owned vehicles parked them there at night and walked back to their quarters, a couple of blocks away. The houses were so old that they were built way before the invention of the automobile! Consequently, there were no entryways or garages attached to each house, nor was one allowed to park a vehicle on the street overnight. The city, as well as many of the old stone houses, was 400 years old!

Peter's office was a third-floor kind of a penthouse over the bedroom of our second-floor apartment. The view from his north windows was spectacular and included a 17,000-foot snow covered peak named

Tunari (pronounced two-nar-ee), as well as some of the city and foot-hills leading to the peak.

There was also a large mechanic shop downstairs and the mechanics hired by the mission would work on the cars as necessary. The property also contained a second two-story building inside the main patio, which housed either another missionary couple or a single lady. That building was later turned into the mission office and a storeroom for the mission bookstore. There was also an apartment downstairs from ours that housed another missionary couple.

The climate was absolutely delightful. It was in the mid-70s by day dropping to a comfortable 65 by night. It took us a little while to become accustomed to the altitude. The oxygen was a little thinner and occasionally when scurrying about, or running upstairs, we would become winded. But that would not last too long.

We now were able to enjoy a daily newspaper, an indoor toilet and bathtub, and well-stocked stores. We did not have hot water, but there were electric heaters that could be submerged in a bathtub or a washing machine, and the water was hot in no time. Drinking water had to be boiled, and all fresh fruits and vegetables had to be thoroughly cleansed with an iodine solution. However, the selection of fruit and vegetables was wonderful, and I was able to use more of my cooking skills due to the wide variety of ingredients that I was able to find. I could get fresh lamb, beef, pork, poultry, and occasionally, even beautiful lake trout from Lake Titicaca. We really enjoyed the local sheep cheese, and the market contained stalls of beautiful flowers. There were many wonderful, imported staples, including olives, many different kinds of pasta, as well as the locally grown mounds of potatoes, carrots, beets, onions, garlic, squash, and dried potatoes, lentils, beans, quinoa, and many other grains.

We were soon put to work and became extremely busy with Peter preaching, teaching Sunday School, helping to edit a local Christian magazine, becoming president of the inter-mission group of Cochabamba, and both of us soon teaching in our Bible school. I began leading the Bible school choir and also became involved with teaching a woman's Sunday school class and various other activities in the mission and church. I was given the responsibility of overseeing a large correspondence school that soon grew to over 700 students. I did have a helper from the Bible school to help me grade the papers and prepare various mailings.

Our baggage arrived quite quickly this time, but unfortunately had been broken into and thoroughly ransacked. We lost a lot of our clothing and household items, but the important things were pretty well replaceable, although expensive.

Peter made a trip somewhere, I can't remember where or why, but Ruth and I were left alone while Karen attended missionary children's boarding school, taught in English, and as I recall it was about 8 miles outside of the city. Ruth was a toddler at the time, although she couldn't toddle very well, but she certainly could creep up a storm. Our kitchen was located off of the little outdoor patio, just a few steps from our living room. I recall having someone make a chicken wire fence, so that I could keep Ruth close to me at all times, because there were cement steps at the end of the patio, which led to a landing that contained my storeroom, and a tiny bedroom for the lady who was our live-in help.

One day it had rained, and Ruth had crept next to a little puddle that had accumulated on the patio. She began sipping some of the dirty water, and I immediately swooped her up, and put her in a safer, dry place. That evening she began to vomit and came down with a dreadful case of vomiting and diarrhea, a dysentery to be sure. I called the pediatrician who worked just a couple of blocks from our home. By then Ruth had quickly become seriously dehydrated. He came over and attempted to give her a dextrose drip in her vein that would rehydrate her. We almost lost her! I recall standing over her crib trying to comfort her while he was trying to find a vein. Ruth was so far gone that she did not even resist the needle pokes or cry any longer, and I feared for her life! He was using the tiniest needle he had, that was ordinarily used for veins in the head of an infant, he told me.

We both knew that it was a matter of life and death and that he had to keep trying in order to save her life. I was sending up some very agonizing prayer, of "Please God, help him find a vein!" It took 28 pokes of the needle before he was able to locate a vein. There was a great sigh of relief when we were finally able to get Ruth hydrated a little. One of the new missionaries, also a nurse, who had just arrived from Australia, offered to stay up with Ruth and hold her arm all night long, while she was being rehydrated. I was emotionally worn out and accepted her kind offer. I did go into her bedroom several times, and it was fun to watch her bounce back. Her eyes opened and soon she was smiling and chattering. I don't recall if she was given other medication or antibiotics of some sort, but I imagine there must have been something in that drip to kill the bacteria.

We never found out what the name of her disease was, although it might've been cholera or some other form of dysentery, which was a very common disease among small children in Bolivia and many died. The infant mortality rate in Bolivia at that time was over 50%. It was considered an enormous victory when the child lived through his or her first year. I recall that in my darkest hour of this ordeal, I was wondering what I would do with her body should she die. It even crossed my mind that I might disobey local law that stated that a body had to be buried within 24 hours of expiring. I thought I might wrap it in a blanket and put it in my refrigerator until Peter got home in a couple of days, so that he could be at her funeral. But happy days soon reappeared, and this was an ordeal of the past, praise God!

We were very busy with the Bible Institute. Peter was teaching more than a full load, enjoying every minute of it because his main gifting was in the area of teaching. In 1963, however, he developed some sort of a cyst on his neck that had to be surgically removed. We had become good friends with a local Christian surgeon, Dr. Roberto Tardio, and his office was in the same building as the hospital where Peter would spend the night after the surgery. Just a few hours after waking up, he suddenly went into what the nurses and his surgeon called "a total collapse." He had lost his vital signs—his heart stopped beating, and he stopped breathing. Dr. Tardio was just opening his door to say goodbye to a patient when the nurse screamed for him from the patio below, and he came dashing downstairs to Peter's bedside. He went to work immediately with some adrenaline shots and giving artificial respiration and got Peter back again! That was a very close call, and the surgeon admitted it.

That meant that thus far in the short time we had been in Cochabamba we came within a whisker of losing both Ruth and Peter. But there's more.

When Ruth was a about two and a half years old, we decided to take her to the city of La Paz to see if they could determine how seriously injured her brain was. There were some brain specialists in La Paz who could administer an electroencephalogram, and this would help us with a diagnosis. Karen stayed at the boarding school, and we took Ruth and climbed on a bus for the 12-hour drive through the Andes.

The mountainous scenery is spectacular to say the least, although the road was very narrow and not paved, and there was a lot of traffic, including very large semi-trailer trucks and huge buses carrying people to and fro. The buses each contained a "copilot" who would jump out the door each time the bus came to a hairpin curve, and with his hands direct the driver how to maneuver the treacherous corner. Since I was seated by the window, I would often look down and not see any road at all because we were so close to the edge. The only seat available on that drive where all three of us would fit was directly over the rear dual wheels. Unfortunately, there was not much legroom for me because of the big metal curve that was over the wheels. To top it all off, there was a hole in that metal and when we hit really dusty spots in the road, the dirt and dust would find its way up through the hole and give us a little shower.

I recall having taken that bus ride once before and remembered well that late in the afternoon the bus stopped at a roadside inn where the passengers could get out, use the bathrooms, clean up a little, and order supper. This usually happened about 5:30 in the afternoon. The inn was located at the beginning of the Altiplano, the extremely high flat plains, before dropping down into the city of La Paz. The Altiplano ranges between 12,000 and 13,000 feet above sea level. We were weaving in and out of treacherous mountains from early morning until about 5:30 in the afternoon.

Then I noticed something strange, because I was sitting by the window. Once we arrived at the Altiplano, we were able to pick up speed and travel along at about 60 miles an hour, I would guess. Then I saw us approaching the inn, which happened to be on my side of the road, we sped right by it! We finally came to a stop down the straight road. The driver notified us that the air pressure hose had somehow developed a leak and we had totally lost the air brakes! I often wonder exactly where it had broken and how long some angel of the Lord who was dispatched to save our lives had to hold it together until we got to a safe place. I really believe in angels, whom God sends to do His bidding.

We had to wait for quite some time until another bus was sent from the company in La Paz, to reload all of the passengers and their baggage and take them down into the city, another thousand feet below the Altiplano, in the beautiful basin that houses the city. It is one of the most picturesque cities in the world, with the city in the basin, and the gorgeous snowcapped Mount Illimani (pronounced Ill-ye-mahn-ee) standing at a majestic 21,122 feet high, overlooking the city. We did not mind the wait at all, because we were in a safe warm place well supplied with food, drink, chairs and a restroom. It gave us a little time to sit and contemplate what might've been and how good God is. So that made another close call for both Peter and Ruth, but this time for me as well.

After completing the electroencephalogram, we were informed that Ruth was not at all mentally retarded, as we feared she might be. That was all that we needed to know for the time being. We headed back to Cochabamba to pick up our duties.

About a year later it seemed as though she began stumbling more and more, and her knees appeared to be bowing backwards at times. Peter and I decided to get a more accurate reading on her and wanted to see if there was anything that we could do to help her.

Since both of us had maintained our permanent residence in New York State, and had voted by absentee ballot in every major election that was held, we were still considered bona fide residents of New York, but living in a foreign country. So, we were qualified to take Ruth to the New York State Children's Rehabilitation Center in Buffalo, New York, for a free diagnosis. In late June, Karen, Ruth and I flew to Buffalo, New York.

By then I was pregnant with our third daughter, Becky, due to arrive in October. Peter's sister, Margo, who happened to live in Buffalo at the time, graciously invited us to stay with her and her family while we were undergoing the medical evaluations.

It took us two months to undergo all of the examinations and lab work as we were attending the center twice a week. When it was all over, the diagnosis was that Ruth indeed did have a mild case of cerebral palsy, she might possibly outgrow much of it, although there was no guarantee, and she was of high average intelligence. It was felt that braces on her legs might keep her from fully developing her potential and that we would just have to put up with her falling so that she would learn to compensate on her own. This was very good news! We then got her fitted with some special shoes and headed back to Bolivia. Oh yes, and by the way, the Jewish doctor who was in charge of Ruth's case admitted that it was a miracle that she was alive and that she did not have a hopeless case of cerebral palsy!

So, since nothing more could be done for Ruth at the time, I decided to hightail it back to Bolivia so that our baby could be born there. It just so happened that Margo was working for an obstetrician at the time. He graciously gave me some pills that would keep me from going into labor because I was only a few weeks away from delivering the baby. He joked that we certainly didn't want the baby born high over Ecuador. He gave me a letter of some sort, as I recall, just in case it was needed, told me to wear a long loose coat, to get my return booked as soon as possible, and get on my way.

As soon as I could, I wrote Peter with all of these details, telling him that I would arrive back in Cochabamba one week later. However, with the mail system as unpredictable as it was, he never got the letter! But he did happen to be at the airport to meet that very plane because someone else from the mission would be traveling on the same plane's last leg from La Paz to Cochabamba. He nearly fainted when Karen, Ruth and I deplaned. Once reunited with Peter, Karen said to me, "Mommy, this is the best place in the whole world!" The letter arrived a couple of days later!

I went back to my obstetricians, a Yugoslavian couple who were somehow able to flee the Nazi invasion of Yugoslavia during World War II. I was told that all was well, and Becky obliged by arriving a few days late. I recall that I went into labor on the morning of October 7, 1964. My obstetricians were being so careful with me they closed their office down for the day and both accompanied me to the hospital. Peter desperately wanted to be present for the birth of our child and was promised that when the time came, he would be allowed in the delivery room, although this was very unusual at the time.

I ran into a complication just as I was about to deliver. The wife of the obstetrical team was checking the baby's heartbeat when she let out a scream and called her husband. The heartbeat had dropped drastically. They both went to work and delivered Becky with forceps, having to cut the cord that had gone around her neck two times! When I first laid eyes on her I thought for sure that she was dead because her little head looked black, she had been strangled so severely. She did not cry, and they gave her artificial respiration. She finally let out a whimper, then a cry! I cannot help but feel fortunate that the problem was caught in the nick of time and that her life was saved. So,

Becky entered the distinguished ranks of our family members who had almost lost their lives.

When Peter found out that Becky was born without his being present, he was furious! I finally did get him calmed down, telling him what a close call it had been, and he survived quite well, but let us all know how disappointed he was.

Becky was a very happy child. She was very easy to raise and was always smiling. Her big sister Karen, then ten years old, so enjoyed having a real-life doll to play with. I found all three of the girls one day playing church, all dressed up in hats, gloves and heels, Karen holding Becky, clutching on to hymnbooks, and singing in their little chairs. I just can't remember if they were singing in English or Spanish.

Ruth had grown very strong in her arms, sort of compensating for her weak legs. She sometimes would slide down the pipe banister from her daddy's office in our third-floor penthouse, and she occasionally would swing like a monkey from the pipe. She loved to climb.

Because our apartment was on the second floor, and by this time I was the proud owner of a washing machine, I did our laundry and hung it from my second-floor kitchen window on a pulley clothesline extending to the other building in the patio. Ruth was toddling around the kitchen keeping me company. I had just picked up the laundry basket when quick as a flash Ruth climbed up on the chair by the open window and leaned out. By the time I dashed to the window, I just caught her by the heel as she was falling out. Another half step and I would not have made it in time to save her.

Our ceilings were very high and consequently our second floor was very high above the first floor. My guess is the fall would've been a good 20 feet onto the cement driveway below had the good Lord not enabled me to get there in just the nick of time. Once again, I had to breathe a prayer of thanksgiving to the Lord for sparing her life. When we moved into the apartment, one of my very first tasks was to hire a carpenter to make screens with a couple of high hooks each for all of our casement windows. It was not to keep the bugs out, since we had very few bugs in Cochabamba, but it was to keep the kids in!

We saw many interesting things from those windows. The walls of the building that faced the street were very thick, between 1 1/2 and 2 feet, I would guess. These thick walls were very handy at times. The windows and doors were set back in, flush with the inside walls of the building. They all had built-in metal bars to keep intruders out. Since the homes were made of adobe, bricks or poured cement, house fires were virtually nonexistent, so sealed off windows using bars were the norm.

Bolivia has always been a land of many revolutions. At the time of our tenure there, Bolivia had more revolutions than years of independence! We had to be very careful to stay inside when there was shooting out on the street, but there was one occasion when things began to get nasty as we were walking home from a meeting at church. We were being accompanied by fellow missionary, Peter Savage.

While we were just a half block from our front door, a group of shouting university students came running down our street, followed by a military truck with soldiers on the back, who were firing live bullets over the heads of the students. We could hear the zing of the bullets flying just over our heads. The three of us were walking on the sidewalk but made a quick decision to start running furiously toward our front door. My Peter outran us with the door key stuck in his hand and quickly opened it expecting us to be right behind him. But in the meantime, Peter Savage had grabbed me and pushed me into one of the deeply indented doorways, and we both stood plastered against a neighbor's door until the students and the truck, complete with machine guns, had passed by. We were only a few doors from home, and Peter was quite dismayed when he turned around and saw that we were not running right behind him. When all of the hullabaloo ceased, it was then safe for Peter Savage and me to finish our walk home!

On October 9, 1967, the then-president of Bolivia, Rene Barrientos, had given the order for Che Guevara who had been captured in the southern jungles of Bolivia, to be killed. The newspapers claimed that he had died in a shootout with the army. A few days later, an army truck carried a coffin through the streets under our window, and we were told that it was the body of Che Guevara heading back to Cuba. I recall that the sunlight hit the casket just right and there were massive amounts of flies swarming around it. We now know that it must have been the body of someone else, because Che was buried in a mass grave near the airstrip of the southern city of Vallegrande.

Years later, in 1997, Felix Rodriguez, a former Cuban defector, was working for President Barrientos at the time in the field of intelligence. He had carried the orders for the execution of Che Guevara from President Barrientos to the army in the south. He revealed that he had been present at the burial and also disclosed the exact spot where the burial place was located. Indeed, the mass grave of seven bodies was located and Che's bones were exhumed and sent back to Cuba. His skeletal remains were quite easily identified because at the time of his death both hands had been cut off and sent to Argentina for positive identification since he was originally from Argentina and the government had his fingerprints on file. After positive identification, the hands were sent to Cuba and probably got reunited with the rest of his skeletal remains in 1997.

It was just a short time later that President Barrientos was killed when his helicopter struck some electrical wires and brought it down in flames. His body was brought to the city of Cochabamba, his hometown, and we were standing in the main plaza as his casket was carried into the main cathedral. There was some mass hysteria taking place, and the casket was jostled about quite a bit with people trying to touch it. We feared that it might fall to the ground, but fortunately it did not, even though it did get tossed around pretty severely. Only a few months before, during the Evangelism in Depth effort, President Barrientos was invited to one of the functions, and Peter got to shake his hand.

On another occasion President Charles de Gaulle from France was a state visitor to Bolivia and also came to the city of Cochabamba. His motorcade passed very close to our home, and a couple of friends and I were able to see him pass by and wave to him.

These were a few of the sights and sounds witnessed from our window and the neighboring street. Getting back to the inside of our front door and patio....

Ruth was very fascinated by the mechanic shop, and when she was allowed downstairs near the shop, she was underfoot and taking in all she saw. One day she made-believe that she was fixing her little bicycle chain. She picked up the bicycle, tipped it upside down so that it was resting on the handlebars and seat, and proceeded to turn the wheels as fast as she could. Then somehow, she got her right hand caught in the chain and it cut off the tips of her two middle fingers. One of them was cut through the fingernail and I thought had broken the bone, and the other tip was severed and dangling. I immediately called the same pediatrician who had saved her life previously. Naturally it was siesta time (when everything closed down from 12 until 2 for lunch and a rest), and by quite a miracle I was able to get him on the phone. He told me to wrap it up in clean cloths and meet him at the hospital right away, which we did. He gave her a couple of whiffs of the ether, cleaned out all of the bicycle chain black grease, and sewed it back together as best he could. When he gave her back to me, he said he was guaranteeing nothing, but that he did his best. To this day, 50 years later, some very slight scarring is visible, if you look hard enough. Her fingers are totally intact, there is no malformation of those fingers, and she is able to use them normally!

At the time, Bolivia was quite an underdeveloped nation. If an individual wanted to attend university, there were not a whole lot of subjects that one could major in. As a result, even though there were not very many people who were turned out with degrees in fields such as science, engineering or agriculture, excellent doctors and lawyers were graduated in abundance, and competed for patients and clients. We had excellent medical care in Cochabamba, but when we lived in the jungle there was not a doctor to be found!

When the director of our mission, Joe McCullough, left for furlough, the direction of the mission was handed over to our field council. One of the perks was that he also handed over to us the keys to his eight-passenger van. This meant that we had to undertake the task of getting our Bolivian driver's licenses. This turned out to be quite an adventure!

There were three parts to the driver's test. Since the city of Cochabamba was over 400 years old, the streets were extremely narrow because they had been constructed for oxcarts, horses and donkeys. Consequently, all the streets of the whole city, excepting for a few wide boulevards, were all one way. The first part of our driver's exam was to memorize the name of every street and to be able to tell the examiner if it went from south to north, west to east, north to south, east to west or diagonally. When the cities were originally built in Bolivia, they were all laid out exactly north and south, east and west, mercifully! So, it's pretty easy to tell directions in the cities and villages. There was another part to the exam that I don't quite remember, but I do remember that I had to be quite familiar with the driver's manual. The only problem was that there were none to buy, and I don't even recall how we finally found one, but somehow we did!

The second and third parts of the driver's tests were open to the public and became quite a spectacle. We all had to get ourselves down to the local graveyard, where there was a paved circle at the entrance. There were numerous cars, buses and trucks parked around the circle. When your turn came, your vehicle was measured from bumper-to-bumper and one extra meter was added to the space between two vehicles, the front one being a wide vehicle and the one behind your vacant parking space being a narrow car. You were given three opportunities to parallel park on that circle with the tires of your vehicle no more than approximately 30 centimeters, or a foot, from the curb. If you did a good job, there was great applause from the crowd, or a corresponding groan for a bad job! Peter had taught me how to parallel park very well, and I got that sucker placed perfectly the first time. This all made very good sense because parking was at a great premium around the city, and when a parking spot was found, it was a good idea to whip into it quickly.

The third part of the driver's test was to head up the steep hill to a monument overlooking the city of Cochabamba. There was a statue of some women on top of the monument, because during the battle of Cochabamba for the liberation of the city from the Spaniards, the women of the city played an important part. There were stones placed in the middle of the road and this created a very narrow, passable part in the road. It was the job of the student to drive his or her vehicle to the place where the stones ended, and then to back down around several sharp curves without touching a stone or running off the pavement. This exam made a great deal of sense and showcased the student's ability to back up accurately. It was because the dirt roads of the incredibly mountainous Andes were very narrow. When you met an oncoming car, and you were headed uphill, it was the vehicle heading downhill that had the right-of-way. It was up to you to back up carefully until you found a place in the road wide enough for both of you to safely pass, and at times, it was a mighty long backward drive.

The roads that we traveled between the cities of Santa Cruz, Sucre, Cochabamba, and La Paz, were extremely dangerous and visibility was dismal. There were no guard rails. At the time we were living in Cochabamba, the only paved road in the whole nation was between Cochabamba and Santa Cruz. Then, even at that, part of it went through an extensive rain forest that never dried out enough to be paved. It was full of rockslides, big muddy holes, and never saw the sunshine, and it was usually raining or misting. Frequently one was driving in a cloud resembling a thick fog because of the altitude.

Once we were able to buy a car for ourselves, we always went with the Volkswagen Bug because they were so reliable and light enough for all the passengers to push out of a mud hole should the occasion arise. We have frequently driven through huge deep mud puddles, especially in the city of Santa Cruz, and later looked at our headlights, noting that the muddy water had just about covered them completely. They were noble, even if a bit ugly! And they were very easy to parallel park in a tight spot while other longer vehicles had to keep searching for a parking place.

Along all of the major roads, which as I mentioned above had no guardrails, there were grim reminders of bad accidents, and these came along very frequently, usually on curves. They were groupings of white, wooden crosses, many with names painted on them, indicating how many people had died in a particular accident at that spot. Often human beings would travel on the backs of open trucks, and when these rolled down a mountainside there were rarely any survivors.

I saw a special on the Travel Channel last year about "Death Road." This is the road that goes from the city of La Paz down to the garden area called the Yungas. It is particularly steep and has many dangerous curves dug out of the mountain. A new road has been in the process of being built for quite some time, but it is an extremely difficult project. While I was checking the Internet for the height of Mount Illimani, I ran across a slideshow with the topic of this "Death Road." You might want to check it out if you're interested. There are many enormous trucks that travel along this narrow road carrying lumber and produce, such as bananas, fruit, yucca, and other vegetables up to La Paz, or other goods down to the Yungas. What makes it especially dangerous is that there are so many very narrow, blind curves. Some of the local residents have taken to helping the travelers, in an attempt to cut down on the accidents. They will stand at the blind curves with signs in the form of big circles about 2 feet across, painted either red or green, indicating when it is safe for people to navigate the curve. They do this all day long just for tips. We have found so many of the Bolivian people to be especially kind. And with this I will conclude the tales of our driving adventures in Bolivia.

One of the events that we enjoyed so very much was the World Vision Pastors' Conference which was held in Cochabamba in February of 1965, when Becky was just four months old. Peter had been named

National Coordinator of this event. His job was to pull together every Bolivian pastor in the nation to meet with the folks from World Vision in preparation for the yearlong event called Evangelism in Depth. The only trouble was that there was not a venue that could house and provide meals for the expected 800 pastors as well as an adequate meeting space. We decided that drastic steps had to be taken quickly, so we borrowed our missionary children's school and the Bible school across the road. We erected a temporary meeting hall on the soccer field of the school and put up a temporary kitchen with eight places for cafeteria lines that would take care of 100 people each. I don't recall what we did for dorms (probably local churches opened their sanctuaries and folks slept on the floors). When everything was over, the slightly used materials were sold to help meet expenses.

Over 800 pastors showed up and everyone had a fabulous time, because it was the first time that we really saw how big the church had grown. Some of the old-time missionaries who had labored so many years with so little fruit burst into tears when they saw one of the trains arrive with 400 pastors. Buses came from every corner of the country where there were roads and many flew in from outlying areas in the jungle. Dr. Paul Rees, vice president of World Vision, was the main speaker and there were several other international inspirational speakers as well. We had a wonderful time and within a week after the event the kids could play soccer once again. It was a very fulfilling experience, although a difficult and demanding job. Peter pulled this off masterfully with a lot of volunteer help from local churches.

Vacation time had come, and we decided that we would leave baby Becky with one of our dear friends for a few days and visit Machu Picchu in Peru. Karen was ten and Ruth was four years of age. Ruth was able to walk off and on, holding on to someone's hand, and we felt that she would be able to get around Machu Picchu, with one of us carrying her when she needed it. We drove up to the city of La Paz, and then crossed Lake Titicaca, the highest commercially navigable body of water in the world on a white ferry boat. As a matter of fact, it is extremely deep, and varies from 360 feet deep to 930 feet deep! Huge, beautiful lake trout are harvested from its cold, clear water. The steamer boat journey was an all-night trip across the huge lake to the city of Cuzco, Peru.

When morning came, we were still quite a way from Cuzco, so Karen, Ruth, and I decided to take a walk on deck. Then a very strange thing happened. While Ruth was grabbing the railing, looking over the lake, the railing gave way, and she swung out over the lake! It's a good thing that she had very strong arms and was used to swinging down railings like a monkey! She just hung on for dear life dangling over the water, until Karen and I were able to swing her back again and fasten the railing that apparently someone had left unlatched! One more time we seemed to be overworking her guardian angels who were right there to save her yet again.

We went on to tour the city of Cuzco and then boarded a train for Machu Picchu. This is one of the most unbelievable sights of Inca handiwork and ingenuity. From the riverbed it is impossible to see that there is an entire city laid out among the high mountain peaks. It was quite a breathtaking experience to tour the ruins of houses, terraced areas to grow crops, and the huge altars of worship to their gods, which included human sacrifices. I read once that upwards of 70% of the bones excavated were of young women, presumably offered up to the gods. I have seen some travelogues of Machu Picchu since and a great deal of restoration has been accomplished since we visited back in 1965. We thoroughly enjoyed our vacation and headed back to our heavy load of work in Cochabamba.

A few months after that, Ruth had yet one more close call. It was after church on a Sunday morning and the family was outside on the sidewalk waiting for Peter, who had apparently gotten engrossed in a conversation with someone inside. I was holding baby Becky, and Ruth was playing with some of her pals. The sidewalk was quite narrow, and there was a row of parked cars. The entrance to the church was about 50 feet from a very busy corner. As Ruth and her friends were playing tag, Ruth darted out between the cars and into the street just as a taxi came around the corner very fast. I had my eyes on her and let out a bloodcurdling yell. Then a very strange thing happened. Ruth's momentum was carrying her into the street just a few feet from the front bumper of the speeding taxi. I saw an invisible someone literally push her back and up onto the sidewalk, and with such force that her hair flew back from her face! I was totally dumbfounded! I told Peter, when he did appear, that I saw a guardian angel or two at work. We thanked God many times over for this miracle.

Later on, that year, one of Peter's assignments was to write a biography about one of our missionaries who had been recently killed in a light plane crash. His name was Wally Herron. It turns out that Wally was one of the very first missionary pilots in the whole world.

Wally and his wife, Violet, were serving as missionaries in the northern jungle province of Bolivia, called the Beni, in a town called Magdalena. On May 22, 1939, when Violet was due to deliver their first child, the birth was very complicated. In the process she died, but the little baby boy, Robert, lived. Wally was grief-stricken over the fact that he was not able to get his wife out of the jungle and up to a hospital for some decent medical care. He decided that he wanted to become a pilot in order to help others who lived in remote areas to be able to receive emergency medical care when the need arose.

Wally went back to his homeland of New Zealand, got his pilot's license, and brought back to Bolivia one of the first small airplanes. He later married Emily, a single missionary who was also a nurse and together and they started a leprosarium some distance out of the town of Magdalena in a place called Lake Victoria. By that time an effective treatment for leprosy was available and many lepers' lives were spared and enriched because of this effort. Wally was highly respected, so much so, he was awarded a medal from the president entitled "The Condor of the Andes." This was in recognition of his humanitarian contribution to the Bolivian people of the northern part of Bolivia.

Shortly after we arrived in Cochabamba, Wally had some business to accomplish in the cities of La Paz and Oruro that involved bringing another plane to the city of Cochabamba. Something apparently went very wrong, and the plane went down on the Altiplano, killing all three passengers aboard. This tragedy occurred on March 7, 1964. Wally had been faithfully serving the Lord for many, many years.

Because his story was so groundbreaking, and because he was so very well known in Bolivia, the mission assigned Peter to write his biography. Peter had traveled around the northern jungles of Bolivia interviewing many people whose lives had been touched by Wally. But then we wanted to make sure that everything Peter wrote was accurate, so it was decided that Peter, Ruth, Becky, and I would spend about a month at the leprosarium where Wally's widow Emily lived. Karen would remain attending her classes at the missionary children's boarding school, where she would be well looked after.

The leprosarium was carved out of the jungle, with a landing strip down the middle. On one side of the landing strip lived the lepers in some very nice housing. On the other side of the landing strip was the missionary housing, and by the time we arrived to visit, there were quite a number of lovely productive fruit trees and other crops growing. Leprosy is only contagious to people who have been in close, prolonged contact with infected individuals. The lepers had to be very careful to take their medication daily.

Peter set about the task of reviewing all of the tapes containing the interviews that he had collected over the past months. There was no electricity, as I recall, and his writing was done on a manual typewriter. His tape recorder was run on batteries.

One thing that I recall very vividly was that the surrounding jungle area contained humongous flocks of fruit-eating bats. They would come out at dusk, and fly in a long stream into the jungle to feed. One evening during our stay there, a flock of bats must have lost its way, or their radar wasn't working very well! There were some vents at the peak of the roof in the house where we were staying, and somehow a large number of them got into our quarters. I felt very much like the children of Israel, but instead of a plague of frogs, ours was a plague of bats. No matter what we moved during the day, it seemed as though a bat was sleeping behind it! Some were in the oven of the iron kitchen stove, others were behind mirrors, and every nook and cranny they could find on the wall had been invaded. They weren't harmful at all, it's just that whenever something was moved, a bat flew out and sometimes flew toward you and whacked your body. The jungle also contained many vampire bats that would feed off of the blood of cattle, dogs, wild beasts, or whatever else they could find. But these invading bats were just harmless fruit eaters.

In the jungle lowlands, a phenomenon occurs that causes the weather to change very drastically in a short period of time. It is usually when a strong south wind picks up from the Antarctic, and the ensuing rainstorm is quite cold. The temperature can drop 20° in as many minutes. This part of the jungle is ordinarily very hot. Once the rainstorm is over and the sun comes out again, the steam begins to arise from the earth and the plants, and you know you are in for a hot time in the next few hours. The storm is a *sur,* meaning "south," because the wind always comes from the south.

One day, after one of the strong storms had passed by, and the sun came out, I thought it would be a good idea to make a very large container full of lemonade, especially for Peter who would be writing furiously, because we knew we were in for a scorcher. I went outside to a nearby rather small lemon tree that was loaded with lemons. However, the strong wind had knocked several dozen of the very ripe ones on to the ground. My mother taught me never to be wasteful, and I recall standing there pondering which lemons I should gather. I finally decided the best thing to do was to pick up the lemons from the ground, because they would probably be the ripest ones anyway.

I had gathered a few dozen in my apron which I held by the corners to form a pouch. I stood up straight underneath the tree and for some reason looked straight up. There, about 4 inches from my nose was the belly of an enormous snake draped across the lower branches! It looked as though it was four or five inches in girth. I don't know which end was the head, and which end was the tail. I got a good look at a couple of feet of its middle! But I do know that I let out a scream and dashed into the house without losing a lemon from my apron. I always wonder what might've happened if I had chosen to pick the lemons from the tree and had my hand or my head up among the branches...

We had another incident that was noteworthy during our month at the lake. There was a girl I had hired to do our laundry in the lake. One day I decided to take the girls down to the lake and stay very close to the shore because I knew there were piranha in the lake. One of the lepers had previously caught quite a string of these fish and given them to us. Once they were fried, they were safe to eat. The fish are only about 9 to 10 inches long and are very bony, by the way. Their danger lies in their huge numbers and once they know that blood is around, they go into a feeding frenzy, devouring whatever is bleeding with their razor-sharp teeth in a matter of minutes, if not seconds. It is not wise to go into these waters with an open sore.

But this particular morning, as I was playing with the children, the girl who accompanied us to the dock suddenly lifted her head and said one word: "Sucuri!" That means "anaconda." I asked her how she knew there was an anaconda nearby, and she said she could smell it. We never stayed around long enough for me to learn what that smell was like. We never saw it and didn't know exactly where it was. Someday, when we get to heaven, I am going to ask the good Lord how close we came to danger or even death, and never knew about it, because we were protected from it. I'm sure that there are multitudes of these incidents.

It took Peter about a month to write the book and Emily would read it chapter by chapter, making necessary corrections. It was a wonderful time. In June of 1966, Peter signed a contract in the name of the mission with Fleming Revell, and the book was entitled *The Condor of the Jungle.*

The entire year of 1965 was spent in the campaign that brought together all of the Protestant missions in the nation. This was called Evangelism in Depth, and the headquarters was located in the then-vacant apartment downstairs from ours. We spent the entire year with various evangelistic campaigns, including many large musical events in which I was involved. There was a major attempt to include everyone somehow, and the flurry of activities was almost overwhelming at times. But it seemed to be very rewarding.

After the Evangelism in Depth program was completed, we continued on with a very heavy load of activities, the Bible School, evangelism, teaching our adult Sunday School classes, working on our local Christian magazine, my large correspondence school, and various musical and evangelistic events.

In July of 1966, the McCulloughs left for their furlough back in the States. At that time Peter was named as Assistant Director of the mission. As I recall, we had about 115 missionaries in Bolivia and had expanded to include a Bible school in Lima, Peru. This is when our job began to get difficult. These 115 missionaries came from seven different countries: USA, Canada, England, Australia, New Zealand, Germany, and Jamaica. It was at that time that some pretty strong anti-American feelings rose to the surface. Many people had been members of the mission for a far longer time than we had and resented Peter's appointment as Assistant Director. The rest of our tenure with the mission was not as pleasant as it had been because we were feeling rejection on the part of many. However, we plugged away doing our assignment as best we could.

Peter was able to move his office to the empty apartment in the second building of our patio, and the office of the mission moved there as well. He was assigned a secretary, Judy Kunkle, a delightful young lady from Canada. Things moved along quite well for a few months. Then Judy decided to marry a Bolivian man and left the mission rather suddenly. That left Peter without anyone to type a letter. He asked me to help him. I remember having signed an agreement when we first joined the mission. The agreement stated that I "would take an emergency assignment on a temporary basis if requested to do so." I could type quite well. I proved to be rather valuable because I could transcribe his dictated documents in either Spanish or English.

It was sort of like being farmers again but this time in the big city, working side by side as a couple. Little by little I had to let some of my other duties go. The day came when I finally had to make a choice between my many musical activities or helping Peter. It was because the emergency assignment had become rather permanent, and I was greatly enjoying working side by side with him again. So, I cut way back on the music—it was rather an easy choice because of my lost finger. I could no longer play as well as I once did anyway. Because the office was just a few steps from our apartment I never really had to leave home or abandon my children because I was always there, and we had an employee to be with the children at all times. If some sort of an emergency arose, I could take care of the situation in my home and then go back to work when the kids were either napping or after they had gone to bed for the night. I was always available to them.

A few months later, Pam Toomey, a short-term missionary from the United States, arrived on the field, wanting to use her secretarial skills. I don't remember exactly how long she was there, but I do believe it was about 18 months. She taught me how to fine-tune my office skills, and it was a fantastic apprenticeship for me. Pam was very pleasant, and we greatly enjoyed our time together. By that time, we did have three IBM Selectric typewriters, two Dictaphones, and a large electric Gestetner mimeograph machine, which at that time was state of the art. Peter had the ability to be able to keep both of us busy from morning till evening, and we got a great deal accomplished.

We devoted many of our Saturdays to outings with our children, usually visiting the open markets in nearby cities, or taking a picnic up to the mountains. We were able to buy rotisserie-roasted chickens to take along. I spent a great deal of time making homemade potato chips, and we usually added a homemade salad or some corn on the cob when it was in season. Fresh fruit or cookies rounded out our picnic meal. Those were fun times with our girls. Peter always tried to save time for his girls, even though our administrative duties and teaching responsibilities were quite heavy. He was a wonderful daddy.

The McCulloughs returned from furlough in 1967, and it was time for us to leave on our furlough.

I will save the conclusion of what I learned from our first term with the Andes Evangelical Mission stint until our move back to America, at the end of the next chapter, and include that in all our years with the Andes Evangelical Mission, since it is all one ball of wax.

CHAPTER 8

The School Of World Mission And Leaving AEM

Peter, who was never one to be idle or take a prolonged rest or vacation decided to study missiology at his old alma mater, Fuller Theological Seminary in Pasadena, California. Dr. Donald McGavran had recently founded the School of World Mission. He had come out with some groundbreaking teaching in the study and practice of missiology, and Peter wanted to catch up on the latest in the field. So, we returned home, met with family and friends, and headed out to California once again. Peter began his studies in September of 1967.

Housing was provided for us by the dear folks of Bell Friends Church in the neighboring city of Huntington Park. Peter commuted the half hour north to Pasadena for his classes, and we enrolled Karen in seventh grade, in a junior high about a block and a half from home. Ruth was in second grade in an adjoining school just across the street from our home.

At first it was quite a fight to get Ruth enrolled in that second-grade class. I had to secure a note from her doctor from the Buffalo Rehabilitation Center stating that she should not be involved in gym class, but she should be enrolled in all of the other classes with other normal children. We finally prevailed and both girls went off to public school. By this time Karen had grown up to be a very attractive 13-year-old, with beautiful long, platinum blonde hair and blue eyes. The entire city of Huntington Park was rapidly becoming Hispanic, and there was a great deal of Spanish spoken in the school. Of course, Karen understood every word, but never let on that she was bilingual until the last day of class!

The closest grocery store was also just a couple of blocks away so that I could get along without a car during the day. We bought one of those "pull-behind-you" grocery carts that carried all the groceries I needed at once. We had some dear friends in the church who worked in grocery stores or the dairy business, and they supplied us with boxes of baked goods and dairy products on a regular basis. Our dentist friends once again took care of our teeth, and we were incredibly blessed to be able to spend the year with our dear friends at Bell Friends Church.

Peter thoroughly enjoyed his studies, and occasionally, I would be able to sit in on some special events. Peter's Master of Arts degree in missiology was crowned off with a thesis that studied in great detail the growth of the Protestant Church in Bolivia. I remember that Peter had a number of obligations, and that he left me to finish the typing of his thesis and to hand it on the specified day while he was off traveling somewhere.

The very difficult part of the thesis is that there were not yet home copy machines around! We had to type the dissertation with five carbon copies! We were able to get some graphs and charts copied at a friend's workplace, but that was all. I remember copies were dreadfully expensive, over $.10 per chart or graph. Since I was missing part of my index finger, I was not a tremendously accurate typist. So, every time I made an error, I had to erase the five carbon copies. This made it quite a laborious task for the thesis that was over 300 pages long. The night before the dissertation was due, I had to pull an all-nighter, and after the kids were in school, grab Becky and deliver the thesis in its five boxes to Peter's mentor in Pasadena.

Peter graduated in June of 1968 with a Master of Arts in Missiology. At the end of his time there, he was offered a teaching job at the School of World Mission to stay on and teach along with Dr. McGavran. We knew that the teaching offer was a huge honor, but we felt that it was not quite time to leave Bolivia, and that we had to go back and finish up many of the tasks in which we were involved and turn our part of the leadership of the mission in an orderly manner. So, in August of 1968 we returned for our final three years in Bolivia. These proved to be extremely fruitful and beneficial for all concerned.

Shortly after we returned to Bolivia in the summer of 1968, Peter was named Assistant General Director of the mission. He reluctantly agreed to accept this position because he realized that his main spiritual gift was teaching, certainly not administration. He did continue on with a light teaching load in the Bible Institute, which had by then changed its name to the George Allen Theological Seminary after the founder of the Bolivian Indian Mission. The BIM had also changed its name to the Andes Evangelical Mission because we had branched out into Lima, Peru, to a theological seminary there. Two of our well-trained German young couples were assigned to the seminary in Lima.

Karen would've been about eight years old when we first moved to Cochabamba to start work with the Bolivian Indian Mission. I had persuaded a girl named Felicia that used to help me when we lived in San Jose to move up to Cochabamba to help me once again. Karen knew her very well, and she was someone I trusted. She would often care for Karen when I was teaching my classes and would help with kitchen work. We lived only about four blocks from a major, very large farmers market that took place every Saturday. Since it was a pretty day and I needed some vegetables from the market, I told Felicia to take Ruth in her stroller and Karen walking close by down to the market to get the vegetables and come right home. Felicia and Ruth arrived home about an hour later, but Karen was not with her! They had somehow gotten separated in the milling crowd, and she was unable to locate Karen. I ran down to the market like a mad woman, calling her name at the top of my lungs. This went on for what I would guess was the better part of an hour. Once again, I was extremely aware of the fact that little girls were frequently stolen, and we had returned to an area that was very foreign to Karen. Finally, one of the ladies who was selling goods said to me that she thought she knew where Karen might be. So, she led me to a strange little back room in a building, and sure enough, there sat Karen with some policemen, and they were broadcasting on the radio that they had a lost little girl looking for her parents. Since we had recently returned to Bolivia, Karen had not yet memorized her address or phone number, and when the policeman asked her where she lived, the only thing she could think of was the name of a subdivision of the city that was way on the outskirts of town. I was overcome with gratitude to God when we had finally located her. Once again her guardian angel had his wings of protection surrounding her—there is no doubt in my mind.

Ruth and Becky settled back into missionary children's school at Carachipampa. They were home every evening and every weekend, and this really suited Becky greatly. Because we had just returned from America, Becky was very accustomed to riding in cars. But back in Cochabamba, between our whole family, we only had the one little VW Bug. Often one of the two of us had to use it to run errands or work on some assignment. We each owned very nice 28-inch Hercules bicycles. When we had to go short distances, we each grabbed our bike and braved the narrow streets to get where we had to go. I remember one time when I was coming back from visiting someone in the hospital, I had a rather narrow skirt on, along with high-heeled shoes. As I was tooling down the avenue, keeping to the right of the cars in my narrow little passageway, someone opened the door right in front of me and I had to veer into the traffic, narrowly missing a taxi speeding along on my left. I admonished the driver of the parked automobile to please look behind before opening his door in the future! He was, of course, very remorseful. Anyway, all that to say we used our bicycles a great deal.

There were times when in the course of going somewhere, we needed to transport a kid along with us. Becky learned the hard way that skill is needed in riding on the back of the bicycle. I can't remember exactly who was driving the bike, but Becky was on the back. In the process of trying to keep her balance, she somehow got both of her heels caught in the spokes hurting them pretty badly! We had to bandage up her wounds and console her for quite a long time after the accident. It was not serious enough for a doctor visit, but it sure did bruise her heels and chew them up some. After that, Becky rode with her toes pointed way out from the bicycle! She had become a master passenger. It was a good thing, because when she was four years old, she went off to kindergarten every day on the back of the bicycle for her morning's schooling. She wore her little blue and white uniform like all of her other classmates. The next year she was able to enroll in first grade at Carachipampa and ride the bus with her sisters.

As Mrs. Assistant General Director, my chores also increased. It was my duty to entertain all dignitaries passing through, and it was also my job to give orientation to the newly arrived missionaries. By this time, I had to cut back on my musical involvements which really wasn't a great loss. But that day did come when I had to make the choice of staying gung-ho with my music, or being Peter's full-time assistant. In that respect, I am so glad that I let the music go. Working side-by-side with Peter was much more fulfilling and rewarding even though the workload was heavy.

Becky would have been about four years old at this time and had not yet been enrolled in kindergarten. She was always such a joy to us, and one of her little quirks was the way she was able to pick up poly-syllabic words, without necessarily knowing how to use them appro-priately. Many hilarious sentences came out of her mouth! She was always the consummate diplomat, trying to express herself accurately, and it was quite obvious that she had inherited her father's gift and would probably one day become a writer. She seemed to understand that I was incredibly busy, but never too busy to lend an ear to her. One day I just about melted when she looked up at me with her great big brown eyes and said, "Mommy, I remember spaghetti." I came to the realization that I had not made it since I returned to Bolivia, because it was such a project. But you can bet that I immediately went to the market, bought some meat, tomatoes, and tomato paste along with the dry pasta, and came home to devote the better part of an afternoon to making spaghetti. It involved grinding the pork meat by hand, making Italian sausage out of it, simmering the tomatoes and tomato paste along with the aromatics down into a proper sauce, and we all enjoyed a fabulous spaghetti supper that night. To this day when the girls want to ask for me to cook something special, they will say something like, "I remember stuffed cabbage leaves."

It was during the middle part of our first term in Cochabamba that we started a school board made up of a group of parents to over-see more closely the on-goings of the missionary children's school at

Carachipampa. The school was extremely diverse, in that there were children of missionaries from many different countries whose educational systems were not all the same. There were also a few English-speaking Bolivians thrown in the mix.

It was the policy of the mission that all school-aged children would be sent away to this boarding school no matter where there lived. The reasoning was that all of the children should be treated alike. Then the day came when the school board made a ruling that the children whose parents lived within commuting distance would be allowed to spend weekends at home. That seemed to work out very well, so soon thereafter the school board ruled that a school bus would be made available to pick up the children every morning from around the city of Cochabamba and they would then commute the eight miles to Carachipampa. This meant that the workload of those assigned to the school, would be cut by quite a bit during the evenings and weekends, thereby freeing up more time to donate to the fewer children in the boarding situation. Some of these children were from homes in which other languages were spoken, such as German, and many of the cultural situations in the homes differed one from the other. There were seven different countries represented in our mission—New Zealand, Australia, England, United States, Canada, Germany, and Jamaica, and these cultures are quite different one from the other. I recall one time when a family from either England or Australia was very upset because their children were speaking English with an American accent! There may have been a bit of jealousy on the part of those parents who were working in remote areas of the nation, who could not have their children home in the evenings and on weekends. There was a little bit of unrest over this for a few years, but it eventually settled down. It was a very convenient situation for parents who had to make trips to other parts of the nation, since their children were well cared for and were in situations with their very close friends when they had to remain in the boarding set up for a few days at a time.

When I checked with my girls and asked them what they wanted me to include in these memoirs, Karen promptly returned a fax with a number of suggestions. One of her favorite memories growing up was our family trips together in our little Volkswagen Bug to places like Santa Cruz or La Paz. It was fun to be able to relax and drive around the cities to see the sights and hear the sounds, to visit the various open markets, and to see the historical and geographical highlights as well as the flora and fauna of these places.

We always tried to take a day off from the office to spend with our girls, and because we were very busy on Sundays, we took off Saturdays. One of our favorite pastimes was to pack a picnic lunch, usually consisting of a rotisserie chicken, some raw veggies, and some homemade potato chips, along with some cookies for dessert. The last few years that we were there, we were able to get drinks in liter bottles, such as Pepsi and Fanta Orange soda. We would spend an hour in the early morning peeling and thinly slicing potatoes, cooking them in oil, salting them, and packing them in a Tupperware container. These were a tremendous treat for our kids. Actually, the Andes area is the home of the potato, and we certainly didn't have any problem finding several heirloom varieties.

Once our picnic lunch was ready, we would carefully pack it in the trunk of our little Volkswagen Bug, grab some heavy sweaters and a blanket, and usually head off to the mountains. We would search out a spot that looked safe and had a good view and have our picnic. The highest snowcapped peak that overlooked the city of Cochabamba was called Mount Tunari and rose to an altitude of over 17,000 feet. The dirt road that led to the mountain pass went up to about 14,000 feet. We decided to head up that way one day because we thought the view would be outstanding. It was above the tree line, and there were just short mountain grasses of various varieties, and probably some short tiny flowers growing in meadows on the rocky hillsides. We found a pretty place and set things up for our picnic. All three of the girls were enjoying exploring the mountainside, as Peter and I were keeping an eye on them.

Becky would have been about four years old. As she was wandering around the hillside, she came across a patch of snow. Since we had spent most of the previous year in California, she was not accustomed to snow at all. She decided to take a walk on this white stuff and promptly sank down in it over her knees. It startled her so badly that she thought she was in grave danger of being swallowed up and began screaming for help. I was not exactly sure what might've happened to her, but at the time I probably imagined she had slipped and hurt herself. Karen was somewhere between me and Becky and the first thing I thought of was stupidly to holler, "Run, Karen!" So as best she could, Karen ran up the steep hill to rescue Becky. It never occurred to me at that moment that we were perched alongside a road probably over 14,000 feet high! Karen got Becky's legs unstuck and proceeded to collapse grasping her heart! It took her quite a few minutes to recover, and I felt terrible that I could have done such a foolish thing. It's a good thing that Karen has a very strong heart! As a matter of fact, when my pediatrician first examined her as a newborn, he listened to her heart and smiled broadly. He said, "This kid has got quite a ticker!"

I remember once when we found a delightful spot to picnic, there was a herd of llamas feeding nearby. Ruth had a ball chasing the llamas about and watching their graceful movements on the steep incline.

They can be running lickety-split but never seem to move their heads at all. We all absolutely fell in love with llamas and when we came back to Colorado and settled in our new home in the woods, there was enough pastureland to sustain a few llamas, so we bought seven or eight.

Llamas are very gentle animals with great big brown eyes, long eyelashes and faces that look like miniature camels, since they are of the camel family, called camelids. However, we lost all of our herd excepting for one named George. A black bear attacked the herd one night and killed one of our prettiest woolly llamas named Buckshot. He had a bad hip and could not quite keep up with all of the rest as they ran to escape the predator. It turns out that this same juvenile black bear was apparently staking out some new territory for himself, and the previous night he had killed another llama a little over a mile away from our home. We contacted the fish and game department and told them about this bear. At the time our daughter Becky and her family were living downstairs in our house, and our 18-month-old grandson was playing in our fenced-in backyard. Becky had just brought Sammy in the house and could not believe her eyes when in the middle of the day, the bear ran across our yard just a few feet from her back door where he had been playing just moments before.

We secured permission from the Division of Wildlife to kill the bear, because he was an apparent nuisance and was just killing for the fun of it. They set a trap made out of a big barrel and a spring-loaded door. They baited the trap with some of Buckshot's meat inside. We had some very important meetings that we had to attend early the next day, but our dear next-door neighbor, who is an avid hunter, volunteered to sit up and wait for him in order to kill him. Sure enough, at about four in the morning he turned up again right in plain view under our big yard light. I happened to be up watching as well, and when he came prancing toward us, he was growling and rolling his head from side to side. However, our neighbor, Brian, is an excellent shot and the black bear met his Waterloo forthwith. The carcass of the bear was the property of the Division of Wildlife, so we were not allowed to keep it to mount.

Shortly after that our llamas begin to die one by one. Our veterinary could not figure out why, so we helplessly stood by as we lost all of our herd except for George, who apparently was a little more fit. Llamas are guard animals, and as such, George sits in the pasture in front of our home guarding it all day long. Llamas are frequently used in Colorado and elsewhere to fend off predators, such as coyote, from herds of sheep. Usually, the only fight that they will lose is against a mountain lion or a bear, and they will fight to the death to protect their herd. They are noble, graceful, and beautiful creatures.

As an aside, there are four kinds of similar animals found in the Andes. These are the llama, the guanaco, the alpaca and the vicuna. While they are all cousins, they vary in size, the llama and the alpaca are domesticated, but the guanaco and the vicuna roam wild in herds high up in the Andes.

The llama stands about 4 feet high at the shoulders, and his head is 6 feet or little more above the ground. These lovely creatures are used as beasts of burden and can carry about 80 pounds divided into two saddle pack-looking bags. Their owners frequently decorate their ears with brightly colored yarn to dress them up and probably to distinguish them one from the other. They can be any combination of colors from white to tan to brown to gray to black and can have large areas of their wool divided up by any or all of these colors, or they can be speckled. A white llama bred to a gray one can give birth to a black baby or a wild combination of any of the above colors. These animals are suited to the mountains, and the cold does not bother them at all. They only need to drink once every few days and can forage on the mountain grasses very well. The bottoms of their cloven hooves are soft, and they can walk among the delicate grasses without harming them at all. None of the llama is ever discarded except for its bare bones. The wool can be dyed or left undyed and spun into yarn. This is used to make warm clothing in the very cold Altiplano and mountainous areas. However, if worn close to the skin, since it is a little hairy, it can be pretty itchy.

The meat can be eaten and tastes very much like a lamb. The hide turns into leather and has many uses including the roofs of houses and to make rawhide straps for sandals. Since these animals frequently live above the tree line, firewood is scarce or nonexistent. Llamas produce manure in cute little pellets that can be dried out and used as cooking fuel. I don't know if this is true or not, but I have been told that if a herd of llamas is taken to market, for example, carrying grain or some similar product to market to be sold, that if they lie down in a circle and a rope is tossed around their necks, they will not stray because they are too proud to lower their heads out of the rope. If I were that pretty I would be proud too!

The alpaca is the second domesticated camelid. These are probably the cutest of the bunch with a sweet lovely face. Their wool is not at all hairy but is soft and cuddly. It is highly prized for the knitting of scarves, hats, sweaters, coats, ponchos, and the like. It is very fine and quite expensive. These animals stand about 3 feet at the shoulders and in recent years have been imported into the United States in large numbers. An excellent breeding female currently sells in the neighborhood of $20,000, and a top breeding male can go for $90,000. This has recently become a hobby of wealthy retirees in America. They all are usually off-white in color, which makes dying their wool quite easy.

The first of the two wild species is the guanaco. They roam in herds along the mountainous and Altiplano areas from Colombia through Ecuador, Peru, Bolivia, Chile, and northern Argentina. The largest herds are found in Patagonia in southern Argentina. They are just a little shorter than llamas, and they stand between 3.5 and 4 feet at the shoulder and weigh about 200 pounds. Some Bolivian Indians have been known to raise these animals to help them regain their population stability. They usually live to be 20 to 25 years old. Their only predator is the mountain lion. These are always the same color, ranging from a light brown to a dark cinnamon shading to white under their bellies and on the inside of their legs. They have very fine wool and it is highly valued.

The second wild species is the vicuna. This is the smallest of the four and they stand at approximately 3 feet at the shoulders and weigh less than 150 pounds. Its long woolly coat is tawny brown on the back while the hair on the throat and chest is white and quite long. Their wool is highly prized because it is extremely fine and very expensive. They are more delicate and graceful than the guanaco and are protected by law. They also live in family-based groups with their own territory. They have a smaller area in which they roam, including the mountainous areas of Peru, Bolivia, northern Chile and northern Argentina. Their wool is sold on the world market for $300 per kilo (2.2 pounds). Because the wool is the finest in the world, it is never dyed because it is so delicate, but is used in its natural coloring. The government of Peru allows the native Indians to round up the animals into corrals and to shear them once every two years. They must be returned to the wild and cannot be sheared again for another two years. This ensures that a large portion of the profits return to the villagers. However, there is also illegal activity involving the exportation of illegally gotten wool. Some countries have banned the importation of the fiber in order to save the animal. Current prices for vicuna fabrics can range from \$1800-\$3000 per yard. Vicuna fiber can be used for apparel such as socks, sweaters, accessories, shawls, coats, and suits, and for home fashions such as blankets and throws. A scarf costs about \$1500, while a man's coat can cost up to \$20,000.

Because we did not live in the highest areas of Bolivia, we never did see the wild animals in their natural habitat, although we wish we could have! (The facts and figures concerning these four animals were taken from Wikipedia.)

When a rainy Saturday would roll around, we had to figure out something else to do. Saturday afternoon was a time devoted to the children. Karen asked me to include a little history of how these days were spent. Our first option was to bake up a storm. The things that stick in Karen's memory most were the cinnamon rolls, apple pies, and making little snails with the leftover scraps of piecrust. We would roll out the pie dough, sprinkle it with cinnamon and sugar, roll it back up, and cut little pastries about a half inch thick. The kids particularly loved to do this by themselves and then eat their finished products. We did make Christmas anise cookies just like their grandmother taught me, and we could always find something new to cook or bake.

Karen said that one of her favorite comfort food dinners was a stack of just plain pancakes. The top one was served with a fried egg, and when it was devoured, the rest of the stack was drowned in cream gravy. This was exactly the way it was served to me when I was a child. Karen says that it was not until she was an adult that she found out that it was because at the end of the month when funds were running a little low, it made a very inexpensive yet satisfying and delicious meal. The egg on top of pancakes harks back to Peter's summers on the farm, because that is the way Shorty, (his host) had them. The cream gravy over pancakes was what I was served in my childhood home. Milk was there for the taking, and occasionally neighbors made maple syrup from the maple trees in very late winter, although it was a treat and scarce. Karen just combined the two for a favorite comfort food.

Sometimes we would get involved with various craft projects. There was not much of a very exciting nature to buy in the stores, but we did locate embroidery thread, yarn, and very pretty shiny colored paper. We made Christmas tree ornaments out of the colored paper by cutting it into various-sized circles using glasses or cups or saucepan lids. We would then fold the circles into triangles and glue the rounded edges outside the triangles together. We could glue a colored string with a knot inside the last glue job and, voila, a very colorful ornament. I also recall making miniature Christmas trees out of cardstock paper glued together in the form of a cone and painted green.

We girls would enjoy going to the market and selecting macaroni in varying shapes, sizes, and styles, painting them and gluing these on to the tree. Their ingenuity was put to the test as they manufactured these homemade Christmas gifts for their friends. We also made boutonnieres for our choir members' Christmas concerts out of evergreen sprigs, red ribbons, and tiny colored glass balls available in the market. These kinds of activities were thoroughly enjoyed—at least by me! Each time we were expecting, I was desperately hoping for a son in order to carry on the Wagner name since Peter is the last of his tribe. But as our girls were growing up and Peter was traveling a lot, I realized how very fortunate I was to have all daughters. It was so easy to think of girl things to do and not be bothered by softball, soccer, football, and the like. We all became very good friends because of this. When

Karen's second son was born, I got a phone call from her from the hospital saying: "Mom, you finally have your Phillip."

The one bedroom that we had for the girls in Cochabamba could have its furniture painted pink. I remember that we shipped a refrigerator from the US, and its shipping crate was a very large wooden box. This box served two purposes. It was painted bright pink and equipped with a pipe to hang the girls' dresses. One of the outside boards was used to measure the height of the girls every year on their birthdays, and names and markings were added very faithfully. It upsets me now to think that I forgot to pull off that board and bring it home with me. It was a one-of-a-kind, and when we left Bolivia Karen was 16, Ruth was 10, and Becky was six years old. It had kept track of their growth for nearly 10 years.

Sometimes our day trips would take us to surrounding villages and exciting open markets which were always held on Saturdays. I recall buying a spinning wheel one Saturday, and we would find all sorts of items to bring back and decorate our home or hang on the wall. One time we were watching a peasant gentleman winnowing a crop of harvested wheat. He would throw the stocks of grain up into the air with a large homemade eucalyptus wooden pitchfork, made out of a tree limb that had three branches. He cut the branches off to form a three-tined fork and it worked beautifully. Peter went over to chat with this fellow and asked him if he would sell him his beautiful fork. He was very happy to do that, and to this day the fork hangs on my dining room wall.

Most of the population in the cities is made up of mixed-blood people who are descendants of the Spanish. However, the Quechua Indian peasants in the countryside were extremely colorful in their dress. This people group is very large, and they extend from Ecuador clear down to northern Chile and southern Bolivia, all along the Andes Mountains and valleys. They are descendants of the Incas. Out of the hand-spun yarn of sheep, alpacas, or llamas, they make pretty skirts and extremely colorful large shawls that serve as backpacks to carry goods or children. Both men and women wore sandals made of leather strips with part of a recycled rubber tire as the sole. Some of the women, however, did wear shoes. As we traveled around the country, we noted that each area or particular geographic subgrouping of individuals wore a distinct hat. The Quechua women that lived in and around Cochabamba wore a very large, stiff, flat topped white hat decorated with a black ribbon in a certain pattern. The pattern of the black ribbon indicated the exact area where they lived.

When we traveled to Sucre, we noticed the women there wore dark blue hats made of felt, but they were the same size and shape as the ladies from Cochabamba. Then we had occasion to go to Potosi and noticed the Quechua women there wore felt hats the same size and shape as the women in Sucre, but theirs were brown.

In La Paz, the Aymara Indians are descended from a pre-Incan civilization. These are some of the heartiest, strongest people in South America. They survive in these extremely high areas and can eke out a living above the tree line! Since they live at such an altitude, they are quite barrel-chested because their lungs are so large. Many of them, once they survive childhood, live to be very old, some over 100. When the Incas were on the march conquering all of the tribes in the Andean area, the Aymara were the only ones who maintained their culture and language and were not conquered by the Inca. It is very interesting that the Christian church has grown vigorously among the Aymara people, but it has been considerably slower to grow among the Quechua. Anyway, the Aymara women wear brown or black or white derby hats. It has tickled me in recent years to see *chulos* for sale all over the place in Colorado, even in my then-local grocery store. These are the brightly colored knit hats, with knit ear flaps, and sometimes strings of yarn hanging from the ear flap. This is the everyday head covering of choice of the men all over the frigid Andes area and has been for generations.

We managed to collect about 20 of these hats and covered one whole bamboo wall of our home. They were often borrowed to use in plays by people who knew we had them. I had the goal of buying a hat right off of someone's head, but apparently, they are too personal and too highly prized to do so. No one would ever sell us his or her hat. We had to buy our souvenir hats in hat shops.

We had also collected a few mementos from the jungle area. One of our pastors in a province called Beni, was an excellent painter. Emu, an ostrich-like large bird, grew wild all the way from our jungles down into Argentina. They laid enormous eggs, each one equaling about a dozen chicken eggs. If the shells were carefully blown out, they provided a decoration that could be hung by transparent fishing line in a corner in groupings. This particular pastor painted the shells in lovely jungle scenes, and we had several of them hanging from a corner in our dining room. Also, there was an abundance of huge turtles that lived in the north-flowing Guapore River, which separates Bolivia from Brazil and is part of the huge Amazon River basin. These turtles are often over three feet long and over two feet wide, have slightly domed thick shells, and their meat is delicious, I am told. The same pastor also painted two of them for us, one with the colorful Bolivian coat of arms, and the other with a jungle oxcart scene. These graced our walls in Bolivia during the time we lived in Cochabamba. We also had a huge oxcart and jungle scene painted on a bamboo curtain that was about six feet by three and one-half feet hanging behind our sofa. The Bolivians who frequently came into our home were very honored that we decorated our home in this manner and told us so!

When we lived in San José, one of our pastors there sold us an incredibly beautiful female jaguar skin. This particular female jaguar had killed several of his young calves, so one night he waited for her in a tree and shot her right through the heart with a 22 rifle. When we returned home from Bolivia, we brought the beautiful skin with us and were allowed to bring it in to America because it was untanned. We were able to get it tanned in the city of Gloversville, New York, very close to our little town of St. Johnsville, in a factory that tanned deer hide and calf hide for glove production. This hide hung in the log cabin in our woods for the 30 years we lived in Colorado. Today it is on the wall of the Peter Wagner Legacy Room at the Global Spheres Center. I understand that it is quite difficult to transport these hides now.

During the first year that Pam Toomey worked for us, I remember our girls asking, as most kids do, for a puppy. We decided that we would head down to the market in search of a mutt. Everything was sold at the open market, so we went over to the live animal section to see what we could find. We did locate a very scrawny, black and white mutt with floppy ears. We brought it home, bathed it, and awaited the girls' return from school to present them with Snoopy. The girls were, of course, thrilled. But shortly after they began playing with it, and I believe it may have been while it was eating, it turned around and bit Becky in the face, with one of its fangs going clear through her nose! I was furious!! As a matter of fact, my mama bear instinct took over. I had a machete in my hand and was ready to send Snoopy to the promised land. However, I did have sense enough to call Becky's pediatrician and he admonished me to keep the dog for 10 days to see if it was rabid or not. After the 10 days were over, and Becky's wounds were healed, there were several Bolivian folks standing in line who wanted Snoopy. The Spanish language is such that Spanish speakers cannot pronounce a word that begins with S followed by a constant, without putting in E in front of the word. No one could seem to pronounce "Snoopy" very well, so when the dog was given away, its name became "Esloopy." All I wanted to see was the backside of that creature headed out my door. By then the girls were ready to say goodbye to him as well.

Once we moved to Cochabamba, I quit cutting Peter's hair and had him blow $.25 every few weeks for a haircut. There were some excellent beauty shops in town, and so it became my custom to leave early Friday mornings for a shampoo and style. That was one thing that could be very well done, so I never looked shabby during those nine years in Cochabamba! It cost two dollars for a shampoo and style, and the girls were excellent at their trade. Sometimes there are wonderful perks that come along with the package of being a missionary. This was right up there with the filet mignon sandwiches and orchids when we lived in the jungle.

With Peter's studies at Fuller, he was able to meet many influential individuals involved in the field of missions from all over the world. He became very involved in a program called "theological education by extension." One of his former professors by the name of Ralph Winter was the program's architect. The whole idea was that most people who wished to train for the ministry were already deeply involved in leading a church, and some of them were bi-vocational and could not leave their jobs because they needed to support their families. They certainly could not pick up and move to a seminary. Ralph dreamed up the idea of taking theological education to them. This, of course, meant a great deal of travel for the professors. They would usually travel by light airplane to remote areas to teach groups of pastors in various subjects, just like the training they would receive in a seminary. This was highly successful, and the ideas soon began to spread to many parts of Latin America, and eventually the world. Peter began to travel, teaching these concepts to groups who could implement them.

It wasn't too long after we returned when Peter was asked to make a trip around the world to teach these concepts in various nations, including Taiwan and India, and probably a few other stops that I can't remember. He was gone for quite a long time, and I decided to meet him on the way home and spend a couple of days resting in Lima, Peru. This was quite an interesting time to say the least. At that time the girls and I shared a single passport. This meant when I left, I took the passport with me and the girls were left without one. While we were in Lima, one of our infamous revolutions broke out. We were in Lima and our kids were in Bolivia! All flights into Bolivia were canceled because of the political upheaval, and we had to hang in there in Lima waiting for things to settle down. We were listening to the radio and devouring the daily newspapers for three extra days as I recall. During that time the government changed hands three times, and during one of those times we actually had "co-presidents" for a day! As soon as we could, we booked ourselves on the first flight back to Cochabamba, and we were met by a glamorous Karen who had her beautiful blonde hair artistically piled high on her head. She had braved the revolution in order to get her hair done to welcome us home! All of the kids were just fine at the missionary children's school and were well looked after. Needless to say, we each got our separate passports soon thereafter. I distinctly remember that Becky's first passport said that she was 36 inches tall. In this way we could mix-and-match Peter's traveling with some of the girls should the necessity arise. It never did.

Late in 1969, Peter was named as press secretary for a large International Congress on Latin American Evangelism (CLADE) to be held in Bogotá, Colombia. It was sponsored by Billy Graham and held for nine days at the end of November 1969. It was an extremely busy event bringing together several thousand people from all over Latin America. There were numerous planning meetings held here and there, all during 1969. I accompanied Peter on this trip. It was my job to mimeograph and mail out hundreds of press releases produced by Peter. I distinctly remember the first planning session that I attended with Peter. It was held in Buenos Aires, Argentina, and it was really one of my first trips outside of Bolivia. It was then that I realized that all of Latin America was certainly not the same. Buenos Aires looked a lot like I imagined Europe would look, because it seemed to have large groups of Italians and Germans along with the native-born Argentineans. It was a beautiful city, very advanced and clean. I learned a great deal about Argentina during that trip that would come in handy in later years as I would visit it over and over again, accompanying Cindy Jacobs as she taught spiritual warfare and prayer.

Our last three years in Bolivia were a whirlwind of activity. I will not bore you with all of the specifics, but it seemed as though we packed everything we possibly could into every day. Peter traveled a great deal all over the country, all over Latin America, and made many trips back to the School of World Mission to teach. It seemed as though we were just getting useful when we were saying goodbye. The girls very much enjoyed their life. We would take annual vacations in our little Volkswagen Bug. We would either go to La Paz or down to Santa Cruz. These were highlights for the kids, and we always had a wonderful time.

Our Christmas times were very special, because Christmas itself was Ruth's birthday and December 29 was Karen's. I remember one time we were in Santa Cruz and were unable to get a cake for Karen's 12th birthday. We did find a big flat loaf of bread and a fat candle and sang "Happy Birthday" anyway. Karen wanted me to be sure to include this story!

What lessons did I take away with me from our tenure with the Andes Evangelical Mission? I learned much more about the cultures of the Spanish-speaking Bolivians and the tribal people groups of the Quechua and Aymara, although we never attempted to learn their languages. Many of our missionaries did learn the languages, however. I learned that it was a complex balancing act to understand where the missionaries from the seven nations represented in the AEM were coming from at all times. There brewed beneath the surface a rather strong anti-American feeling, now and then. Some of the Americans resented the fact that we had to raise our support entirely but those from some other nations did not. Our mission operated on the "pool system" and all income was equally shared among the families. Some of the time the leadership was American and when new leadership came on board that was American also, resentment surfaced. We all got along with the Bolivians in great fashion and they were oblivious to the fact that there may have been discord brewing. But that all was left behind and we chalked it up to experience when we were able to turn over our responsibilities to others and tie up all our loose ends in preparation for Fuller School of World Mission, our next assignment.

Peter and I loved working together. Pam Toomey had taught me many office procedures and I was very comfortable with my newfound skills. When the invitation was extended to Peter to become an assistant professor, he informed the Fuller administration that he and his wife were one package. They had to hire me also, or neither of us. They really wanted Peter, so they very reluctantly agreed, being careful to inform us that it was against seminary policy for us to work together. Wives could work for another professor, or in the library or cafeteria, but not in the same office. However, Peter stood his ground and prevailed. We worked together in the seminary for twenty years and had great success. We worked together many more years running the worldwide prayer movement during the 1990s and for even more years after that. We were a team.

CHAPTER 9

Fuller Seminary School Of World Mission

I was very happy that Peter was taking up a position at SWM. It seemed as though we had made all of the mistakes possible that young missionaries could make. If we could spare someone else some grief because of our experiences, I felt it would be very worthwhile. Peter would be holding down two full-time jobs—one as a professor and the other as the missions' director for the Fuller Evangelistic Association. More about that later. Besides, Peter informed those that were hiring him that I was part of the package and that we would need to continue to work together. Although it was considered odd, saying that it smacked of nepotism, they agreed after Peter said, "If you want me, you take Doris too."

During our last year in Bolivia, 16-year-old Karen befriended a young man who was a fantastic guitar player. He helped us with our church services and street meetings. As a matter of fact, on one occasion they let us know that they were thinking of eloping! This was a proper age for marriage of girls in Bolivia. Peter and I took them out to dinner and did some very fast talking. Peter fully employed all of his diplomacy skills! They wisely decided to call it off, but that did not make saying goodbye any easier for Karen. I just read a very sad article from *The Journal Missiology* (The Lost MK by Kietzman, Pike, Jones and Lingenfelter, Missiology, Vol. XXXVI, Oct. 4, 2008). It was a study of missionary kids in later life. The sample was very broad and consisted of the type of mission very close to our situation. I knew one of the authors, one who had spent some time in Brazil as a child. There were 16 kids and missions that were studied. All 16 of these participants had rejected their parents' faith at some time during their adult lives. Over time three are gradually returning back to faith and two have already returned to faith. Nine actively rejected their parent's faith, two of these have chosen Eastern meditation and mysticism, and one developed a personal philosophy of God as Wisdom. The remaining two participants seem to be adrift, passively rejecting faith yet missing the sense of community that faith provides. All of these kids were deeply affected by the notion that their parents considered the pagans to whom they had been called to ministry more important than the kids. Many of them struggled deeply at boarding school and the long periods of time away from their parents. Many of them suffered trauma and abuse related to their MK experience; many of them were stressed by the political turmoil for extended periods of time in their adopted countries. Some were struggling with the fact that they lost relatives during their time away. Many were impacted by the abrupt changes. Some were not told that they were going to be dropped off at boarding school following furlough and this presented great trauma. One even felt that it was impossible to forgive parents for abandoning him for a supposedly higher cause.

One of the enormous benefits that we enjoyed was being out of the country for the most part during the turbulent 60s. Karen, who would've been the kid that was raised through adolescence on the mission field, does not hold resentment to this day. When I asked her one time if she felt cheated because she was not raised in America, she responded by saying that she felt it was an advantage to be raised abroad and to have a second language and understand a second culture.

She is probably highly unusual according to the study above. As an adult she has chosen to serve others in the field of medicine by caring for seriously ill patients, as well as serving those suffering from severe trauma in her intensive care unit, where she has served for about 45 years. She is very valuable as a bilingual nurse in the Los Angeles area. We understand that this is somewhat unusual and can but thank God for His faithfulness to us through the years, and for answering prayer on their behalf. As of today, Ruth has served God with us in Global Spheres organization using her skills in technology and remains as my 24/7 caregiver since my severe handicap episode. Becky is the mother of three children, two of whom are autistic, and she and her husband have a ministry of reaching out to parents of handicapped children and ministering to them, Children of Destiny. They planted and are pastoring Lake Effect Church in Grand Rapids, Michigan. We still remain a very close-knit family after all these years, and we can but thank God once again for this.

I personally learned two very important lessons from our mission field experience of 16 years. First: God never asked me to do something but that He equipped me to do it with the knowledge, and the physical and the spiritual strength needed to complete the task. And secondly, although we were often living in hostile surroundings, the safest place to be is in the center of God's will. There were many close calls with life and death situations but God healed, blessed, and often miraculously saved and brought us through them ALL.

So, we got rid of most of our earthly possessions in Cochabamba and returned to the U.S. in the summer of 1971. I gave my accordion to Martha Buitrago, a fine musician who had gone through the Bible School and was also my assistant in the correspondence school. She was a very dear friend.

We stopped in Mexico City for a couple of days to visit friends, and it was there that we somehow got word that my mother was very ill and hospitalized. We hurried home only to find her terminally ill. Her kidney cancer had spread to her pancreas and liver and the cobalt treatments had weakened her and closed off her intestines.

My brother Buddy had another serious heart attack just a few days after we got home to the farm. The hospital was quite small, so strangely enough, my mother had to be moved out of the intensive care unit to make room for him. As it turned out, he did not survive the first night there. With my mother on her deathbed, we buried Buddy. He was only 43 years old and left behind a wife and five kids, the youngest two were about five and ten years old.

Mama continued to languish in the hospital and although we stayed as long as we could, the time came for us to leave New York for California. Unfortunately. children were not allowed in hospitals during that era, so our girls never got to see her or say a final goodbye. She adored our girls, and this made my heart hurt. The school year was about to start, and we still had to buy a house and a car and get the girls enrolled in school and Peter ready to teach his classes. We said our tearful goodbyes and headed off for Pasadena.

Mama lived for another few weeks. Peter had to be in a conference in Illinois, so he left that to continue on to New York and officiated at her funeral. I was unable to go. It was very hard to lose a brother and a mother in one month's time, but at least we were not in South America, and we did get to see them both alive for the last time.

Dr. and Mrs. McGavran (both well into their 80s) took us into their home while we were house hunting. We later found out that Dr. McGavran was sleeping on the floor and Mrs. McGavran was on a lumpy sofa during the several weeks we were there getting our business done! Horrors!

With all the money we got from selling everything in Bolivia, we were able to put a down payment on a Datsun station wagon. We were tough missionaries, so Peter decided we could forego the accessory of an air conditioner. However, buying a house was something else. Once again, Bell Friends Church people came to our rescue. We located a Spanish style house close to the seminary but couldn't quite swing the down payment, so a dear couple in the church loaned us what was lacking, and we were able to pay it back within a few months. Bell Friends people also gathered up dishes and furnishings and we had enough to get along on. I still use some of the baking pans they gave us all these years later.

Peter's memoirs detail these years, so I will just do broad brush strokes here, and tell a little more about the kids and me to fill in.

Peter had two jobs. He worked with the Fuller Evangelistic Association (FEA) as their coordinator of mission projects, and he also taught a full load, sometimes more, in the Fuller School of World Mission. We both soon got offices in the FEA building. I was allowed to flex my hours by coming in early and leaving early in order to be home when the kids got out of school every weekday.

Early on during these years, Peter was asked to serve on the Lausanne Committee for World Evangelization and traveled all over the world to attend meetings. He especially enjoyed the Strategy Working Group which began the difficult task of pinpointing the unreached people groups of the world.

Peter became well versed in the field of church growth as Dr. McGavran's understudy and did a great number of seminars and consulting sessions where he was invited. He worked to bring these teachings to the U.S. and also worked with the Fuller School of Theology in the Doctor of Ministry program. He so enjoyed teaching these classes because it meant working with mature pastors. His classes were very large, sometimes over 50 or 60, and we became friends with many denominational executives through this means. He eventually became the Professor of Church Growth.

He was invited to teach church growth at the summer school of Wheaton College in Wheaton, Illinois, for nine straight summers. This was a great time for us and our girls, because instead of a plane ticket, he asked for the equivalent in cash, and this was enough to buy gasoline and allow us to drive to Illinois every summer. This was a highlight in our girls' memories.

We took a different route each of the nine years and tried to see the sights in a different state every summer. The summers had a name. They all began with "Know...." One year would be "Know Utah," or "Know Colorado," and one year it was "Know the Native Americans," and we visited as many of those people groups as we could, eating their food and studying them as well. We visited the cliff dweller ruins and the Navajo reservations. We traveled for a couple of years with a tent on the roof of the car and camped all along the way.

Then came the day when one of Peter's books, *Look Out, the Pentecostals are Coming,* produced a royalty check that was enough to buy a small pop-up tent-trailer on sale at the end of the season, and we no longer had to spend an hour driving in stakes for the tent and using the fold-up camp stove. We had graduated to wheels and propane!

During the two weeks of Peter's summer-school teaching, the girls and I would now and then drive back to New York and sometimes Massachusetts to visit my remaining brother and sister (Herbie and

Irene) and Peter's father and stepmother. Sometimes the girls got a summer pass to the Wheaton public swimming pool, complete with lifeguard, and enjoyed that greatly.

I remember one summer after Peter's teaching, we drove down the Appalachian Mountains and spent a couple of days in Nashville at Opryland amusement park when it was still open. Many country singing stars had shows there, and one time we got tickets to the Saturday night Grand Old Opry. I don't remember who was singing that night, but I do remember that we were in the second balcony in Row XX, the very top row. As a matter of fact, we could put our drinks on the wide railing behind us! Since then, we have become friends with a few of those fine, Christian entertainers and now get to go backstage. Times have changed. Some of them attended a spiritual warfare conference we had at the Opryland Hotel, which has since become a Gaylord resort. We had a dinner once with Connie Smith, Barbara Fairchild and Sharon White Skaggs. We have since befriended Ricky Skaggs, and he and Sharon visited us at our home in Colorado. We love the classical country music. Growing up, we always had a radio on in the barn listening to country music. The story we heard is that it made the cows relax and give milk better. Besides, as Peter says, "We wanted to expose our children to some culture."

Ruth would have been about twelve during that trip to Nashville and suffered a horrible accident. I was frying sausages for breakfast and as she walked by the camp stove, her shoulder clipped the frying pan handle and it flew right over her neck and chest with the searing grease. A sweet lady in the next campsite heard her scream, ran quickly and grabbed her Foille ointment and came running with it. We applied it to the burn after we had cooled it down with ice for about five minutes. It healed perfectly with no scar left behind, for what I thought for sure were third-degree burns. I always keep Foille on hand for burns ever since and can only find it on Amazon, but I am two tubes ahead at all times.

One summer we finished up at Wheaton and had to hightail it to Oregon where Peter had either a conference or a teaching stint that began two days later. We could overnight only once as we drove. We then returned home through the redwoods and the beautiful agricultural areas of northern California.

I don't recall if it was on this trip or another one, but we had another close call. (Earlier in the spring, back in Pasadena, as I was driving home from work one spring day, I had been broadsided by a car that ran a stop sign and got a dreadful whiplash. So, I had to wear a big spongy neck-supporting collar for about six months.) I recall that we were heading south on Route 99 in northern California near Chico, and we were pulling the tent trailer. We always chose Route 99 because it takes you through the spectacular farmland and fruit trees of plums, peaches, nectarines and vineyards. I even remember we could buy five melons, including watermelon, for $1.00 at the time. It was a blessing to these old farmers. Peter looked very tired, so I offered to drive so he could get a little rest. Ruth and Becky were in the back seat. It was August and beastly hot.

It was during the gas crisis of the mid 70s, and the speed limit was 55. I may have been exceeding the speed limit by three or four miles per hour, so I was going full tilt. I heard a strange squeal coming from the back of the car, and I asked the girls what they were doing back there. Before they could say anything, the wheels of the car locked up, and the car began swaying drastically from side to side with the trailer slapping the back bumper and rear of the car. Then the steering wheel totally locked up and I couldn't steer it at all! I had totally lost control.

We began skidding sideways down the four-lane road. I thought for sure we were going to start rolling over and over! When the car finally came to a halt, we were perfectly parked on the shoulder totally out of the traffic lanes just beyond the outside solid white stripe, facing the wrong way and the oncoming traffic. It felt like an old Abbot and Costello movie, but everything looked so perfect! We had avoided hitting any other vehicles. And wouldn't you know it—we were just a couple of steps from a rest area and a telephone (before the days of cell phones!) and were able to call a tow truck.

It turned out that the transmission went out on the car that had only 55,000 miles on it. The tow truck took us to the closest town, Oroville, where we rented a car and got our crippled car to the Datsun shop. They said it would be five days until they could get the new parts from San Francisco. The tow truck took our tent trailer to a campground and we set up shop there. I was somewhat traumatized and trembling badly, but Peter made me get right behind the wheel of the rented car to "get over it." And I did in a matter of minutes.

We found a church to attend Sunday night and a couple there was on their way back to Pasadena and offered to take Becky and me back home. Ruth stayed behind with her dad and promptly made friends with some people who owned an almond orchard and were in the middle of the almond harvest. She had a ball helping them and learning something about the almond industry. Figs were in season also, and Ruth remembers to this day being able to eat her fill of all of those sweet, perfectly ripe figs. Ruth adores the heat; she is my jungle baby.

Finally, the new transmission came, the car was repaired, and we all got home safely. I have often wondered if an angel took over steering that car when I could not.

We really enjoyed being part of Lake Avenue Congregational Church and especially the 120 Fellowship adult Sunday School class that Peter taught for 13 years. He rarely missed a Sunday. During all of that time we studied the Book of Acts. Out of that came his commentary on the Book of Acts, which, I personally, feel is one of his best books.

Peter enrolled in the University of Southern California and, as well as carrying two full-time jobs, earned his PhD in the USC School of Religion. His field was Social Ethics, and his dissertation eventually became the book, *Our Kind of People.* It was about the "homogeneous unit principle" first taught by Donald McGavran. The thesis is that "People like to become Christians without crossing cultural or social barriers." In other words, people are most comfortable worshiping with others of their own cultural and social class. This, of course, is true, but not really politically correct these days, so folks don't like to hear it. But, deep down, it is true.

What did I learn from this transition? Probably the greatest lesson was the demonstration of God's love and kindness to us. He allowed us to see and say goodbye to both my brother and my mother, just about in the nick of time. He introduced us to many denominational executives and influential pastors and worldwide leaders, who would later join forces with us in the prayer movement. He provided everything we needed to set up our new home. Actually, our home was quite spacious and allowed us to host many large gatherings for the School of World Mission. We were able to spend quality time with our girls every summer and build deep friendships with them as well as showing them around our beautiful country. He protected us when the transmission in our car failed. Peter was able to complete his PhD studies, debt-free, and thus qualify him eventually to become a full professor. We met and formed lasting friendships with a myriad of

Peter's students who would co-labor with us for years to come. Peter was becoming well known with his contacts with the Lausanne Committee and met a different group of worldwide leaders. He was able to lead the Strategy Working Group that would later identify the task of evangelizing the remaining unreached people groups of the world. It was a very pleasant, labor intensive, but wonderful time. We had found our best niche yet! As a bonus, we greatly enjoyed worshipping and teaching the 120 Fellowship adult Sunday School class at Lake Avenue Congregational Church, and we gained many lasting friendships with these wonderful people.

Peter was never one to show affection toward me publicly very often, although we held hands a lot. During this period in October of 1971, he attended an international meeting of Christian leaders in Wheaton, Illinois. Ken Taylor, the author of the Living Bible Translation attended that meeting and gave two full copies of the whole Bible, first edition, that he had autographed, one for Peter and one for me. Peter wrote on the inside of mine: To My Pearl of Great Price: There are many fine women in the world, but you are the best of them all Proverbs 31:29. He signed it just "P." and dated it October 3, 1971. In private he was profuse in his written and spoken words of affection toward me and on one occasion I remember him telling me, "Man has never loved a woman as I love you!" We just never fought, and our lives together were what most people only dream about, but we lived them. We laughed a lot, labored long and hard together, and Peter had a finisher's anointing. He always set goals and didn't stop until he got the job done. On one occasion he even likened us to Siamese twins who were such a team and were together so much in every assignment that we just couldn't live any other way. How I thank God for my wonderful life with Peter and our three girls!

CHAPTER 10

John Wimber And Power Evangelism

It was in the 1970s that we met John Wimber. He was a student of Peter's in the Doctor of Ministry program at Fuller. He knew so much about church growth as a practicing pastor that Peter soon had him give some lectures giving examples of the practical aspects of church growth.

There seemed to be a demand for church growth teaching and consultation, so Peter set up a Department of Church Growth in Fuller Evangelistic Association to facilitate the seminars and teaching as well as consulting with churches and denominations that was requested. Peter hired John Wimber and was his boss for two years.

However, John soon got restless and wanted to start another church. Peter gave him permission to start a new church, and he left his consulting job with us eventually. Out of that rapidly grew the Anaheim Vineyard and the whole Vineyard Christian Fellowship association of churches.

John had a phenomenal gift of evangelism. I often think of a story he told us about the time he became a new Christian. John had been in the big-time music business, actually with a famous group called The Righteous Brothers, and was earning a great deal of money. But his marriage and his life were falling apart. When he was converted, things got salvaged, and he wanted to serve the Lord. But first he had to learn about the Bible, so he attended a Bible study that met every Tuesday.

He was offered a job managing the very first Beatles tour through America in the 60s. That would have brought him a pile of money, but he refused because it would have made him miss at least one, or maybe more, Tuesday Bible studies. The people discipling him at the time told him to come out from the world, and not to get involved again.

Coming back to John's extraordinary gift of evangelism: He had the gift of leading people to Christ quickly, easily, and thoroughly. He was an excellent musician, being partial to the keyboard. I once asked him how many instruments he could play and he blithely replied, "All of them." He wasn't bragging, just stating a fact.

So, John missed out spending time with the Beatles at the very beginning of their career. I have often wondered what the world would look like today if he had been told to take Christ with him into the field he knew so well and excelled in. The Beatles had so much influence over young people of the day. They led many young people of the day into Eastern religions, drugs and rebellion. What kind of music could have come from them if they had become believers in Christ in those early days? I have no doubt in my mind that John could have won them to the Lord if he were encouraged to be "in the world, but not of the world." But we new Christians were all told to escape the world. That's why I didn't go to nursing school.

Many years later I had a lovely conversation with Carol, John's widow. She said that the Lord told John to gather up all of his music from past years, arrangements, CDs, sheet music, and absolutely all memorabilia, load it in the back of the station wagon and drive it to the dump, which he did. If the Lord told John, I believe it. I was just speculating in my mind the "What if we had the 7 Mountain teaching back in the 60s."

Mercifully, things are changing in the church and we are now encouraging Christians to stay in their profession of choice and gifting and to influence that area for Christ, even to become the top people in their field. The world needs God's best leading every area of what has been called the "Seven Mountains": Family, Religion, Education, Media, Arts & Entertainment, Business, and Government. If Christians were at the helm in these areas, our nation would look much better.

So, John moved on, but it was wonderful working with him. After establishing the Anaheim Vineyard, he soon felt the Lord asking him to begin to pray for the sick. It took some months of tenacious prayer before they saw their first healing. But soon they saw many miracles of healing.

Peter figured that this might be something of interest to his many Doctor of Ministry students as well as a handy, dandy tool for his many students in the School of World Mission who would be heading back to the mission field. Peter invited John to teach some sessions on how to pray for the sick in his classes. He would serve as "resource personnel" and Peter was "Professor of record" in Peter's missions' classes.

These classes soon became the talk of the seminary and the pre-service younger students in the Master of Divinity program enrolled by the droves. I, personally attended every single one of those classes. The classes were taught in the evenings and we had to move to nearby churches to accommodate the size. I recall one of the classes had around 250 students enrolled, and other students would sneak in during breaks. They really wanted to learn about and witness the miraculous. That class broke all records for attendance in the history of the seminary. It caught national attention and was written up in national Christian magazines at the time.

Finally, the administration asked me to stand at the door and not allow anyone whose name was not on the class roster into the class-room. I once turned away a young professor on crutches, with a broken ankle, asking him to leave a healing class! I didn't know who he was. I was just carrying out orders!

In addition to the classes on healing, John also began teaching on the subject of the casting out of demons. This began to fascinate me personally, and I picked up a call to minister in this area. It was very plain to me that in praying for the sick, sooner or later demons will surface that are often connected with physical infirmities. One of the students, who was with the mission organization Youth With a Mis-sion, somehow found out I had an interest in the topic of casting out demons. He procured for me a wonderful "how to" book by an elderly Australian couple, Noel and Phyl Gibson. I began studying voraciously, and started practicing the casting out of demons. I was personally men-tored by Noel and Phyl Gibson, using fax. Email had not come into use. This couple taught me just about all I know. Eventually I found myself quite busy. I discovered there were many people with demonic bondage who were seeking freedom. I often ministered at least three or sometimes even more times per week in this area. The people who came to me for ministry were usually the ministerial students, the mis-sionaries, or pastors who found out that I worked in this area. This ministry then grew us into other areas of spiritual warfare that were territorial in nature.

These topics greatly interested the student body. I remember once when I returned from a ministry time in Argentina, a demon appeared in my bedroom in the middle of the night. I was in California and Peter was teaching a Doctor of Ministry course in Philadelphia, so I returned to an empty house since our girls were all married and had moved out of the house. It was a very large grayish figure, about three meters tall with bright green eyes and teeth. Oddly enough, it did not frighten me and when I started blasting praise music and ordered it out of my room, it went immediately. Later on, I had occasion to spend some time with my now-deceased good friend Omar Cabrera in Argentina and described this grayish figure to him, and he had encountered the very same thing. I was also with David Yonggi Cho of Korea, pastor of the world's largest church. One time he was recounting an experience he had in a hotel room in Tokyo and talked about how "...the devil came and sat at the foot of my bed." I asked him what this figure looked like, and he described a three-meter-tall gray figure with green eyes and teeth. Hmmmm! Somehow this story got out and was copied on the bulletin board downstairs from my Fuller Seminary office window. I recall seeing students standing five to ten deep reading it. This all sparked a great deal of interest and became quite the hot topic around the seminary.

Then, a strange turn of events occurred. The next few years were the most painful of our time at Fuller. What apparently happened was that a number of the students from the School of Theology began to hold some discussions in their classes that the school of theology professors did not want to deal with or did not appreciate, as near as we can figure out. This eventually led to a series of discussions in the faculty and the upshot was that some of the school of theology professors (of cessationist theology, that the miraculous gifts went out with the death of the apostles) were asked by the administration to help teach the class to bring another point of view into the topic of healing. This was really a great disappointment, because we felt that some of the academic freedom that Peter was promised as a tenured professor was taken away. To say the least, the topics of praying for the sick and casting out demons were greatly watered down and compromised.

Things got even worse when the faculty discussions turned into what could have been interpreted as a heresy trial! Peter and I also felt that underneath the foment was an underlying desire to have him fired or to make it so uncomfortable on him that he would resign his teaching position. In order for a person to be fired from the faculty, proof had to be forthcoming in one of three areas: doctrinal heresy, immorality, or financial impropriety. Search as they might, they were unable to pin anything on Peter. There was nothing in the Fuller statement of faith against praying for the sick, and it certainly was impossible to prove that it was scripturally wrong. What had probably come up was the belief on the part of a number of the faculty that things such as signs and wonders had ceased to exist with the death of the apostles at the time of Christ. This cessationst view was standing in the way of the faith to believe in signs and wonders for today on the part of some of the faculty. They were drawn so far out of their comfort zone that a battle ensued. Part of it may also have been that we were perceived as charismatics and, in the midst of a school of reformed doctrine, that didn't fit very well and so gave rise to friction.

It was very interesting to Peter and me that the School of World Mission faculty was very supportive of us. One of the School of Psychology professors also stood with us wholeheartedly. All of these were people who had cross-cultural experience in ministry and totally understood the importance of what we were teaching. Several of them had been involved in the casting out of demons on the mission field. Dr. Charles Kraft, who had served as a missionary in Nigeria, really picked up on praying for the sick and inner healing and was a staunch ally of ours. He continues deeply involved in this ministry up until today. After Peter and I left the School of World Mission, Dr. Kraft carried on with the teaching of some of the classes having to do with inner healing and the casting out demons. John Wimber was deeply hurt, and I don't think he ever really recovered before his death in 1997. John was a special, deeply committed man who did the world a lot of good. I am only sorry he was not fully appreciated by the academic community. John was not approved because he did not have the academic credentials the leaders felt necessary in order teach in an accredited seminary. The class got so watered down by other professors disagreeing with our point of view that Peter gave up teaching it, much to the dismay of many. Praying for the sick is a handy dandy tool for missionaries to have, but the theologians overruled us unfortunately. This is probably why Peter entitled his memoirs "Wresting with Alligators (which he did in the jungle), Prophets (he sought to bring credibility to the modern-day prophetic movement), and Theologians (a well-fought battle that he could not win because of doctrinal issues). And that last one was the worst of the wrestling, to be sure. But we do thank God for the large classes that were exposed to the teaching and went out and practiced it. One of our missionary students in a difficult area of ministry in the world, told us of his raising a child from the dead! So, some good was accomplished. This was also excellent training for us to later teach very large and fruitful seminars to thousands of individuals when we ran Global Harvest Ministries.

That era was very unpleasant for both of us, but since we felt we were in the will of God, we fought it through to the end. My personal observation is that Peter was extremely gracious throughout it all. I felt as though we had been branded as "weird," and viewed with suspicion. I do know that our most outspoken critics from the faculty and administration left the seminary within just a few years for one reason or another. I felt that in the end a truce was called. It may have been because the large classes were bringing in a hefty amount of tuition, and it could have been for expediency's sake. But things were never the same for me after that sour experience. I personally felt Peter was being treated rather shabbily. By then, it was the decade of the 90s, and I had moved on to more fun things to do in the Prayer Movement and, therefore, tried to put it behind me.

We made the move to Colorado Springs in 1996, and Peter continued to teach at Fuller while commuting back to Pasadena for his classes, which often lasted two weeks at a stretch, until 2001 when he resigned.

What did this period of time teach me? Our friendship with John Wimber was a priceless treasure, and he taught and demonstrated so very much to us. I got my feet wet in the field of deliverance and have since prayed for and taught thousands of pastors and men and women from all walks of life and on most continents of the world. I so thank God for Noel and Phyl Gibson, now both deceased, but they spent hours mentoring me in a rock-solid foundation of deliverance that has stood me in good stead. I praise God for Youth With a Mission. I found another true calling and loved it. I find it to be so gratifying to see a person freed up from bondages, many of which have been lifelong. I watched Peter fight the good fight of faith with grace and humility and respected him even more for it. I watched him teach the Book of Acts to our large adult Sunday School class, and they were very anxious, as was the early church we studied, to pray for the sick and cast out demons. We determined to live out the Book of Acts in our day. Those in the Sunday School class were such an encouragement to us as other battles were raging. We always felt like we were in the center of God's will, and with this assurance, we kept pressing onward. As long as Peter and I were together in mind, body and spirit, not much else mattered, even though at times we felt like it was "You and me against the world." But those times were few, and we never disagreed with each other; we knew God would see us through, as He certainly did. Little did we know that our best days were still ahead!

CHAPTER 11

Catching Up On The Kids And Our Most Productive Ministry

Let me backtrack a little to fill in some of the blanks. We moved from Bolivia to California in August of 1971. It was right after a major earthquake. I believe it was the Simi Valley quake in June, and over 60 people were killed, as I recall. The majority of those died in a veteran's hospital. In light of those events it seemed as though there were houses for sale on every block. Since we had been missionaries in South America, the Spanish-style houses particularly appealed to us, and we looked at house after house until we were virtually cross-eyed. We finally settled on one in the city of Altadena, which was a great bargain at the time. It was just three miles north of Fuller Seminary, and perhaps four miles from Fuller Evangelistic Association. The Altadena elementary school was just a couple of blocks from our home, and Karen's high school was maybe five miles away, but since she was 16 years old, she would soon be driving. Lake Avenue Congregational Church was also about three miles from our front door. It was very close to a grocery store, a bank, a pharmacy, the cleaners, and all sorts of convenient shopping. However, even though it was a spacious and beautiful home on a corner lot, it was in a rather rough, integrated neighborhood. We had to be very careful to keep our doors locked and keep a watchful eye at all times. We were told that, at that time, about 10 blocks from our home was located the highest daytime crime rate in the state of California, and that's saying something! We knew there were drug dealers that lived very close to us, and it was not unusual to hear gunshots especially at night.

On one occasion there was a movie shot down the street just a couple of houses away from ours. It starred the then-famous actor Christopher Reeves while he was still very healthy before the tragic accident that left him a quadriplegic. The movie company came to our front door with a paper for us to sign, agreeing that it would be okay with us to do the movie. They explained that much of the movie would be shot at night after dark and that we would hear gunshots. They assured us that the bullets were all blanks and we did not need to be worried. We explained to them that gunshots were not uncommon in our neighborhood and those were the ones we were really worried about! We assume that none of those were blanks.

It took a little getting used to the new environment and the occasional earthquakes. We seemed to get a good shaker every few years. However, there was a nice space for a vegetable garden, which I started and Peter took over a couple of years later. We planted a few fruit trees and got some harvest. A pretty and productive lemon tree survived the change from a vegetable garden to a "prayer garden," and in later years, because we traveled so very much, we landscaped the area into flowers, shrubs and a water feature. It was lovely. The kids had married and left home, and Peter and I both traveled extensively, and two people can eat just so much zucchini!

I adored my flowers. I could plant both winter flowers (primroses, pansies and snapdragons) and a second batch of summer ones for two crops of flowers in our front yard around our three-tiered Spanish fountain per year. We grew some water plants in the pool at the base of the fountain. I once tried fancy goldfish in the pool, only to discover that they made a marvelous appetizer for the many raccoons that lived nearby somewhere. They managed to wiggle in the courtyard between the iron gate uprights. Peter added to the gunshots in the neighborhood on several occasions and managed to kill a few of them from the balcony off of our bedroom. They were very large coons!! We estimated one of them to weigh 40 pounds.

We had enormous deodar trees along the road, as did the entire street, over a mile up and down hill. Our street, Santa Rosa Avenue, was a historical landmark. The trees were over 100 years old, had been imported from the Himalayas and resembled the tamarack (wispy limbed evergreens) that could be found in my native New York State. They were decked with colored lights every Christmas, and our street was also called "Christmas Tree Lane." We were told that in the earlier days of Pasadena, chariot races were held between the trees.

Beneath the four or five deodar trees planted on our property, I planted hundreds of impatiens that bloomed profusely. When the job of planting got too much for me, I hired some Mexican help. They were delighted that I could speak Spanish with them, and the job got done quickly and efficiently. I sometimes saw people slow down to enjoy the flowers; to share their beauty brought me joy as well. Bird-of-paradise grew like weeds, and I enjoyed making tropical looking arrangements out of them. We had a couple of camellia bushes and azaleas as well. Two other flowers were my specialty: Roses (I had 42 bushes and took blossoms by the armful to work to give away) and also cymbidiums that look so much like orchids. I had several rows of pots of them on the top of a wall by our carport and when the time came for them to bloom, I put them by my front door entrance. They were very showy, if not downright elegant.

Because our home was large and we had a particularly big living room, it fell to my lot to be the hostess for many activities and large parties. I dearly loved to cook and entertain and had a great deal of experience from my days in Bolivia. I recall that on one occasion we had invited over all of the missionaries and faculty that were Spanish-speaking, and there were about 80 people in attendance. Many of them were eating their meal sitting on our stairs that lead up to our bedrooms. The dining room, living room, and outdoor patio were jammed, but it was great fun.

We also had a post-wedding reception party for daughter Ruth and her new husband Alex when they were married in 1985. I believe that crowd may have been just slightly larger and was probably in the neighborhood of 90 to 100 of their closest friends. But those entertaining days are now gone, as I am pretty well confined to a wheelchair and can no longer cook up a storm as I would like!

Getting back to our move to California from Bolivia. The three girls settled down in their schools. Karen could pretty well take care of herself because of her background. The one thing that helped a little bit was that our children were always accustomed to being part of the minority and knew how to act accordingly. She was always interested in nursing and went into the field as early as her senior year in high school. She attended nursing school at Pasadena City College and did very well. She has been employed at Huntington Memorial Hospital in Pasadena for over 40 years, working in the Surgical Intensive Care Unit. She eventually met and married a young man from Lake Avenue Congregational Church. He came from a very fine family and showed great promise but had some major moral flaws. The marriage was terminated after the birth of Christopher, Phillip and Jennifer, and 24 years of an unhappy marriage. Karen carries on very well as a single mother. She has worked very hard to provide for her two sons and has even put her daughter through college. It has been extremely difficult, but she has done an admirable job. She is a wonderful mother and grandmother.

The one who probably suffered the most was Ruth. She had not yet outgrown her walking disability and was a little feisty herself. On one occasion around the sixth grade, as I recall, she was jumped by a gang of girls who wanted to steal her lunch money, and in the ensuing melee, her knee hit her ear and her eardrum was broken. That proved to be quite costly, but it was able to be pretty well repaired by using some of the tissue behind her ear to form a new eardrum. It seemed to serve her very well until unfortunately some shooting practice without earplugs damaged her hearing as an adult. She also struggled with scuba diving when she was a teenager. When she was about 20 feet below the surface, a drop of water penetrated that ear drum and she suddenly did not know which way was up. It was an extremely frightening experience for her and she gave up scuba diving.

Probably because Ruth was raised in a mechanic shop, her interest in automobile mechanics and related topics led her to enroll in Pasadena City College with a major in welding and auto mechanics. She discovered during the course of her studies that she had been severely dyslexic all of her life and could have gotten state aid to assist in coping with this disability. But she managed to be an average or above student despite all of this.

She loved welding and even beat out all the other guys in her graduating class by winning the welding prize that year. She then worked for Southern California Edison Electric Company and repaired brakes on their large trucks for two years. She then got a fun job welding the infrastructures of the floats for our very famous Pasadena Rose Parade.

Because she was so much smaller than the guys who were her co-workers, she was sometimes harnessed with safety gear and hoisted to the taller spots that needed welding. In 1981, Ruth was selected to take part in the actual Rose Parade that occurs each New Year's Day in Pasadena. Her float-making company, Festival Artists, built the float entry sponsored by Baskin Robbins Ice Cream. There was a medium-sized float followed by 31 miniature floats, which were built over golf carts totally covered with flowers, of course, and appropriately decorated to represent their 31 flavors of ice cream. She was dressed as a ladybug with a big red speckled Styrofoam hump on her back and strolled among the miniature floats. She had to walk the entire route of the parade, which is 5.5 miles (9 kilometers) from start to finish. She got blisters under blisters on her feet by the end of the parade.

At the time, we had five television sets in the house. They were all pretty small, but we lined them up and watched for her to appear on the major networks on national television. Then, when she had passed all the cameras, we drove down to the parade route. We had our personal parking space saved at Fuller Seminary, just one short block from the parade route, and watched her in person. We were yelling to her from the top of our lungs! An estimated million to a million and a half persons crowd the parade route, some in paid spots in bleachers, but most folks just take folding chairs and set them up as close to the blue line painted on the street, close to the curb for a front-row seat all along the parade route. Someone has to guard the chairs and spot all New Year's Eve night, as others will shove them out of the way and usurp the few square feet of real estate if left unattended. Poor Ruth had to soak her feet for hours after she got home at the end of the parade. But, in a sense, it was a huge victory considering that in her childhood we were told she might have struggles walking at all! God is good.

It was during her studies at PCC that she met Alex Irons, the man she eventually married. They moved to Wyoming to a large ranch. Alex's parents moved to Wyoming with them. His mother was a medical doctor and worked at a veteran's hospital until her retirement. Ruth and Alex spent something like 20 or more years together. Three children were born to them, Katie, Josh, and Herbie. They have been separated for over 10 years, but are still friends. Ruth has lived with us during that time, and because my health has been fragile, Ruth cared for me in order to enable her father to continue on in his ministry. Since Peter's death, she has been my 24/7 caregiver, for which I am very grateful. She visits their farm in Wyoming every now and then, and she and Alex talk on the phone multiple times every day.

Becky has always been our easy-going child. I think it's because we all sort of raised her together. She had a way with words ever since she was a child and always used very large words from an early age, many times not knowing exactly what the definitions were. It often caused great amounts of laughter in those days when she was in grade school. She began working after school in our office at Fuller Evangelistic Association when she was very young and learned many office skills and computer skills by apprenticeship and did a great job at it. She is following in her father's footsteps as a writer. She has co-authored eight books with Chuck Pierce and really got him started on his writing career. He no longer needs her help. She has also co-authored one with Bob Beckett and one with Tommie Femrite. The material is Tommie's, but all of the beautiful writing is Becky's. Writing just comes naturally to her. She has skillfully produced the index for a dozen or more of her father's books. Unfortunately, currently she is unable to use her gifts as much as she would like to because she is the mother of two autistic sons, and that job is all-consuming. She met and married Jack Sytsema, a very fine young man who was in several of Peter's classes at Fuller Seminary. Jack often volunteered at our office and endeared himself to us during his seminary days.

Jack and Becky were married in 1996 just one month after we made the move to Colorado. I think one of the saddest days of my life was when we buried their first child, a beautiful stillborn daughter named Anna Jean. I carefully looked after her grave all of our remaining years in Colorado; they had moved to Florida to get better care for their autistic sons, Nicholas and Samuel. Nick is profoundly autistic and cannot talk or function normally. He is over 20 at this writing and still at home being cared for by his parents. A suitable group home has not become available for him, according to the State of Michigan, where they now live. They have a third son, William (nicknamed "Trey" because he is the third son of a third son and a third daughter). He is very bright and at an early age was identified as "gifted." His personality is much like Becky's, in that he has a way with words and often makes us laugh. He does amazingly well living with his two handicapped brothers and is very well adjusted and an enormous blessing to us all. At this writing, their recent church plant, Lake Effect Church in Grand Rapids, Michigan, is doing very well. Jack is an excellent pastor and preacher. Becky is very active in the church, functions as a co-pastor and does the brunt of the administrative work. They are very happy in spite of their difficulties.

Back to California and our time at the School of World Mission and A.D. 2000, which I personally consider to be some of our most productive days of ministry. We settled in our new home in Altadena, California, and actually stayed there 30 years. The 1970s were spent with Peter's working at Fuller Evangelistic Association and Fuller School of World Mission and earning his PhD. I had my office at FEA and worked on their mission projects. Peter's office was there also, where he met with his individual students when necessary. I believe I worked from my office at FEA for about nine years, and somewhere in the early 80s, I moved over to the School of World Mission where I got a cubicle right outside Peter's office. I served as his assistant and "moat dragon," making all of his appointments. I also served as research librarian, so I kept track of every thesis and dissertation, made sure they met literary standards, sent them off to be bound, and looked after the entire research library. I had to sign off each student for graduation, making sure he or she had jumped through all of the appropriate hoops in regard to their thesis or dissertation.

It was also my duty to help produce our alumni newspaper, keeping track of all alumni, giving them news of the school and passing along the alumni news to all grads. Maintaining an accurate list of the whereabouts of a few thousand alumni was a challenge because missionaries are always on the move. Peter and I were also in charge of publicity, so I placed ads for the School of World Mission in the various mission journals and Christian magazines.

The notorious flap with John Wimber took place in the 80s, and Peter became more widely known and was traveling extensively. One by one our girls got married and left home, and I was a little freer to get around myself. Peter was very active in the Lausanne Committee for World Evangelization during the 70s and 80s. This required travel to many parts of the world for meetings.

It was during the time when Peter and John Wimber were working together, and Peter was so very active in the Lausanne Committee that he became afflicted with a horrendous headache that lasted 70 days and 70 nights. Nothing would bring relief for more than brief interludes. John felt that somewhere, somehow, Peter had been subjected to a curse and the headache was caused by an afflicting demon. So, John prayed healing over Peter and suddenly the problem was gone. Having seen Peter suffer so with that headache and seeing him healed in an instant was another reason that spurred me on to learn more about demons and how to cast them out.

Then came the 90s and the first decade of the new millennium. Those 20 years were what I consider to be my most productive years before becoming handicapped. I was able to work harder than ever before and things become simpler with just Peter and me living at home.

We agreed to work with AD2000 coordinating the United Prayer Track. We really enjoyed working with Luis Bush, a native-born Argentinian, who understood and could easily work alongside charismatics.

As a personal aside, I have sought the Lord concerning the gift of tongues, but it never came. Many people have prayed over me asking God to download it to me, but to no avail. John Wimber once joked telling me I was the only "dud" he ever had, and everyone else he prayed for spoke in tongues. I am okay with that, figuring that I have enough other giftings to serve the Lord and keep me busy. It has not kept me from casting out demons or ministering in other ways. I realize that I am looked at with a jaundiced eye by some of my charismatic colleagues, not quite as though I had a slight case of leprosy, but that something is wrong with me. That doesn't bother me a bit. I have asked, it has not come, and I am content. Scripture says that God gives gifts *as He will* and that's good enough for me. I take solace in the words of Paul in I Corinthians 12:29-30 "Are all apostles? Are all prophets? Are all teachers? Are all workers of miracles? Do all have gifts of healings? Do all speak with tongues? Do all interpret?" I believe the obvious answer to all of those questions is "No!" That being said,

I admire and feel very comfortable working alongside my colleagues with strong gifts of prophecy, tongues and interpretation and healing, and thoroughly enjoy working with them. I feel equally comfortable with my evangelical brothers and sisters. However, I never quite know what to do when a leader tells everyone in the audience to pray in tongues or to prophesy to a neighbor. I guess the leader figures that if you are in the audience, you are automatically a tongues speaker and a prophet.

The details about how we got involved with AD2000 are spelled out in Peter's memoirs, so I won't repeat them here. The upshot is that I had to leave Fuller School of World Mission and administer our new organization we had to form to house the worldwide prayer movement. We called it Global Harvest Ministries and found an office just a few blocks from Fuller seminary. Dr. Charles Van Engen was another professor at Fuller Seminary and was a missionary to Mexico along with his sweet wife Jean Van Engen. Peter and I took them out to dinner and offered Jean the job of office manager for the prayer movement. I love Jean. We both were Spanish speakers, and she was a cheerful and delightful coworker. I can never recall a single argument or disagreement in all the years we worked together. She helped grow Global Harvest from the very beginning into something huge.

God had set us up very well for the 20 years that I worked for Fuller. We had become very close friends with many worldwide leaders when they were students at the School of World Mission from scores of countries around the world. I had their names and addresses and knew about many of their ministries, and even their families. Many had been in our home for various get-togethers. Peter and I especially enjoyed working with the mature, experienced missionaries and national leaders, and since we were friends, they all responded positively to us when we asked if they would help us enlist a prayer army for about ten years in order to concentrate effort and energy on the unreached people groups. The A.D. 2000 initiative was an effort for the decade of the 1990s only and was to end at the turn of the century. Talk about a supernatural setup! I don't think anyone turned me down, but they all jumped on board, and we immediately got an army of intercessors chomping at the bit to get to work.

If our own personal contacts weren't enough, those persons would often know someone in authority in their or a sister network who could be recruited, often bringing in whole large mission organizations and prayer groups from foreign nations. The main purpose would be prayer. Young and old, men and women, and boys and girls— there would be something for everyone to do. Everything was on a volunteer basis, and our job was to provide information and instructions and coordination from our office at Global Harvest Ministries. Whole organizations joined in, such as Women Aglow (active in over 170 nations of the world, led by Jane Hansen Hoyt), Youth With a Mission (an enormous organization also active all over the world, led by John Dawson), Concerts of Prayer led by David Bryant, Campus Crusade for Christ's World Prayer Crusade, Intercessors International led by Beth Alves, The Prayer Room Network led by Terry Teykl, The End Time Handmaidens led by Gwen Shaw, Heal the Land led by John Dawson, Generals of Intercession led by Cindy Jacobs, Every Home for Christ led by Dick Eastman, Christ for the City led by Paul Landry, Marches for Jesus led by Graham Kendrick, Harvest Evangelism led by Ed Silvoso, many large mission boards and prayer organizations all over the world, far too many to list here. We had a large group of children called the Esther Network led by Esther Ilnisky, and I think, if I remember correctly, a group of YWAMers called King's Kids joined in.

Some of the kids traveled to international meetings with us and prayed right alongside the adults.

I especially enjoyed helping set up the Marches for Jesus around the world.

In addition, Peter and his strategy-working group divided up the whole world into geographical sections and major unreached people groups and data was collected for prayer purposes and to inform mission organizations of the remaining task of world evangelization. For several years books were published entitled *Unreached Peoples*. These were produced by World Vision's MARC (Missions Advanced Research Commission) and Peter's Strategy Working Group, part of the Lausanne Committee on World Evangelization, of which Peter had been a member since its beginning. The books started in 1979 and carried on publication for three years until the major research had been completed.

Peter and the Strategy Working Group also divided up the world into smaller geographical areas, and many of our students from the School of World Mission were already laboring all over the world, and they willingly accepted overseeing the cause of evangelization in their part of the world, as well as raising up an army of intercessors to pray in the harvest. The Intercession Team out of our office was led by Chuck Pierce and Bobbye Byerly. They usually accompanied us as we led seminars all over the country and were an invaluable asset to us. They often had special intercessor teams praying in a back room somewhere during the seminars.

This was a massive, expensive—I dare say multi-million-dollar undertaking—and each person or organization paid their own way. It gave new meaning to Psalm 110:3, "Your people shall be volunteers in the day of Your power." Our budget remained small; we were responsible for a few salaries and office expenses and many mailings and printings, since not everyone was set up with computers and email at the time. And there were volunteers to help pay for it and volunteers to stuff envelopes. It was a massive job, but it came together easily and well. To advertise our upcoming seminars, we would often mail post-cards. Our mailing list got so large that I remember signing a check once for a mailing house to print and mail small postcards for one seminar of ours, and the cost was $38,000!

One of Peter's students, part of a wealthy business family, greatly helped us in setting up the office and helped us get a start until we were able to build up our own donor base. When his family found out that Peter was friendly toward our charismatic brothers and sisters, our support was suddenly and totally cut off, and he disappeared from sight. But God used him to get us started, and we are very grateful.

So, we had an enormous army in place ready for marching orders! By the time we finished our last prayer thrust in 1997, it was conservatively estimated that there were 50,000,000 believers "Praying Through the Window." By the time we came to our last event in Ephesus in 1999, Peter declared that the prayer movement was "out of control," and we have no idea how many millions of brothers and sisters were part of that praying army!

When we began, our first job was to scope out the remaining task of world evangelization by identifying significantly large people groups yet totally unreached or that the Christian beachhead was so small that it remained without a church large enough to be capable of evangelizing their own group.

Peter had been working with the Strategy Working Group of the Lausanne Committee for World Evangelization, so the work had been begun. After a few grueling meetings with the researchers involved, it was decided that we would use the figure of 1,739 unreached people groups.

Let me put in a disclaimer at this point. When the project was over, we gathered up all of our files and sent them to the Billy Graham archives for research and safekeeping. Therefore, copies of our mailings, etc. are no longer here in my office. So, I will paint broad brushstrokes, as best I can remember them.

As I recall, the Strategy Working Group of the Lausanne Committee for World Evangelization, World Vision, and Ralph Winter's group at the U. S. Center for World Mission had input here. At first it was difficult to arrive at an exact number, because Ralph's group wanted a very large number, but we needed a workable, realistic, accurate number. It's all in how they were counted and where they were located. Ralph included groups like "Iranian taxi drivers in Paris" when the Arab peoples were listed elsewhere and already counted. As I recall, Ralph's original figure was upwards of 16,000 unreached people groups, and that included many small sub-groupings. But, after a great deal of work and refining by all of the research leaders, they agreed that the final number we were to work with was 1,739 significant unreached people groups. This was manageable.

Larry Stockstill's church, Bethany World Prayer Center in Baker, Louisiana, single-handedly undertook the enormous task of producing a brief four-page profile of every one of these groups with the information they could glean from mission, country, encyclopedia sources, etc., including photos of the people when they could find them. It was a massive job and the finished profiles (of only one 8 1/2 by 11 sheet of paper, folded in half like a pamphlet, per people group) filled three white boxes that measured in length just about 13 inches on my bookshelf! What a labor of love!

Luis Bush had noticed that the majority of the unreached groups were located geographically across Africa and Asia from 10 degrees latitude to 40 degrees latitude! It began a bit above the equator in Africa and went directly east to Indonesia and stretched north nearly to France on the west and cut straight east to Japan It included most of China, all of India and the Middle East. It also included the seat of the world's non-Christian religions, the most deserts, the most poverty and hunger, the worst treatment of women, etc. This rectangle on the map needed a name, and Doris Bush, Luis' wife, came up with the word "window" so it then became the 10/40 Window. Our prayer events were called, "Praying Through the Window."

We then produced occasional calendars with various prayer efforts. We gave information on how unreached for the gospel the various nations and people groups within them were. Many churches adopted an unreached people group and prayed for them. Some even sent teams to the group to pray on-site and sent missionaries to evangelize. They tried to meet physical needs of their adopted group and a good deal of humanitarian work took place over the decade. As mission boards, denominational mission boards, and even churches became aware of the need, they could focus in on the need and help get the job done. Coordination seemed to be the key, and the intercessors dearly loved to pray for something and see action take place. At this writing the number of unreached people groups has dropped from 1,739 to about 550! Those 550 are being worked on and are in the most difficult places, or the ones located in closed nations that have to be reached by other means. During the 1990s, if Americans or Europeans were unable to reach them, there were strong churches or businesspeople in Africa, Asia or Latin America that had no restrictions on entering those areas to pray or work. All people needed was information and suddenly a huge army appeared to, as Larry the cable man says, "Get 'er done!"

It was during this ten-year period of time Peter and I lived in Colorado Springs and began holding seminars. Our first set of seminars was on the subject of intercession. I loved these seminars because it finally gave credence to the gift of intercession and encouraged this precious group of, oddly enough, mostly women, to have their gift recognized and to encourage them and give them fodder for prayer. These were held all over the country and in many foreign nations. Then we became very involved in spiritual warfare, which included the more experienced and advanced intercessors, and those seminars took off. We led large seminars on the topic of transformation since we desperately wanted God's people to see His "Kingdom come, on earth as it is in heaven." We also began doing seminars on deliverance and the interest was unbelievable. The first one we had in Colorado Springs drew over 3,000 participants. Dear friend and colleague, Frank Hammond, who wrote one of the very first books on the topic, *Pigs in the Parlor,* taught in our seminars occasionally until his death.

Somehow God has seemed to gift me with the ability to help people get free from sexual bondages, an extremely pervasive problem in today's world. So, we bravely moved ahead to have an entire seminar entitled "Finding Freedom from Sexual Bondages." Then it hit the fan!!! We got a myriad of requests from persons all over scolding us for addressing the topic and asking to be removed from our mailing list. But this proved to be a blessing in disguise because dozens and dozens asked if we could get the seminar online, and it was the beginning of our getting out to our constituency over the internet. In retrospect, my guess is that folks feared if they attended the seminar they might be branded as those with sexual bondages and they didn't want to take that chance, even if it might be true. It was out of this effort that the International Society of Deliverance Ministers was birthed and continues to thrive today. Peter and I started the Society in the year 2000 and led it until 2010. Thereafter, it had been capably led by Bill and Sylvie Sudduth until Bill's untimely death due to COVID-19 on November 1, 2020. But it certainly will continue on vigorously. Membership hovers around 300 deliverance ministers who meet yearly and share new insights into what God is teaching us.

There were very long stretches where we were doing a major seminar, sometimes even two per month, all over the country. I was thrilled with the response and felt very fulfilled, although dog-tired at times.

It was during February or March in the early 90s, in our busy seminar season when we were recruiting our army of intercessors, that Peter had another very close call. He was preparing the preliminary figures to send to our tax man, and he climbed up to a loft we had over our cars in our garage in Pasadena. My guess is that the loft was about twelve feet off the cement floor. It took our longest step ladder to get up there, using the top step. Peter needed some information from his tax return from the previous year, stored in a trunk in that loft. He retrieved the information and as he was about to descend, he said he felt he was pushed. The ladder flew out from under him, and he fell flat on his back on the cement floor. The bulk of his body would have fallen from about 14 feet. I was ironing his shirts, preparing him for a ministry trip to Brazil in a day or two. I heard the ruckus and ran out the back door to the garage to find him dazed and lying flat on his back. I screamed, "Don't move, don't move!" I feared he might have broken his neck or back. Our dear neighbor came running over and called 911, and they got him to the emergency room on a stretcher. It turned out he suffered severe bruises, but no broken bones. He left for Brazil on time, but it was a terrible trip. It was a very long, uncomfortable airplane trip both ways. He was at some sort of a conference and had to sleep on a thin, straw mattress with some of the worst pain of his life. His back, ribs and shoulders were black and blue for several weeks. We both firmly believe a demon pushed him off the loft. But we also believe an angel cushioned his fall enough to prevent his death or some paralyzing injury. We later learned that one of our intercessors was at a movie and felt an urgency to pray, that someone, not of her family, but a close friend, was in severe danger. She immediately left the theater, hung out in a corner in the lobby and prayed protection over whomever it was that was in danger. Peter thought that may have saved his life. We love intercessors; they hear from God. But then they have the good sense to stop and pray during the emergency.

I do not recall exactly when, but it was while we were living in Pasadena that Peter made a trip to Japan. I believe it was with Dr. Paul Yonggi Cho, pastor of the world's largest church in Seoul, Korea, at the time. I had been suffering from severe degenerative joint disease and needed some foot surgery to correct some major problems with my foot breaking down. My problem was called Charcot Foot. Ruth says she distinctly remembers the orthopedic surgeon say he counted either 21 or 22 fractures in my foot. The surgery went well, I was in a cast for a time and when things were healed, it was time to remove the cast and pins that had been in several hammer toes. When the pins were removed, I noticed that I was bleeding pretty profusely but was bandaged up and sent home.

Peter had already been in Japan a few days doing a seminar for Japanese church leaders. The growth of the church in Japan was always a disappointment to us. There were no large churches and those that were planted all seemed to be very small and struggling, quite the opposite of our Korean friends just a few hundred miles away. We were praying fervently for a revival in Japan.

I awoke the morning after the pins were removed and could not breathe. I was alone in the house, but I called Becky who lived nearby. She had a key to the house, so she came over immediately and called 911, and I was transported to Huntington Memorial Hospital in bad shape. My family doctor came rushing over telling me I had a severe case of pulmonary emboli (blood clots in both lungs), and I was breathing with a tiny part in the bottom of one lung the size of an orange. The rest of both lungs was coated with blood clots. I was immediately put on blood thinners. We managed to get a phone call through to Peter (remember, these were the days before cell phones), who wanted to drop everything and rush home because my life was in the balance. I remember Pam Marhad (this was the same Pam Toomey who had served in Bolivia with us and was my dear friend, now married to George Marhad) was sitting at the foot of my bed for hours praying for me. I remember telling Peter that all that could be done for me was happening, it would probably take him two days to get home, and "We will not give the devil the satisfaction of pulling you away from ministry in Japan." I encouraged him to stay, and he did. It took me quite a few days to get well again, but I did. My degenerative joint disease has been so bad that to date (2021) I have had exactly 50 surgeries including both knee replacements, both hip replacements, one shoulder replacement, multiple foot surgeries, and a mid-thigh leg amputation. But I feel fine and at this writing in 2021 am wheelchair-bound, but I get to where I want to go and continue to teach as opportunity arises and minister deliverance weekly. God is good, and once more, "To the Lord belong escapes from death."

Ruth and I recently purchased an R.V. and have begun to travel all over the country doing seminars on deliverance and praying for those in bondage. Ruth is the driver and mechanic and I have a hospital bed in the back, a wonderful platform with a hydraulic life to get me up and down and in and out of the R.V. in a few seconds. We travel the country for weeks or months at a time, and I am determined to keep on in ministry as long as I possibly can. After all, I am only 89 years old at this writing.

Probably our most dramatic escape from death occurred sometime in the early 90s, and unfortunately, I cannot recall the year. I do recall that we were studying signs and wonders still, but were focusing on territorial spirits and how to defeat them. We had formed a group of specialized intercessors and spiritual mappers and called it the "Spiritual Warfare Network." Our job was to figure out how to identify and defeat these territorial spirits that seemed to hold the local people captive to sin and degradation.

We heard about an indigenous small city in Guatemala that had defeated a pagan god named Maximon (pronounced "Ma-she-moan," accent on the last syllable). There was even a pagan idol by that name that was worshipped, which was located the next town over just a few miles from Almolonga. What we call "a people movement" had begun in Almolonga, formerly a city of vice, drunkenness, wife-beating and immorality. But a few people somehow came to the Lord, then little by little the vast majority of the inhabitants got saved and large churches were built to accommodate the crowds. I do not remember the exact percentage, but somehow the number of close to 90% seems to stick in my mind, but that is just a guess. The local jail was closed due to a lack of inmates.

These people were vegetable farmers and God seemed to begin to bless the very land of the surrounding hills, and their vegetables began to increase in quality and quantity. It seemed as though the soil was being supernaturally watered and nourished. The people became wealthy and began to transport their huge harvests down to Guatemala City, and even other Central American nations, in Mercedes trucks paid for in cash! When I visited Almolonga for the first time, just to witness firsthand the total transformation of the place, I recall seeing not a square meter of ground being wasted. I witnessed onions growing close to the path leading up to the front door of one of the houses. The terrain is quite hilly around the city and the hillsides were ablaze with gorgeous fields of flowers in bloom and rows and rows of every kind of vegetable imaginable. That blessed this old farmer's heart, and I uttered an audible "WOW!" We were to visit once or twice again and held a large event there to show people what transformation looks like. Peter and I had been to Guatemala on several occasions and became good friends with Harold and Cecelia Caballeros. They pastored a large church called El Shaddai in Guatemala City and had some of our most active and effective intercessors during the Praying Through the Window initiative. Their university conferred an honorary doctoral degree on Peter a few years later. For some reason, I was unable to attend that event in person.

Peter and I, along with Harold and Cecelia, were on our way to the city of Quetzaltenango in the mountains of Guatemala. We were in a six-passenger twin engine Cessna, as I recall. We were coming in for a landing on a dirt runway. One of Harold's intercessors, Filiberto Lemus, was waiting for our arrival, and he noticed the landing gear of the plane did not come down, so he prayed fervently for us all. Then it happened— we crash-landed! The belly of the plane split apart, forming sort of a plow that scooped up bushels of dirt and spewed it all over the four of us that sat facing each other. The wings cracked and came loose and the propellors bent into right angles. I happened to be sitting next to the door. When we finally came to a halt, I found myself overtaken with a fit of laughter. Peter screamed at me, "Open the door, Open the door. Get out! Get out!!" Of course, he was fearful that we might explode in flames, which, mercifully, we did not. We were all laden down with dirt and could see nothing because our glasses were totally covered with dirt. We celebrated that afternoon dining on homemade tortillas and chicharron (fried pork belly). After all, not very many people walk away from a plane crash. I think God must have dispatched a whole army of angels to protect us that day as our feet were dashed against a dirt runway (Psalm 91). In the event we had crashed on a paved runway, my guess is that sparks would have, indeed, set the plane on fire. The strange thing is that the plane had undergone a total maintenance check just a week or two prior to this incident. The devil had failed again, and we had, one more time, made an escape from death.

I recall one other close call I had. Peter and I were both ministering in Malaysia and Singapore. I had a deliverance seminar in Kuala Lumpur, Malaysia, and there was a very large group of about 800, as I recall, for that three-day seminar with translation, of course. During that time, the water was shut off for some reason that I do not remember. I was teaching when a bug of some sort bit me on my right shin and I automatically bent down and scratched it. I had been to the bathroom a couple of times that day, but there was no water to wash our hands. I finished the seminar the next day and we moved on to Singapore where Peter was teaching and had radio interviews for a few days. I suddenly came down with a high fever and was violently ill. I usually accompanied him to many of his speaking engagements but opted to stay in the hotel that day since I was feeling poorly. As the day progressed, I got weaker and weaker.

I was able to get in touch with one of Peter's former students (Ed Pousson, a missionary to Singapore) who rushed over with his lovely wife. In Singapore because of the traffic congestion, cars with odd-numbered license plates can drive on odd number days, and even-numbered license plates could drive on even number days. They had the wrong license plate for that day, but found an Australian missionary friend with the right one, and they came and immediately transported me to Mount Saint Helen's Hospital, which I later discovered to be considered one of the finest in all of Asia. By that time Peter had finished his obligation and Ed picked him up and brought him over to the hospital. When I was put in a bed, they took my temperature and the nurse gasped loudly. That did not sound very good. They got a doctor there who diagnosed me with a flesh-eating bacterium in my shin where the bug had bitten me in Malaysia. My whole shin was red and swollen. I was very, very ill. They immediately gave me a number of antibiotics intravenously, but I was burning up with fever.

A beautiful Chinese Christian couple stayed by my beside and fanned me with a palm fan and kept placing cold, wet washcloths on my forehead. It took five days for my fever to come down. Peter and I decided to get back home as soon as possible. It was the worst international trip of my life. I was very weak and still violently ill but not contagious. Daughter Karen met us at the Los Angeles airport with her station wagon, with the back made into a bed for me. She drove us directly to her Huntington Hospital in Pasadena where I was immediately admitted. I was placed on the "last ditch" antibiotic, vancomycin, twice daily and remained there for an entire month. I enjoyed being on the top floor right under the helipad so I could watch the severe cases arrive by helicopter. It served as amusement and helped pass the time.

I often reflected on the Chinese couple who were desperately trying to make me comfortable. I never got their names and never got to thank them, sad to say. Maybe they were angels. Anyway, thank you, whoever you were. I think that was the closest scrape with death I ever suffered, and it was not pretty, but God saw me through one more time. And it was back to work at Global Harvest in due time. Jean Van Engen held the fort very well in my absence.

Let me add a brief summary of a bittersweet experience we survived next. The devil did not like what we were doing much, as we were invading his territory and seeing millions snatched from his kingdom of darkness to God's kingdom of light. So, he put a big bump in our road when things were going so very well.

During the early 90s, we were invited by Ted Haggard of New Life Church in Colorado Springs, to build a World Prayer Center on the property of his beautiful facility across Interstate 25 and opposite U.S. Air Force Academy, in view of majestic Pike's Peak. It was gorgeous. It was to provide a home for the very active prayer movement. We packed up our office and home and moved to Colorado Springs. We found temporary space and subleased enough to house our staff. But we discovered that the person who subleased to us had done so illegally, so we were out on the street, or would have been had it not for our friends at David C. Cook Ministries and Publishing House. They had a large, beautiful building with more space than they needed and there was an entire unfinished floor that was vacant. They took us in and leased the space to us for a dollar a year in exchange for finishing off the office space on the top floor. We were no longer homeless and remained at that facility at least a year until our new building at the World Prayer Center was finished and ready to occupy.

Peter and I arduously raised 3.5 million dollars from intercessors and churches all over the world who desperately wanted prayer for their own nations. With this we paid for by far the majority of the construction of the World Prayer Center. As I recall, it was 55,000 square feet and contained rooms for intercessors to come for days at a time to fast and pray. It had a beautiful chapel with circular large windows facing the snow-capped Rockies including Pike's Peak, and it would seat something like 800. We held many small events and prayer meetings there, and when Peter started Wagner Leadership Institute, classes were held in that beautiful chapel. We started a small publishing company called Wagner Publications and produced a few small-run books useful for spiritual mapping, intercession, spiritual warfare, starting a prayer ministry in a local church, leadership, prophecy, holiness, divine healing and other specialized topics. We had a large bookstore in operation, which was eventually managed by Becca Greenwood. Both she and her husband, Greg, were employed by Global Harvest Ministries. Becca had great gifts of intercession and deliverance as well as doing a bang-up job in the bookstore. Our new offices were complete with kitchen, laundry facilities, a beautiful lobby and the gorgeous chapel as well as the hotel rooms.

George Otis and the Sentinel Group from Seattle were to have moved in with us, but something came up and they changed their minds and decided not to move down to Colorado Springs. That was a bit of a disappointment, since they were working with the unreached people groups and transformation theme. But it was not to be. We grew to 53 employees so needed all the space anyway.

A few years later, friction arose between Ted and Global Harvest and we were informed by a janitor that "We had worn out our welcome." We later discovered that Ted was undergoing a moral failure and would be forced to leave the church. He was quite uncomfortable around Peter and me and even said in our last meeting together, "I never invited you to Colorado Springs." This was just before his problem had hit the news and apparently, he was struggling. As Peter and I were driving away from that sad meeting, Peter said to me "Ted is trying to rewrite history."

In any event, we had to look for another office and located a fine, spacious building closer to downtown. While Peter was on a mission trip, I found suitable quarters for us, and bought it on the spot, because it was being offered at a ridiculously low price. Our two new buildings were even more spacious than the World Prayer Center and cost only 1.5 million, as the owners were anxious to sell. However, the whole uprooting and moving experience was a nuisance to have to endure at the time, a bump in the road that expended valuable time, energy, and God's money.

What were lessons learned from this wonderful chapter in my life? I learned that Peter had a God-given power of convocation, and whenever he called a meeting or offered a seminar, or asked to recruit persons for a specialized task, people appeared in droves to join him in the project at hand. Remember, this was all a volunteer work, so they did it for the mere privilege of accomplishing a specialized task. Peter always loved to set realistic, measurable goals for the tasks assigned to him. We loved to rejoice when those goals were met. It seemed to help people work harder and feel rewarded by seeing those goals achieved.

Peter had earned great credibility and was constantly involved in some cutting-edge assignment for the Lord. All of our missionary experience and cross-cultural studies were put to good use, and the myriad of students from all over the world that had endeared themselves to us were anxious to help in this massive undertaking. I especially enjoyed the many seminars we sponsored on several continents that reached thousands of people and trained many in intercession, spiritual warfare, deliverance, praying for the sick, and other relevant topics. We got to meet many worldwide leaders and strategize with missions and evangelism workers. How we loved what we were doing!! The devil was nipping at our heels every now and then, but God met us with great success in our efforts. He kept us both alive through some close brushes with death and the "many dangers, toils and snares" John Newton so beautifully describes in his immortal hymn "Amazing Grace." We felt angelic presence and protection when the devil tried to kill us. We enjoyed the blessing of our wonderful girls, church friends, intercessors and colleagues, as well as God's provision for the work. True, there were a few disappointments and bumps in the road, but we survived them all and felt blessed and privileged to be in the center of God's will.

CHAPTER 12

A Highly Successful Experiment In Argentina And Nepal

It was during the decade of the 90s that we became close friends with Mike and Cindy Jacobs. Cindy had a lot to teach us. As I became more involved in deliverance, I started to teach it to anyone who would listen. It was closely related to intercession. Cindy was called to pray for nations. Peter was called to evangelism and church growth, and we began to feel that all of these fields were closely connected.

Ed Silvoso of Harvest Evangelism was one of the most effective evangelists and brilliant strategists among all of Peter's students. He was from Argentina and was very influential in that nation, although his headquarters was in San Jose, California. Peter and I became close friends with Ed and Ruth. Ed was strategizing on how to reach cities for Christ, while at the same time bringing transformation to the city and its environs. At the time, certain parts of Argentina were in the midst of a vibrant revival. Peter and I went to Argentina and traveled all around that large country on a grueling week with Omar and Marfa Cabrera, a superb evangelist and one who saw signs and wonders. If I recall correctly, John Wimber bought our tickets in order to investigate what was happening there. We had a ball because we could speak the language well and adored the people and the Argentine culture. We returned home thrilled with seeing the revival firsthand.

We became fast friends with Omar and Marfa and met a bevy of other wonderful evangelists who were working a revival like we had never seen in our lifetime. But there were pockets of territory where the revival had not hit and seemed to be very resistant to the Gospel. Ed chose the hardest city he could find and mapped out a plan to evangelize that city, but it was also felt that there were unseen demonic forces that were holding this back. Ed chose the city of Resistencia in Chaco, the northernmost province of Argentina, close to the Bolivian border, not so very far from the jungle area where Peter and I first were sent as missionaries.

Ed, Peter and I conferred, and we felt it good to get Cindy down to Argentina to teach intercession. Ed did not know Cindy and I vividly recall his asking, "But can she preach?" To this I simply smiled and replied, "Trust me, Ed!" This was early 1990. Cindy was not a Spanish speaker, so I was invited to accompany her, to be her roommate, to translate for her and show her around. Marfa Cabrera, whose English was impeccable, would translate her messages. Marfa was a beautiful Argentine lady, who had many connections all over the country since she and Omar were traveling evangelists. She and I stuck close by Cindy all the time we were visiting. Ed was taking a big risk doing these intercession meetings, because at that time, 1990, women ministers were not readily accepted in Latin America. But he took a chance on Peter and me and our judgment and went out on a limb with the whole project which he dubbed "*Plan Resistencia.*"

Ed is a native Argentine, and he also had a local headquarters in Rosario, Argentina, with a team of coworkers on-site. He dispatched a couple of them to Resistencia to do a difficult job, that of researching the history of Resistencia in order to discover why the inhabitants of that city were so resistant to the Gospel. They diligently searched all sorts of documents, meticulously studied the history and came up with the treasure we needed for the spiritual warfare in a few months' time.

I could go into the spiritual atmosphere of Argentina at that time in great and sordid detail, but don't have the space here. To be brief, several decades earlier, Peter and I visited Argentina with the leaders of CLADE (The Lausanne Committee's Latin American Council on Evangelism) for a strategy meeting with the top evangelical leaders of the day from all of Latin America. We had been living in a pretty underdeveloped country, Bolivia, and the city of Buenos Aires looked like Europe to me. It was so clean, prosperous, there were no beggars, they were hard-working people, very well dressed, and there were so many stands on street corners selling flowers. I love flowers, so this caught my attention. People were carrying bunches of flowers in their hands as they went home from work. And I must say that the beef we ate there was the most tender, delicious, flavored beef ever to pass my lips. The animals were totally grass-fed and the flavor is very different. No corn or grain was ever fed to them. As workers were building high-rise apartments, a person was assigned to build a fire, and slowly roast certain cuts of beef over the hot coals for the laborers and that smell was permeating the atmosphere every morning in the streets of Buenos Aires. The workers took a two- or three-hour *siesta* to eat and rest and worked until later on in the day at their jobs.

Then Peter and I returned to Argentina in 1985 when John Wimber sent us down to look over the signs and wonders being reported at Omar and Marfa Cabrera's meetings. That was sixteen years after our first visit. I could not believe my eyes! Everything was dirty, the streets were in disrepair, there were dirty children begging, food was rationed, the newsstands had porn magazines openly displayed, and I saw just a few dry flowers, nothing fresh. I looked at Peter and said, "Where did Argentina go???"

I will try to make a long story short, but these are the notes I wrote down at the time as Ed Silvoso told me. He lived in California, but his mom and extended family lived through it. During the time the famous Juan Peron and his beautiful wife Eva Peron were in power, one of his cabinet members (the minister of social welfare), was a known warlock, named Jose Lopez Rega. He openly invited spiritualists to come to Argentina. A short time later there was a military takeover and Lopez Rega lost power. He cursed the nation of Argentina. Then came the terrible "Dirty War." Figures differ, but somewhere between a minimum of 30,000 and as many as 80,000 influential men "disappeared." They were the cream of the crop intellectually, the doctors, lawyers, wealthy persons in business and industry, etc. It is said that they were rounded up, taken in airplanes way over the ocean and pushed out so their remains would not be found. Then in 1982 the Falkland Island War erupted when Argentina fought Great Britain over the islands and lost the war. The Argentines are very proud people and between the "Dirty War," followed by the Falkland Island War, their pride was broken, their morale plummeted, and a huge economic setback ensued.

When Cindy and I went in June 1990, there was 1,900% inflation. No item in a store window had a price because that price was likely to change once or maybe more per day. I was heartbroken over that beautiful nation that was now so sad. But God was preparing the people for the great revival of that decade that was breaking out. There were a handful of evangelists that God was raising up to preach in theaters, in vacant lots and stadiums. The churches in Buenos Aires were growing rapidly. The people were ready to hear the Gospel and respond.

But because the northern province of Chaco, containing the city of Resistencia, was more secluded and underdeveloped, it remained very resistant. Resistencia was targeted, a city of about 450,000 inhabitants, with a miniscule church of, at the most, 5,500 believers in about 50 or so small, struggling, congregations. When we called all the pastors together, all did not come, but 35 did.

We asked the local Harvest Evangelism team in Buenos Aires to call together a one-day meeting to teach intercession and to pray for Argentina. It was to be held at a Christian campground an hour outside Buenos Aires in the beautiful countryside. We were hoping for about three or four dozen people to turn up. To our amazement, there were six gigantic busloads of people who wanted to learn and pray, and the crowd topped off at 450!! The chapel could not hold them all, so the very elderly sat in the chairs first, then it was first come, first served in the chairs that remained. Mostly the men stood against the walls, and as many as could fit, sat on the cold cement floor (it was June, winter in Argentina, and plenty cold, but no snow). The rest of the overflow of men stood outside and watched and listened through the open windows. Every hour the crowd dutifully swapped places and those who had been standing got to sit. Fortunately, there were no fire marshals to stop the meeting. It was a day of fasting, so no one had to worry about food, folks brought their own water and we just needed a potty break every few hours. The eager crowd was very orderly, and it was an intense day of learning about intercession and spiritual warfare, and carried on until after dark, when we headed back to the city. Cindy and Marfa did a superb job, and everyone left ready to pray for revival in Argentina.

Ed's team had been busy researching the history of Argentina and Buenos Aires, the capital. It was felt that we should do some major warfare in the main plaza of Buenos Aires before heading north on the day's journey to Resistencia. Bear in mind, I am condensing this to the bare bones because the history of this is a yearlong, very complicated endeavor. A strategy was laid out by the Harvest Evangelism team, Cindy and Marfa and me. A precious friend, Jane Rumph, was a writer and editor and she served as our scribe. She was accompanied by her husband, Dave, an engineer who had taken a vacation to come along and pray with and for the team. After the year was over, she produced an 87-page, detailed document of our day-by-day activities.

Let me put forth a disclaimer and warning at this point as to why it was felt that document should not be published yet. This type of high-level spiritual warfare is for the very few definitely called and anointed to take on territorial principalities and powers. It is a very specialized and dangerous undertaking. Our fear was that some might move into this type of warfare prematurely and in presumption and severely harm themselves and others and set back the movement. Only those few definitely called and anointed for the task and backed by an army of intercessors to protect all concerned, should even think of undertaking a task such as this. The backing and blessing of local spiritual authorities must be secured as well. Ed and his Harvest Evangelism team had the blessing of local pastors and evangelists in Argentina. We had secured the intercessory backings of hundreds of friends back home and we kept this endeavor very secretive in the U.S. and very little has been mentioned about it for the above reasons.

The Harvest Evangelism team, Cindy, Marfa, Jane and I, along with local pastors and key intercessors numbering about 80, gathered together at 7:30 a.m. on the cold morning of June 15, 1990, in the Plaza de Mayo in central Buenos Aires. It was winter south of the equator so we were bundled up. I was totally amazed that no one seemed to pay any attention to us whatsoever as we prayed aloud and even sang and worshipped. It is though we were hidden, that large group of 80 people! We prayed, decreed and sang until about noon.

Long story short: We prayed at 5 different spots around the perimeter of the plaza, as research revealed the spirits at work in the country:

1. The Cabildo was the very first governmental building set up after freedom from Spain. We were led to pray against a strong spirit of division and strife prevalent since its founding

2. The *Casa Rosada,* or the Pink House, the current presidential offices. Here the Argentines led in prayers of repentance for corruption and injustices of the past, and prayers were offered for the then–President Menem.

3. The National Bank. Here we prayed against the financial crisis and a spirit of greed. Argentina had a huge national debt, and we prayed concerning that.

4. The Ministry of Social Welfare where Jose Lopez Rega had his offices and had invited in witchcraft. We lingered here and prayed against two very strong spirits, both witchcraft and a spirit of death. Prayers were offered begging God to cleanse the land from the power of the occult and to remove from power those involved in it.

5. The Ministry of Economy. Here a spirit of poverty was discerned as well as an antisemitic spirit. Argentina accepted many Nazis during and after World War II and in so doing, were approving of the hatred of the Jews. So, several Argentine pastors repented of that evil deed of allowing many Nazis to happily live out their days in Argentina and harboring so many of them. A spirit of death was discerned here also, so we prayed against it.

6. We discerned that there was a very strong spirit of the Queen of Heaven and idolatry, but Cindy, Marfa, and the Harvest evangelism pastors felt that was adequately dealt with for the time being when we were praying against the witchcraft and false religions at the Ministry of Social Welfare, so we let that one go for the time being.

We left the next morning by car for the daylong journey north to Resistencia. It is a large, primitive city of about a half million inhabitants, with just a very few paved streets in the center of the city at the time. It had an unusual central plaza. Instead of having a central plaza of just one square block, it was an enormous four-square blocks, with weird murals of strange painted artwork. Many of the streets had sculptures of metal of odd creatures and what looked like modern art, which I personally could never appreciate. I recognized the people group as being very similar to those in Santiago, San Jose, and Bolivia—they even spoke with the same Spanish accent and idioms! These were my people!!

Resistencia was a hard place. It was started by the government mainly to protect the higher class of residents across the mighty Parana River in the city of Corrientes. It has a good-sized indigenous population and was quite poverty-stricken. Most homes were adobe mud blocks with tile roofs. Clean water was hard to come by. When the river would swell after heavy rain, Resistencia would flood because it was on a bend in the river. The inhabitants of Corrientes were known for their pride. Life was a struggle.

Ed had sent a member of his team, Victor Lorenzo, up to Resistencia months ahead of our arrival to research the history and spiritual problems of the city. It is a very long, complicated story, but I will get to the bottom line quickly. Dave and Jane Rumph accompanied us again, and we have the full, accurate report in her essay.

Six strongholds over the city were identified:

1. Spirit of Death. Death was worshipped, and a woman served as the high priestess of the cult of Death. Actually, people had skeletons carved out of human bones implanted under their skin in the hopes of having a good, easy death.

2. Pombero was the name of the spirit of strife and division. That was a main reason why the Protestant churches were not getting along. The pattern was that they grew to about 50 members, had a fight, and split. ALL of the churches had this history and were very small.

3. Kurupi (pronounced Coo-rue-pee, accent on the last syllable). This was a filthy spirit of lust and sexual perversion. Incest, rape, homosexuality, adultery, wife beating, fornication, bestiality, abortion, and child abuse permeated the city. It was horrific.

4. Freemasonry. San Martin was the founder of the north of Argentina and he, as well Simon Bolivar and others of the liberators of South America (as well as almost all of the founding fathers of the U.S.A., for that matter) were Freemasons. There is a great deal of literature written on the subject of how Freemasons curse themselves, their families for generations on down, and their churches and communities. There are statues of San Martin and Bolivar in most central plazas in most cities of Latin America. Sure enough, there was a huge statue of San Martin in the plaza of Resistencia.

5. The spirit of Religion and Idolatry. On every plaza is a cathedral where the inhabitants come to worship. In most instances, the Triune God of Father, Son and Holy Spirit is not what is worshipped, but the spirit of the Queen of Heaven has invaded,

and the false worship of Mary and various saints has replaced it. People are not taught that Jesus died for their sins, but a false teaching had crept in of Mary as a co-redemptrix, a perpetual virgin, and that she did not die, but ascended into heaven as Jesus did, and that Queen of Heaven spirit wants to get the worship instead.

6. Witchcraft seemed to be the biggest, most powerful spirit and seemed to rule over all the others. Much of it came in from neighboring Brazil and indigenous forms were prevalent. Curses were common. A person handed me a piece of paper once and I began to read it to Cindy, assuming it was in Spanish and I would need to translate it for her, when she screamed: "That's a curse, STOP." I am glad her discerner was working that day; it may have been something awful. As I recall, we burned the paper.

We held an intercession seminar in a theater about 8 blocks from our hotel. It was huge; an estimated 700 hundred people turned up for the event. Cindy was her magnificent self, teaching with Marfa translating. The audience was not made up of intercessors, but just some church people and many unbelievers willing to listen. It was very hard, and we all struggled that day. It was the time when the paper with the curse was handed to me, so there were undoubtedly some infiltrators present.

A very small group of us went out to the main plaza early the next morning to do the actual warfare. There were a couple of the Harvest Evangelism team, Cindy and I, Dave and Jane, and maybe a dozen pastors. We did the bulk of the praying at the huge murals, where every clue we needed had already been painted. Here we confronted and prayed against the spirits of death, witchcraft, Pombero and Kurupi.

We prayed against the curses of Freemasonry at the statue of San Martin and against the Queen of Heaven across the street from the cathedral.

Let me briefly explain a sad story. There was a man on Ed Silvoso's team who drove one of the vans to transport us around. Inwardly he objected to us women leading the group of warriors but had been in on the information and strategy sessions with us. He decided he would go to the plaza himself to confront the spirits alone the night before. The morning when he had planned to go, a terrible thing happened to him and he went completely out of his mind. He got the Argentine team home, but died a year or two later, never having recovered from the trauma of being attacked by the spirits and never being in his right mind again.

Ed decided to do a summer of evangelism right after we finished our prayer thrust. He built a good number of wells and water tanks throughout the city to help meet the need of clean water to eliminate the need for women to carry water great distances in clay pots on their heads. He brought American college kids down by the droves to hand out tracts and play tape recordings (the communication medium of the day) of a presentation of the gospel to all who would listen. We held a week of evangelistic meetings at the close of the yearlong effort. Most of the evangelists from Buenos Aires came up to hold magnificent meetings. Hundreds of people were saved and baptized in a mass baptism and the churches began to grow.

On about the next to last trip to Resistencia that Cindy and I made together that year, we were greeted at the plane by an enthusiastic group pf people, saying, "You will never guess what happened." It turned out that the High Priestess of the cult of Death was smoking in bed and, unfortunately, she fell asleep and three items were consumed in her adobe mud block (non-combustible) home: Her body, the mattress she was sleeping on, and several meters across the room, the statue of San La Muerte, the idol of death that the cult worshipped. I was informed in 2018 that there were three men meeting in a home in an attempt to revive the cult of San La Muerte (the Spirit of Death). The tile roof suddenly caved in on top of them and all three men perished. The vigorous growth of the church has apparently kept the territorial spirits pushed back since the 1990s.

Cindy and I went down again to Resistencia for the final week of evangelistic meetings. There were about a half dozen very successful evangelists from Buenos Aires who led the meetings: Carlos Anacondia, Omar Cabrera, Ed Silvoso, and a few others whose names slip me just now. The meetings were held in an outdoor soccer field, and we made known that we wanted to help the believers do some housecleaning. So, we got a big, used, open and vented 55-gallon drum and told people to bring their items that did not please God, wrapped up in newspapers to protect the identities, and toss them in to the barrel as an act of obedience. Each evening the barrel was full to overflowing, kerosene was poured on the contents, and we had a huge bonfire during worship.

Cindy and I made 5 trips to Argentina that year. We did some warfare in the city of Mar del Plata with the local pastors also. There were about 300 of us praying in the main plaza. As in previous trips, we had pastors identify the ruling territorial spirits over the city. I don't remember all we were praying for, but I vividly remember that we prayed against the spirit of witchcraft at exactly 4 p.m., because the clock on the plaza struck four times. The next morning, we had breakfast with Omar and Marfa Cabrera, and Marfa said once again, "You will never guess what happened yesterday." She and Omar had a large association of churches all over Argentina. She said that one of their pastors in

Mar del Plata felt led of the Lord to stay and pray from home instead of joining us at the main plaza. He called them to let them know that at precisely 4 p.m. the leading witch of the city who lived near him dropped over dead and was carried off to the mortuary. It is never our wish that anyone lose his or her life because of spiritual warfare, but for believers, this is a dangerous business, and one must be called to the warfare. Also, my personal theory is that there just may be some folks who are so sold out to Satan and following him that they might reach the point where God gives up on them as being irredeemable. And the judgment of God simply does away with them.

So, does this stuff work??? That is the question. Let me continue on with my story of Resistencia and bring my part to a close.

I am informed by my Argentine friends that massive transformation has come to northern Argentina. Edgardo Silvoso told me that whereas the hot spot of revival used to be the Buenos Aires area, it has shifted up to the province of Chaco and there seems to be a people movement toward Christ currently. Google "Pastor Jorge Ledesma" and watch a portion of his church service. It may still be in his old building. COVID had hit Argentina pretty hard, and they were forced to close for a time. They have the latest in technology that allows him to webcast, and there are electronic musical instruments. The people are very well dressed, and the ladies are made up and folks look worshipful and modern. Jorge was a 19-year-old kid who drove one of the vans around Resistencia during some of Cindy and my trips to Resistencia. He saw what we did and later took up a pastorate there. I could not believe my eyes when I first saw his church service a few years ago. I cried. The crowd did not at all look like illiterate peasants, such as Peter and I first worked with just across the Bolivian border, although their facial features were just like our Bolivian friends. This crowd was enormous, and the membership of his church was, a few years ago, in the neighborhood of 23,000 members—just one of the churches in Resistencia. Jorge's wife said they now have 45,000 in their data base. There are four other large churches with memberships of 4,000, 2000, and two of 1,000. They estimated the total Christian evangelical population to be 150,000 in the year 2020 with about 500 congregations. The current population as of the last census was 438,000 persons. Jorge is in the process of constructing a sanctuary the size of a football field. I don't know if COVID has forced them to postpone its dedication, but it is in the works. And will seat in the neighborhood of 18,000. Cindy will be going down for the dedication, but my age and severe handicap prohibit international travel for me. And that part of the country would not be handicap friendly at all. I noticed the streets around the new structure are not yet paved let alone have a sidewalk for a wheelchair. I feel so privileged to have been a small part of this great move of God among the people I have loved since the early days of missionary work.

CHAPTER 13

Mount Everest Adventure

In 1997 a good friend from Mexico, Ana Mendez, felt the Lord was leading her to do a prayer journey to the highest point in the world, Mount Everest, (29,032ft. high) in Nepal. The mountain is actually on the border of Nepal and China. Peter and our team had been researching some of the most difficult places for the growth of the Gospel left on planet Earth, and north India and the nations around Nepal surfaced in that research. We did not have the luxury of taking a scribe along with us, so I am writing things as I remember them, over 20 years after the fact.

Since the mountain is worshipped by many surrounding people groups, we felt that the Queen of Heaven had invaded that worship and it was one of her thrones. We also wanted to push her back out of the way to enable the inhabitants of those hard-to-reach areas to be more open to hearing the gospel. The headwaters of the Ganges River start out in the melting snow and that river is considered sacred by many Hindus who go to the river to bathe in its sacred waters, which they believe will wash away their sins. There is a special feast time when the Hindus observe this tradition, and it is called the *Maha Kumbh Mela*. There are four major spots along the river where millions congregate to observe this festival. The year before we went to the mountain there were an estimated one million at one of these stations.

The team consisted of Ana Mendez, Pastor Rony Chavez from Costa Rica, and me, along with Bunny Warlan, Charles Doolittle, (who was a wonderful police officer from Glendale, California), Becca Greenwood, another lovely lady from Colombia whose name I don't remember, and another friend of Becca's from Texas whose name eludes me also. One of my employees, Rich Danzeisen, and his pastor, Kreg Vaughne, a Christian and Missionary Alliance pastor from Colorado Springs, were part of the climbing team. However, Rich and Kreg got up as far as Base Camp One, and Kreg came down with a life-threatening cerebral edema that almost took his life. Fortunately, a team from Spain was camped there also, and there was a medical doctor on that team. They had a portable hyperbaric chamber they placed Kreg in. After his crisis was past and he was stable enough, Kreg and Rich returned to the hotel and left for home as soon as transportation could be arranged. We were so glad Kreg's life was spared.

There were some others, and I can't remember their names. On their way to Nepal, Bunny's team was stopped on their layover in Delhi, India, on their way up to the mountain and were pulled into a back room. They were told they could not continue on their journey until they paid a fee, which turned out to be $1,000. We were tipped off that I was going to be kidnapped, and I think the extraction of this extortion money may have been the result. Bunny had to pay it or turn around and go home. Charles Doolittle accompanied me on a different flight. He is an African American well over six feet tall, an extremely fit police officer and if there were plans to kidnap me or anyone, my guess is that his presence intimidated the much smaller locals. There were three other people who should not have been with us and who were a downright distraction if not "plants" from the dark side. Perhaps they may have invited themselves for the adventure, who knows? But it was not up to me to choose the team, so I had no say in the matter. I was just there to help lead the prayer team.

We divided up into those that climbed and those that stayed in a rather rickety, rustic hotel in full view of the mountain; all the while we worshipped and prayed. We actually read the whole Bible aloud, facing the mountain. We had the whole Bible recorded on cassette tape and planted portions of it in many different places along trails and beside the streams that would flow into the Ganges. There was a balcony facing the mountain, and we daily sang, worshipped and prayed in the open air facing the mountain. The climbers were Ana, Rony, and the lady from Colombia, Rich and Kreg. Rich and Kreg were only going to climb up as far as Base Camp One. I don't recall if there were others or not. They may have had Sherpa guides, but my memory is dull here. Ana had gone mountain climbing in Chile and maybe other areas of the world to prepare for this. She was very fit. The rest of us were the prayer team which I led much of the time.

It was an adventure in itself to get to the hotel that was at an altitude of over 13,000 feet. We flew into a small village and were transported by helicopter to the spot where the others were dropped off to climb the little trail to the hotel. It was about a one-hour tough climb in the altitude. Because I was already handicapped and needed a cane to walk, I paid extra and was helicoptered to the grounds of the hotel. I made it up in under 10 minutes.

Mount Everest is considered sacred and is worshipped by the local indigenous people. There are triangular Hindu prayer flags flying in many places. We had some Christian banners and we paced them along the balcony, as our team were the only occupants of the hotel at the time.

It is estimated that over 200 people have died in an attempt to climb Mount Everest. (I just asked "Alexa.") Bodies are not brought down. The locals feel that these have been sacrificed to the holy mountain and their bodies are strewn, probably frozen under the ice, snow and avalanches. We felt that this was another form the Queen of Heaven evil spirit was taking to receive worship.

Ana and her team got up as far as Base Camp One. It was felt that they needed to take some other side trips to locate the seat of the Queen of Heaven, which they did and they performed many prophetic acts to bind her influence so that she would release those under her domain to be free to hear and respond to the Gospel of Jesus Christ. Both teams remained in a warring mode, and we stayed and prayed and warred for the unreached peoples in that part of the world for just about three weeks. We then felt a release to head for home.

The report arrived at our office that year that the festival where folks wash in the Ganges River at one of the spots was much smaller than expected. An estimated 600,000 people would be participating when there are usually a million or more.

Getting back down the mountain was exciting. We had to go to a very small village airport by the name of Lukla. As I recall, we traveled a few at a time by helicopter and hung out in Lukla until the small plane arrived to take us back to Katmandu. While we were waiting, quite a crowd of locals met to get a good look at us, strange people from far away. Charles Doolittle was the center of attention. I doubt some of the short Sherpa people had ever seen such a tall black person with such a wonderful, winsome smile. He and Becca Greenwood put on a skit explaining the Gospel, and I can't remember how it was translated, but the crowd enjoyed it greatly.

Then the plane arrived and the first batch of passengers boarded. I waited for the second flight. I lived in the Andes of South America and have navigated the high airstrips in the thin air a lot, but this was different. We had the advantage of the Altiplano, a vast area of land about 13,000 feet high and flat. Our airstrips were very long while the plane gathered the speed that it needed for liftoff. I actually remember one time when we were returning home from La Paz, and I thought I'd use the restroom just before takeoff, when I realized the plane was taxiing toward the runway for takeoff. It taxied so long that I had time to vacate the restroom, get back to my seat and get buckled in before it had left the ground! The Himalayas don't have such a luxury.

As the plane was about to take off, all available manpower grabbed the tail of the plane and held it back with all their might until the pilot revved the engine and finally signaled them to let go. The plane left the very short runway and disappeared down into the deep canyon below. We all held our breath until we could see it climbing upward between the mountains gaining altitude. Everyone broke out in applause. I must say, when our turn came to go, it was by far the most exciting takeoff I have ever experienced. When we came to the edge of the cliff, the plane dropped what seemed to be hundreds of feet until it gained enough strength in the thin air to climb between the tall mountains on either side of us, but God protected us, and we left the mountain behind. We all met at our hotel in Katmandu and praised God for safety and that our assignment was over. We went home to the other side of the world, weary, but rejoicing.

I am writing this in the year 2021, 24 years after the fact. Spiritual warfare of this territorial level was viewed by many with a jaundiced eye, so we kept things very quiet. We wanted to see what results this initiative might yield. My apostle, Chuck Pierce, was invited to meet with a group of pastors in North India in 2019. He was thrilled to report that the north part of India that had been almost impenetrable was now welcoming the Gospel and that churches were now being planted and growing in what had previously been very hard soil. He met with 1,500 *pastors*! That probably translates into many hundreds of thousands of believers. The spiritual climate of north India has changed! Chuck was able to encourage them. When he came back, he told me that the Mount Everest initiative played a key role in opening up that area for Christ. Once again, I cried. I knew it would bring forth results, but to hear it confirmed from a man of God and recognized prophet and apostle was very encouraging. It was not in vain!

CHAPTER 14

Another Fun Initiative: Marches For Jesus

Some of our most enthusiastic participants in the prayer movement were the organizers and participants of the initiatives of "Cardinal Points," and "Marches for Jesus." Many were from Youth With a Mission and the organizers of Marches for Jesus out of England. Let me explain about Cardinal Points first. We encouraged believers to travel to the points that were the most northern, southern, eastern and western points of many geographical areas: the continents, every nation, every state, every county, and every city, face the center of that geographical area and pray God's blessings into it. They were to pray into the unreached people groups, pray for governments, pray for the believers and the lost. They were to spend a whole day or more if so led. People enjoy a challenge, so this initiative was very successful. Reports came in from all over the world with hundreds participating in many initiatives on many continents.

Then we encouraged all the believers everywhere to gather and march through the streets on a certain appointed day, usually in June, singing and praising God, and end in their main plaza or government building and pray for their city or village. We encouraged them to pray for their government leaders, their nation, the unreached, the believers, using their local pastors and Christian businesspersons to lead. We called these Marches for Jesus Day. We called one year's effort "The Day to Change the World." Peter got this idea from Psalm 86:9 which says, "All nations whom you have made shall come and worship before you, Oh Lord, and shall glorify Your name." So, for a whole of 24 hours or more, starting at the date line in the Pacific and heading west and clear around the globe, there were parades of Marches for Jesus. Since it was in June and winter below the equator, we got a photo (or video, I can't remember) taken at one of the most southern cities in Chile of people pulling their kids in sleds through the snow. Their march was a cold one but on a beautiful winter day.

Actually, some of the most enthusiastic folks in the world are the Brazilians. Latin Americans are used to going to the streets for their Mardi Gras, so it is nothing new for them. Instead of glorifying Satan and sin, we made a valiant attempt to glorify our wonderful Lord and Savior Jesus Christ. We encouraged the playing and singing of hymns and lively worship music, carrying flags and banners, families being together pulling tots in wagons and other creative ways of lifting up the name of our wonderful Savior. Permits had to be secured, and the marchers ended at their City Halls or a park to pray for their cities. But we had a problem in the huge city of Sao Paulo, Brazil. So many people, over a million strong, showed up that the traffic got in a total snarl, and it was a disaster that Saturday. Finally, the officials of the city gave up after the first couple of years, and declared a national holiday, "Marches for Jesus Day!" I am not sure if they are still carrying on these many years later.

I was sent on a fact-finding journey to Israel to set up the first March for Jesus in Jerusalem. There was a lot of enthusiasm for this, especially among the Korean brothers and sisters. A Korean-American travel agent got me a free trip, hotel and meals included, as well as a tour of all of Israel. The upshot is that we were given all necessary permits and held the first "March for Jesus" through the streets of Jerusalem with over 10,000 people from all over the world, about 5,000 from Korea alone. Peter, some A.D.2000 executives, and local pastors led the parade. We ended on the lawn of the Knesset, praying for the peace of Jerusalem (as we are instructed to do in Scripture) and Israel and for God's chosen people to be open to hearing about the Gospel of the Lord Jesus Christ. For many, it was a first visit to the Holy Land and a blessing for everyone. During those few days, we had a prayer and praise meeting and had lunch at the Sea of Galilee where Jesus fed the 5,000, visited the Via Delarosa and the Garden Tomb, Mount Carmel, and many historical sites and museums. That was impressive to me. It was much more fun with the believers than with the unbelieving tour guide who showed me through the land, gave many historical facts and figures. He told me he was not a believer, but he sure had the facts.

It was always interesting to me that as we participated in so many of these events that we were never heckled or persecuted in any way whatsoever. We carried banners, sang, prayed, read Scripture; all was looked upon as a peaceful demonstration, I guess.

What did I learn from this slice of my life? I adored my trips to Argentina and Nepal. I learned a great deal about territorial spirits and saw firsthand the exciting exponential growth of the church once these nasty spirits are pushed back. But the local church must not relax its efforts and must continue to keep them pushed back. I praise God for allowing me to be a small part of these wonderful yet daring adventures. We knew we were entering Satan's territory, but God gave wisdom, grace and protection. I often heard Peter jokingly say, "I am the one who writes about spiritual warfare, but then I send Doris out to do it so I can see if it really works." No joke, my precious Peter, it really does work!

CHAPTER 15

The Last Hurrah: Celebration Ephesus

As I said before, the A.D. 2000 movement was designed to be a 10-year thrust, lasting the decade of the 1990s. I am an old farmer. Difficult tasks are to be undertaken only one way. You start the job, do your best, give it all you've got and lift your head when the job is finished. Then you may rest. (This especially applied when shoveling manure from the drops behind the dairy cows when they were in the barn in the wintertime.)

We were trying to figure out how to have a "grand finale" for the prayer movement. Peter decided we should go to Ephesus in modern-day Turkey. He wrote a brilliant commentary on the Book of Acts, and also he taught the Book of Acts slowly and methodically for 10 years to our adult Sunday School class, the 120 Fellowship. On a former prayer journey to Turkey, we had visited the ruins of the churches that were the birthplace of Christianity. Ephesus stood out to us. Acts 19 tells the story of Paul in Ephesus: He taught boldly, for three months in the synagogue, the things concerning the kingdom of God, and "unusual miracles" were worked by Paul's hands with healings and demons being cast out. The phrase "unusual miracles" always tickled Peter. His reasoning was that if there were "unusual miracles," surely there must have been many "usual miracles" also.

Then there was the worship of the "Great Goddess Diana" (another manifestation of the Queen of Heaven, in our estimation). The silversmiths were suffering a great loss in selling their images of the goddess, and they feared that the people might shift their worship to Jehovah God as the church in Ephesus grew. The idols of Diana were not particularly pretty. The statues vary slightly, but Peter coyly said that he was curious enough to count her many breasts, and the idol he studied yielded a count of 21 breasts, so it was a rather atrocious-looking figurine. The silversmiths feared for Diana's magnificent Temple, one of the grandiose Seven Wonders of the Ancient World, as you may remember from your world history class in high school. Part of the worship of this goddess was animal sacrifices to her, as well as temple prostitution. (Later on, in Scripture, Paul tells believers how to handle the eating of meat offered to idols in 1 Corinthians 8: If you need meat for a meal, go to the marketplace, buy and enjoy it. If you are invited to eat in a pagan temple, do not do it. If you are invited to a home, eat what is put before you, ask no questions, but if you are informed that it was meat offered to idols, do not eat it. That is for the sake of unbelievers who are watching you.)

Then there was a major riot and Paul's two traveling companions, Gaius and Aristarchus, were dragged into the huge open-air theater, where, for two hours, the local citizens shouted, "Great is Diana of the Ephesians!" Paul wanted to join his companions, but other disciples did not allow him to go, probably fearing for his life. Some of the city authorities came into the gathering and told the citizens to disperse, which they did.

The sturdily constructed open-air theater still stands today, firmly built of huge rectangularly cut stones. I am guessing many were granite. I believe the theater holds between five and six thousand comfortably.

Of course, everyone sits on the stone tiers. Some of the stones have shifted somewhat over the years, and no handrails are there, so one must carefully walk to arrive at a seat.

Peter's idea was to hold the grand finale of our 10-year prayer effort in this theater. He single-handedly put the program together. The plan was that we would occupy the theater for four hours, not just two as the silversmiths did, and we would worship and praise God from 2 p.m. until 6 p.m. Many Christian leaders of large organizations joined us in leading 20-minute segments of worship, praise, and prayer. I cannot locate the program because all of those papers have been gifted to the Billy Graham Library in Wheaton, Illinois. I do not want to offend any of my friends by not remembering they were there. Many of the leaders previously mentioned in the list of organizations that joined the prayer movement were there, all at their own expense, of course. It was glorious!

The local Christians managed to get us a use permit for the day with the proviso that we buy accident insurance. The insurance cost $3,000. If I remember correctly, I gave someone two Advil and two others needed band-aids for blisters on their feet from walking. People poured in from all over the world. I searched for a long time and finally found a prayer letter I wrote after coming home with the facts and figures. Over 5,000 (I think closer to 5,500) people poured into the theater from 62 nations of the world! Just days before our event, there had been a massive earthquake in September of 1999. Our event was held on a picture-perfect day, October 1, 1999. My good friend, Charles Doolittle, who was part of the Mount Everest Prayer team, served as my bodyguard. Because we wanted to bless our host nation, I had a big basket and we announced that we would be taking up a collection for the folks who had become homeless due to the quake.

As I recall, many hundreds of persons died in that disaster. We were able to collect $75,000 that day, and we turned it all over to the Christian pastors in Izmir (Ephesus). They were buying over 100 winterized tents for the homeless.

Our precious friend from Korea, Pastor Kim Sundo, put together an orchestra and we concluded the event at sunset by singing Handel's "Hallelujah Chorus." Once again, I cried. Just looking over the crowd, there were friends from every continent and people of every skin color, and it seemed like a foretaste of what heaven will be like. Pastor Kim researched the history of the original orchestra with its number of members and the particular instruments that had performed and duplicated it precisely. Koreans are marvelous musicians.

Also, Pastor Kim was a dear personal friend and happened to be the pastor of the largest Methodist church in the world in Seoul, Korea. He had a beautiful Prayer Mountain where parishioners came to pray for hours or days on end. He hosted a gathering of our Prayer Track Planning Committee a few years before the Ephesus event at his Prayer Mountain, with about 300 prayer leaders from around the world. Koreans are used to sleeping on mats on the floor, but when he discovered that our sissy crowd needed beds, he made a phone call to some military executives, and 300 beds were delivered by the first night. Our crowd seemed to know how to get things done fast. In this case, when all else fails, call out the army!

Let me quote a couple of paragraphs from Brian Kooiman, one of my very dearest friends and Chuck Pierce's assistant, taken from a prayer letter in October 1999:

Our time in Turkey was almost beyond words. The Celebration Ephesus on October 1st was absolutely incredible from beginning to end. Altogether nearly 5,000 people from over 60 nations attended the four-hour worship gathering in the ancient amphitheater in Ephesus. The weather was warm, but the Lord provided a breeze. Chuck helped open the event by asking the Holy Spirit to come. When the Apostle Paul first visited the city of Ephesus nearly 2,000 years ago, he asked the people if they had already received the Holy Spirit. They didn't even know what the Holy Spirit was. The Lord told Chuck that if he would invite the Holy Spirit to come, that He would. Chuck shared that he has never been in a meeting where the Holy Spirit was so present from beginning to end in everything done.

Lora Allison brought a dance team that was fantastic. The accompanying banners were phenomenal. The praise and worship team led by Ross Parsley and David Morris along with the New Life Church worship team were wonderful. Larry Brown coordinated the shofar players. The closing "Hallelujah Chorus" by a choir from Korea was so anointed. Even the Turkish press provided completely positive reports, and the local believers were greatly encouraged. Chuck believes it was totally worth the last two years of effort.

As I was searching for the program, which I could not find (it obviously is resting among the archives at the Billy Graham Library in Wheaton, Illinois), I did run across a schedule of activities for the last quarter of 1999, which I will copy to give you an idea of what kind of whirlwind lives we led when we were in our prime—Peter would have been 69 and I would have been 67.

- Sept 1999 21-25 Prayer journey driving through Basque country in Spain (praying for that unreached people group)

- 27 Peter and Doris travel to Turkey

- 30 Celebration Ephesus leaders meeting

- October 1 Celebration Ephesus 2:00–6:00 p.m. (Turkey time)

- 2 Peter and Doris travel to Frankfurt, Germany

- 3 Peter travels to Korea

- 4 Doris travels to Colorado Springs

- 4–10 Peter speaks at Church Growth International, Seoul, Korea

- 11 Peter travels to Colorado Springs from Seoul, Korea

- 13 Peter—Radio interview, P. McGuire, KBRT, Los Angeles 3–4 p.m.

- 15 Global Harvest Ministries Board Meeting, Colorado Springs

- 18 Peter to Orlando, FL, Antioch Ministers Group

- 18–20 Peter speaks at Antioch Men's Conference

- 20 Peter travels to Santa Rosa Beach, FL, with Bill Hamon's group

- 20–21 Christian International Conference, Florida

- 22 Peter travels to Colorado Springs from Florida

- 21 Doris travels to Rochester, NY

- 22–23 Deliverance Conference, Doris and Chuck Pierce

- 24 Doris travels to Colorado Springs from Rochester, NY

- 27 Peter and Doris travel to Portland, OR

- 28–30 Building Foundations for Revival at Frank Damazio's church

- 31 Peter and Doris travel to Colorado Springs from Portland

- November 1–13 Wagner Leadership Institute Fast Track, Colorado Springs

- 1–3 Peter teaches Spiritual Warfare Today for WLI

- 3 Peter travels to San Jose, CA, in the evening

- 4–6 Peter teaches at Impact School (David Cannistraci) San Jose
- 7 Peter travels to Los Angeles in the evening
- 3 Doris travels to Hemet, CA
- 4–6 Doris and Chuck Pierce— Deliverance Sem. Bob Beckett's
- 7 Doris travels to Colorado Springs from California
- 8 Peter travels to Colorado Springs from California
- 10 Peter travels to Indianapolis, IN
- 11–13 Peter speaks at American Society for Church Growth
- 14 Peter travels to Colorado Springs from Indianapolis
- 17 Peter and Doris travel to Dallas
- 18–20 International Conference on Prayer and Spiritual Warfare
- 21 Peter preaches at Shady Grove Church, Dallas, TX
- 21 Peter and Doris travel to Colorado Springs
- December 1999 1–4 Int'l Intercessors Convocation at World Prayer Center
- 7 Generals of Intercession Board Meeting, Colorado Springs
- 9 Peter travels to Fayetteville, NC
- 10 Peter speaks at pastors' meeting, Fayetteville
- 11 Peter speaks at Grace Leadership School
- 11 Peter speaks at Michael Fletcher's church, Fayetteville
- 12 Peter travels to Colorado Springs
- 13 Peter and Doris travel to Los Angeles, CA
- 14 Peter teaches at Roberts Liardon's school
- 15–16 Peter and Doris do early Christmas with daughter Karen
- 17 Peter and Doris return to Colorado for Christmas
- 24–31 Global Harvest offices closed for holidays
- 31–Jan.1 Prayer vigil at Colorado Springs World Prayer Center

It makes me tired to read this. But at the time we were in excellent health and really full of pep. Our kids were all married and gone, and we were free to work long hours, which I often did to catch up when Peter was gone. We were doing about a five-million-dollar budget and that took careful bookkeeping. I had a marvelous bookkeeper, Thea Corder. One year I recall that after the books were done, we were thrilled to report to the board that she was off by 50 cents. One of the board members threw 50 cents on the table and told us to balance the books!! Our bookkeeping was so meticulous that we only got audited by the IRS once, and they were in and out in two hours, finding all to be in excellent order. I have always been very careful with finances, have hired excellent bookkeepers, and tried to account for every cent. I hate financial mismanagement.

You will notice on the above itinerary that Peter and I split up in Frankfurt, Germany, after doing Celebration Ephesus. He had an obligation in Korea and I had to head for home. The devil was not happy with what we had just done.

My life has been spared from death so many times. I have scribbled down a list of a few I remember and am going to write a short chapter at the end recounting some of my escapes from death, which have been quite a few. One of my favorite passages in the Bible is Psalm 68:19-20 which says "Blessed be the Lord, who daily loads us with benefits, the God of our salvation. Selah. Our God is the God of salvation *and to God the Lord belong escapes from death."* There is no doubt in my mind that Satan tried to kill me and our daughter Becky, her husband Jack and their baby, Nicholas, who was about 15 months old, and even their golden retriever, Abby.

The night I arrived home from Frankfurt, October 3, 1999, just after doing Celebration Ephesus, dog-tired from the international trip and jet-lagged, I looked forward to sleeping in. It was a cold, crisp October evening in Colorado, not much above freezing. I was so exhausted that I didn't even unpack my big suitcase. I just jumped in my nightshirt and in bed as fast as I could and fell very sound asleep.

In the middle of the night, I awoke with a start when I heard Becky screaming in the backyard and crying uncontrollably. Jack was rushing up the stairs to Peter's and my part of the house. He immediately slid open the door of my bedroom to the deck and said "We have got to get out NOW!" The carbon monoxide detector had gone off. When I grabbed a coat and headed for the front door to get out, the smell of natural gas was overpowering. Apparently, a furnace had malfunctioned and spilled the carbon monoxide. We called 911 and were transported to the hospital, where we were all put on oxygen. The fire department shut off the furnace. I learned that when a furnace malfunctions and the flame goes out, the carbon monoxide settles down low but the gas pours out and rises. The kids downstairs had got the brunt of the carbon monoxide, but I got the "skunked" gas upstairs. My part of the house upstairs was filled with the overpowering odor of gas, and I feared an explosion ignited by pilot lights in the stove and fireplace. Fortunately, that never happened. Had some angels kept the pilot lights from causing an explosion? (When we built our home in Colorado Springs, we buried Bibles in the cement of all the corners of the foundation. We drove stakes in the ground of the four corners of our 8 acres with our favorite Scripture verses printed on them. We poured olive oil along the fences all around the land, dedicated it all to the Lord, and invited the presence of the Holy Spirit to surround our new home and to protect all within its walls. God prevented a major disaster at this time, no doubt in my mind.)

Poor Jack, in an attempt to get his family out of the house and run upstairs to wake me up, somehow stumbled and broke his ankle. My guess is he was weak and overcome by the carbon monoxide. So he was hobbling in great pain as he came to rescue me. We were released from the hospital after becoming stabilized through breathing oxygen and went home many hours later to grab some belongings and move out to the World Prayer Center hotel rooms, where our offices were anyway. That was the one and only time my not unpacking was a blessing. I just needed to pick up a heavy coat and grab my suitcase. The repair people fixed the furnace and waited to test it for several days, so we were misplaced from home about a week as I recall.

But wait! There's more!! Let me copy a prayer letter sent out to our intercessors on October 19, 1999, just a tad over two weeks later:

Dear Intercessors:

I can't believe it!

I can't believe that this morning at 6:30 AM our carbon monoxide detector screamed at Jack, Becky, Nicholas, the dog Abby, and me. We all immediately evacuated from the house, and it was cold outside—the firemen said it was 23°. Jack hobbled out in his nightwear already on crutches from the broken ankle from October 3 when their little family was severely overcome with carbon monoxide and needed hospitalization for some hours on 100% oxygen. To say the least, we were all somewhat traumatized to think what might be in the same boat again. The firemen even commented, "Weren't we here just a few days ago?"

This time it was the second furnace, a new propane system that heats the addition that we were building. It was just hooked up a short time ago and when the gas company got there, they were able to detect and locate the problem immediately—a gasket had blown, leaking propane into the area where Jack and Becky and the baby sleep. The gas company said that the leak was so bad that we probably would not have lasted more than 15 minutes this time! All of the gas and electricity in that part of the house are now turned off and the furnace people are on their way to fix it.

It is really rare for one family to experience a problem with carbon monoxide poisoning in a lifetime. We have two close brushes with that, 16 days apart with carbon monoxide problems from two different furnaces in one house, that seems altogether diabolical to me. We are very grateful that we were able to detect it rapidly and to clear out. So, everybody, be sure you have functional carbon monoxide detectors; they saved our lives TWICE!

Please continue to pray for our family, that God would be so kind as to assign a few extra angels to our crowd since it appears to me that evil forces have our address. I must admit that I get somewhat angry when the devil picks on my kids and grandkids, so please pray extra protection over them for the foreseeable future. Pray that we will have peace of mind to be able to sleep without fear. We are all a little traumatized and fearful. A group of our employees is going out to the house today to pray over our property and ask God to seal it off from trouble. Please remember all of our kids and grandkids.

Peter is ministering in Florida next week and won't be back until Friday night. He missed out on the excitement both times, and we are glad.

Thank you so much for your prayers and concern. We love and appreciate you more than we can say!

Doris Wagner

Might it be that the devil was still fuming over our glorious event in Ephesus??

We kept very busy during the next decade. We kept having the Praying Through the Window thrusts with various targets for the next several years. We continued to be very busy holding seminars. Peter carried on his teaching both at Fuller Seminar in two week increments and taught heavily in Wagner Leadership Institute. We had matured greatly in the apostolic, prophetic, deliverance, signs and wonders, and Peter used his incredible gift of convocation to pull together leaders in each of these fields.

He was invited to assist John Kelley with the leadership of the International Coalition of Apostles. This pulled together the main apostles from all over the world to meet and share what they felt God was saying to the churches in these days. He served for about a decade as the lead apostle of this growing organization. Since 2010, John Kelley now is in that leadership role. I attended the annual meeting in 2019 and was very pleased with the direction it was taking.

Peter also pulled together the educators in our field with similar doctrinal beliefs in an organization he named The Apostolic Council for Educational Accountability. Then these brothers and sisters shared curricula and what was cutting-edge in the field of theological education.

Probably the most fun group we were involved in was the Apostolic Council of Prophetic Elders. Peter and Cindy Jacobs pulled this group together. Peter was never able to run those annual meetings with his usual Roberts Rules of Order. He often referred to those gatherings, with a twinkle in his eye, as "the closest thing to herding cats he ever experienced." Prophets are unusual, wonderful people. Peter served as the apostle of this group from 1999 until he turned it over totally to Cindy Jacobs in 2010, the year he turned 80 years old. It has grown vigorously over the years and become much more international in scope. Cindy continues to do a magnificent job in pulling together what the prophets are hearing and releasing it at the beginning of that year.

In the year 2000 Peter and I called together a "Roundtable of Deliverance Ministers" so we could get to know one another. Then, in about 2004, Peter and I thought it good to pull together all the deliverance ministers we could find in order to become acquainted and share information concerning what they had learned. This was very fruitful, and we called the organization the International Society of Deliverance Ministers. Our membership hovers around 300 and we get together every year and over 200 deliverance ministers usually attend these meetings. They are so very profitable. The moral standards of America are dropping quite rapidly, and there are so many people trapped in addictions, moral failures and emotional distress. Deliverance is needed to free them from these problems. I attend each of these annual meetings and find them very informative. A couple of years after Peter's death, I started doing deliverance conferences and personal deliverance sessions with needy people as opportunity has arisen. I intend to keep on doing this as long as I am able as the need is great.

Teaching and education were part of Peter's life since he completed his formal education. He wanted to help pastors be encouraged and teaching and preaching the most relevant messages possible for the moment, including pre-service as well as in-service pastors and Christian workers. He always taught in Bible schools, seminary and started his own Wagner Leadership Institute. When he turned over all of the organizations he had been leading in 2010, he turned Wagner Leadership Institute over to one of his outstanding students, Che Ahn, who became chancellor. Che chose Benny Yang to be dean, and since they have received university status, we are now Wagner University. I often teach sessions on deliverance, and the subjects dear to Peter's heart continue to be taught: the apostolic, the prophetic, signs and wonders, spiritual warfare and other cutting-edge topics. Some of Peter's recorded teachings are still required courses. I am pleased that it seems to be moving forward vigorously.

Then we met yearly with our dearest, closest friends and colleagues in ministry in a group Peter named Eagles' Vision Apostolic Team (EVAT). Peter was considered by this team of about 25 very well-known and influential leaders of worldwide ministries to be their apostle and those were special to me. We shared vision, experiences, prophetic revelation, and prayed together. I won't share their names, but they were all very well-known leaders of large ministries who didn't have an apostle over them. At Peter's passing, that group disbanded, but I miss them all very much. Most of them traveled from afar to be at Peter's funeral and a later memorial service. They were our dearest friends.

CHAPTER 16

The Move To Texas And The Beginning Of The End

As was Peter's custom, he continued to travel all over the world to teach at his Wagner Leadership Institutes. One of the most thriving centers was in South Korea, just outside of Seoul. I get my dates mixed up, but I believe it must have been in January of 2013 that he went over to teach and returned home violently ill with a lung infection. It refused to heal and finally we went to specialists at the National Jewish Hospital in Denver to seek help.

They came up with a diagnosis and put him on some very strong antibiotics he had to take three days a week, but they made him nauseous and violently ill those days. He became weaker and weaker. An oxygen machine was prescribed, and we had tubes strung all over the house so he could breathe a bit more easily. At that point, Chuck Pierce intervened and invited us to move to Texas near him so he could keep an eye on Peter and seek better treatment. Our beautiful dream home was 7,300 ft above sea level, and Chuck offered to move us. A myriad of people showed up out of the woodwork, and we packed up our most precious possessions and left the rest to the movers. We drove down the driveway, and I dared not look back; we just kept looking forward. I could not shed a tear, just look forward to the next phase of life—caring for Peter. Many of our friends helped, and volunteers drove our vehicles down to Denton, Texas. We shall forever be thankful to Chuck

Pierce for offering to care for us for the rest of our days on earth. He is a model son in the faith and treated us as his own parents, out of the kindness of his heart. It's a debt we can never repay but for which we will be forever grateful.

We stayed in a hotel for a month while we went house hunting. I was already confined to a wheelchair, and a very fine realtor from Glory of Zion church worked diligently to find handicap-friendly homes to show us. We sent daughter Ruth, who was living with us, out with the realtor because she has a good eye and could see possibilities. She looked at about 35 houses close to the church, but there were only three that might qualify. I needed a home with space enough to drive my wheelchair around islands in the kitchen, and I needed to have a laundry room big enough for me to use the washer and dryer. A spacious bedroom and bathroom on the lower floor were also requirements because of all of my handicap equipment. We finally chose one in the nearby town of Argyle and had to go to work on ramps for me, so that took more time. But Peter loved the house and his new office right outside our bedroom. The only thing I was not too fond of was that it came with a small swimming pool. Although that meant much more maintenance, Ruth and friends enjoyed it. It also was a lovely spot for outdoor activities and barbeques when the weather was not unbearably hot in the summer.

We had a close friend who was a doctor and worked at Baylor Heart Hospital, and she recommended an excellent heart surgeon to look at Peter. He diagnosed Peter's problem as chronic heart failure and open-heart surgery was performed to replace two valves and repair another one. In addition to that being very traumatic, he began collecting fluid in his plural cavity. On several occasions, I watched as doctors tapped his plural cavity from his back and removed three liters of fluid that had been squeezing his lungs and making it difficult to breathe. We now feel that the problem had been chronic heart failure all along, and the heavy antibiotics made him become more distressed.

Peter loved our new home although it took a year to get sheds built for our tools and fix up the 40-year-old house. Peter continued to plug along at his desk day after day and started to write a final book on the topic of the six major things he learned in life and how he planned to finish well. But he only got about half of it done before he became too ill and weak to continue. After his passing, I finished the book using his extensive outlines and lecture notes he had already prepared on the topics addressed in the book. At this writing, it is under contract with Destiny Image Publishing Company.

One more lung surgery was performed on him with the hopes of making his breathing easier, but it continued to become worse. Once again, we had tubes running all over the house for his oxygen, and he did come to meals as he was able. He was able to do his daily shower and tried to act as normal as possible. He never was really bedridden until the last week of his life.

It was during the 2016 elections. From day one, Peter favored Donald Trump and I believe he willed himself to live long enough to get his absentee ballot and vote. The day finally came when the ballot arrived, and we have a video of him proudly voting, signing his name and licking the envelope. It was about a week before he died.

The doctor had placed him on hospice and basically said nothing more could be done. He asked to have our beds moved into his office, the room he loved, surrounded by all of his books and files. I slept next to him and all he asked was for me to hold his hand. He was content as long as I was there holding his hand. A little at a time, he became weaker and weaker and could eat only small servings of yogurt or applesauce. His communication lessened and he was in a semi coma, I believe. The last words he uttered to me were, "I love you, Baby."

That was on a Wednesday, October 14, 2016. Our 66th anniversary was the next day. But he had become silent. He continued to breathe, and he had a pulse, so we let him rest. He had ordered Ruth to get me a huge planter full of orchids for our anniversary, which were delivered with the usual Happy Anniversary card and "I love you, Happy 66th" written thereon. Finally, he continued to languish until October 21, but was unresponsive or did not talk at all. We called daughter Karen in California and asked what to do. I told her I didn't think anyone was at home in his body. She has worked well over 40 years in a surgical ICU unit and is used to cases like this and is the one specified in our directive to "pull the plug if necessary if and when the time comes." I was convinced that he was gone since there was no response what-soever. She instructed Ruth to go in the bedroom and shut down the oxygen machine. She said he would continue to breathe if he was still there. Ruth did so and came back to his bedside with me. He let out a little sigh, and immediately stopped breathing and his pulse became faint and finally disappeared. I glanced up at the clock and it was a little after 2 p.m.

I am convinced that he died a day or maybe even two before. So, we called hospice, and he was declared dead. Then the funeral home people promptly arrived and his body was gone within the hour. Son-in-law Jack immediately put the house back in order, removing the oxygen tubes and we moved the beds back into the bedroom and by sunset all was done, over with and quiet. Now, I had lost my lifelong companion, friend, lover, provider, protector and felt like half of me had been torn away. We had been so happily married and working together for 66 years and six days. Death is an enemy.

Our wonderful long-time assistant, Brandon Larson, helped enormously with all final details, and we picked out a lovely spot in a very well-kept cemetery only 10 minutes from our home. We had prepaid our funerals and picked out our caskets and even had a headstone engraved, but that headstone was at our burial plots in Colorado. Grandson Chris Potter, who lives in western Colorado was able to pick up the headstone and transport it down in his pickup truck and it now stands on our new gravesite. The old one in Colorado sold very quickly. I actually got a refund from the funeral because I did not need to use the prepaid limo service.

The next week the family along with many friends from all over the country, congregated for the viewing, burial and memorial service, which Chuck Pierce did so beautifully. I will be forever grateful. A larger service was planned for the end of December when more friends could come, and it was to be the day before the large Starting the Year Off Right conference the last days of 2016. The kids and grandkids all came, and we enjoyed the memorial service when hundreds more of our friends from all over the country participated. Peter was either loved or not liked. He had many who loved him that day.

The next day, December 29, 2016, was daughter Karen's birthday and she decided to take the family to Medieval Times as a celebration. I felt it an obligation to stay and attend the first day of the conference so I could personally meet and greet the many who had come for the memorial service. I had our wonderful assistant, Brandon Larson, who had been both Peter's and my assistant for several years and had been working in the Global Harvest office since Colorado Springs. At the time I was getting around using a small travel scooter that came apart in several pieces. I can't remember why, but instead of going to the Chinese restaurant for dinner that evening in a car or van, we went in Brandon's truck, which was rather high off the ground. When I went to get out of the truck, my feet were about two inches shy of reaching the ground, so I just let go and bailed out. Then I heard a terrible "CRACK" and immediately knew what it was. I had broken my femur just above my artificial knee in my left leg. I never fell to the ground, but I hollered to Brandon, "Get my scooter, I just broke my leg!" He got ahold of 911, and I got my first ambulance ride to the Presbyterian hospital not very far from the restaurant. I was given some sort of an injection to make me happy and put me in la-la land. I think the most excruciating pain I ever experienced was lying on the x-ray table and turning over and over while they took 21 X-rays of my leg. Finally, we had confirmation for what I already knew: I had a broken femur. Because it was a holiday weekend, I was unable to get a surgeon there until January 2, so I just laid in bed and suffered greatly when I needed to use a bedpan. It was awful. My kids had to return to Michigan and California, and Ruth and I were left alone to see the ordeal through.

We got a wonderful orthopedic surgeon who decided to not do a cast, but to use an exterior stabilizer, a huge heavy metal rod that had screws and was fixed into the bone in my shin and thigh. I was forbidden to put any weight on it for six months and had a stiff leg that stuck straight out from my body. Ruth welded me a metal cradle to hold my foot and leg steady and attached it to my electric wheelchair and I survived the next six months waiting for the bone to knit together. The sad thing is that it refused to do so. It was decided that I needed to have my leg amputated, mid-thigh, in June of 2017. Then I was really wheelchair-bound. After some months I was fitted with a prosthesis, but it is far too uncomfortable to walk with, so my days are now spent in the wheelchair. I am still able to get where I want to go.

Learning to live without Peter was really hard. I was deeply enveloped in grief for months and felt like half of me was gone, never to return. I couldn't think of the upcoming holidays alone, so Ruth and I decided to make Thanksgiving go away and take a cruise to the southern part of the Caribbean over the holiday, which we did. It was awful. We never went ashore at any of the ports of call. Ruth managed to rearrange our stateroom on board the ship so we could get my wheelchair and commode positioned correctly for my ease and comfort. It worked great. I can't even remember what we did over Christmas, I was so emotionally numb. I bungled through the next year feeling very alone and heartsick.

The next summer, June 2018, I decided to scratch off the remaining thing left on my Bucket List. Having always been a farmer and gardener, I often wished I could see the gigantic pumpkins and cabbages at the Alaska State Fair. Peter and I had taken a cruise to Alaska probably in the 80s. We wanted good R and R because Peter had been working so hard. So, we got a great travel agent who admonished us to travel up by boat, but get a balcony on the side looking toward the land, which we did. Peter spent most of his time writing one of his 75 books, I can't remember which one, but I stayed on the balcony thoroughly enjoying the beautiful evergreen trees and watching the eagles.

Then we ran into a rather large group of lovely Lutheran tourists led by a pastor who knew of Peter, and he spent a lot of time picking Peter's brain at mealtimes. Peter has always been extremely gracious, so he spent hours with this group on the way north. I remember I picked up a bug of some sort and had terrible diarrhea, so Peter went ashore several times in search of Imodium and was successful. When we arrived in Alaska, we did the whole tourist thing of visiting Fairbanks and observing the gorgeous flowers that grew huge blossoms because of the many hours of daylight. We took a train up to Denali State Park and back down. When we discovered we were leaving the day the State Fair was opening, I was bummed because I lost out on seeing the monstrous cabbages and pumpkins.

But since those many years ago, Peter, Ruth and I were invited back up to Anchorage for a conference and got invited into the homes of dear Christian friends. Peter always wanted to taste some of the exotic native foods, so our dear friends, Robert and Eleanor Roehl put on a feast for us and Lee Grady (at that time was with Charisma Magazine), and we had the time of our lives. Our dear Alaskan friend Mary Glazier was there also. I can't remember all of the things they prepared, but I recall a huge baked salmon, which they caught, of course, some fish eggs laid on evergreen boughs that hung in the water and tasted better than caviar, blubber, wonderful wild berries, and many other things that evade me. It was a feast fit for royalty!

Daughter Ruth was with us, and I recall it was Mother's Day. I had somehow gotten another serious infection in my leg and needed attention immediately. Because I have all my major joints, except one shoulder replaced, if an infection settles in an artificial joint, I might lose the joint or worse, so infections need to be attended to posthaste. It was a Sunday and I was taken over to an emergency room and never treated better in my life. I got an antibiotic infusion and all that I needed and was in and out in 90 minutes. God bless Alaska!

I have had a lot of hospitalizations and nearly lost my life many times over. I have had exactly 50 surgeries, most having to do with my serious degenerative joint disease and joint replacements. I began feeling weak a couple of years ago, around 2018, and found my pulse had dropped into the 40s, so it was decided I needed a pacemaker. It works hard most of the time, keeping my heart rate up to 60. I have arrythmia also, so need that checked out frequently. But so far, I have always bounced back and been able to carry on. Once in Bolivia, I had a serious blood clot in the inner thigh of my right leg. I was placed on blood thinners and had to spend three weeks in bed. I had a special table built that could hold my electric typewriter and Peter's dictaphone, and I carried on from that spot. The blood clot refused to dissolve, so I had to have that vein surgically removed from my groin to my ankle since the vein itself was beginning to deteriorate. I once got a serious infection in an artificial knee that almost took me out. I had to have the appliance removed and wait for a couple of months before I could get it replaced. When an infection settles in an artificial joint, it is very dangerous, since the joint cannot cleanse itself, as a natural one does. That is what happened in Singapore. I have been on "last ditch" antibiotics several times, but, so far God has always seen me through to wholeness again. As Peter often used to joke, "Her motor is working fine, she just needs a little body work." Now with the pacemaker, I may be at the beginning stages of needing a motor job as well.

Getting back to that last item on my bucket list. I made a bold move and removed some funds from our meager retirement fund, and we flew to Vancouver and took a cruise to Alaska via Princess Cruise lines, which was full of old people. I later learned that it is often said jokingly that they serve the "Newlywed or the nearly dead!" Their music and shows were the old 50s love songs. One time in port, they brought aboard a bunch of sled dog puppies, and there were piano concerts of soothing music. I thoroughly enjoyed the cruise. When we got into Anchorage, Ruth rented a car and we drove to Robert and Eleanor Roehl's house and stayed in a nearby hotel. They took her deep-sea fishing one day, but it was raining and rather miserable, as was their luck.

The bright idea occurred to Ruth that with all the prices being so astronomical, maybe we could rent an R.V. and save the hotel and car rental money. While we would be able to drive ourselves and go at our own pace, we would also save money because we would be doing our own cooking. That was one of the best ideas she ever got. Alaska has a lot of U.S. military, active and retired. We found a great rental R.V. for the daily rental of less than our car, owned by an ex-military man, so she grabbed it. She spent a day making a frame for the door that would hold a handrail for me and we got me inside. My seat was on a sofa that was marshmallow soft, and it was my bed also. I had my portable commode and travel scooter and was right at home and far more comfortable than in the hotel. So, we took off and drove on every major paved highway in Alaska except one. The glass windows were enormous and the view from my sofa was spectacular. It was almost September and the leaves were turning and the scenery was superb.

Ruth is the proud owner of a Class A license and has often driven an R.V. before, so it was nothing new to her. We were instructed that we were forbidden to use any gravel roads of which there are a myriad. The snowcapped mountains were so very beautiful. We found wonderful R.V. campgrounds during that long trip and we made it back to Anchorage in time for the fair. When we were in Anchorage, wonderful Robert and Eleanor Roehl allowed us to park in their driveway. We had a wonderful time together. It was pretty nippy by then, since it was the very end of August. But at the fair, I got to see the cabbage weighing. It proved to be a poor year for cabbages, and they weighed less than usual. I believe the winner weighed about 90 pounds, but the record cabbage from previous years was 130 lbs! It's interesting to note that the pumpkin that year was the largest one in Alaskan history weighing 1,471.5 lbs. I must say, the shape was not round and pretty, but that does not count. What counts is the weight. Also, it must not have any cracks whatsoever, so each one is examined carefully in order to qualify. I learned that the pumpkins are broken up and given to the wild moose to enjoy after the fair is over. Possibly the other vegetables are as well. Moose can be a nuisance and are the reason that most trees have heavy wire around the trunks and small trees are entirely surrounded by heavy wire mesh.

Ruth and I always enjoy fair food. But I must say this was the first time I have ever eaten a pork chop grilled on a stick, and we had some of the best raw oysters that ever passed our lips. Also, there were gigantic cream puffs that were delicious.

I was surprised at the lack of farm animals. My guess is the bitter cold winters precludes raising them, hence there were very few horses, pigs and cows. There were some cages of rabbits and chickens and a meager flower display. They did have a contest where the little kids were riding sheep (mutton-busting) and that was fun to watch.

The time came when it was getting to be dusk and we had to figure out how to get me back in the R.V. Ruth said, "Let me look for the haircut." I didn't know what she meant, but she was looking for some military kids. She soon found four sweet young men and asked them if they would slip out into the nearby handicap parking lot and help get her mother back into our R.V. They readily obliged and were more than happy to help. The R.V. had four or five high steps. The boys were all dressed in civilian clothes and as kind as they could be. When we got to the door, one of them took charge. He sent two up the steps inside and asked how much I weighed. I had to confess that I weighed 160 pounds. "Piece of cake," he said. The remaining two squatted down as I put my arms around the neck of each, and with a "One, Two, *THREE!*" they hoisted me up like a feather. They were so strong, and the two inside guided me to my marshmallow sofa, and it may have taken all of five seconds to complete. We found out they were from Puerto Rico, Florida, New York and California. Ruth slipped them a hundred-dollar bill for some food and/or drink, and they thanked us and walked off into the night back into the fairgrounds. Once more yet, when all else fails, call out the army!

We flew back to Dallas (man, it is a long flight from Anchorage!) and Ruth started out on a quest to locate a suitable R.V. so I could travel more freely once again. After Peter's death, it took almost two years for me to recover, but when I did, I wanted to get back into ministry again. I let Chuck Pierce know that I fully planned to die with my boots on, and I began a deliverance ministry again. Chuck gave me a little, but very adequate office at church and I did deliverances there most Monday and Wednesday afternoons after working out in the beautiful gym with a magnificent personnel trainer. I have to keep my upper body strength up, being so disabled. I began teaching seminars again and the summer of 2019 was very busy.

I finally got the courage together to pick up the book that Peter left half written. The topic was the six major things he had learned in life and how he planned to finish well. He had written a little over half of it but had lectured on all of the remaining chapters, so I had those lecture notes and his outline of chapters. It was with a heavy heart that I picked it up and wrote what I think he would have said. I was never the literary genius and wordsmith Peter was, but I got through it and one of his former publishers immediately snatched it up, sight unseen. I finished it in the summer of 2020. It was due for publication in the fall of 2021.

Ruth located a "toy hauler" R.V. in Evergreen, Colorado. It was 10 years old, so it needed a lot of attention since it was kept outside all the time and Colorado winters are harsh. But it had a hydraulic lift on the back (originally meant to load 4-wheelers, motorcycles, dune buggies and the like) and I could drive my wheelchair on the metal floor. Ruth would push a button and it would lift me like an elevator up and I could drive right into the back of the vehicle. Oddly enough it was owned by a former American Airlines pilot named Wagner, who had a very unfortunate automobile accident, broke his neck and became a quadriplegic. We decided this would be a good vehicle for me to get around the country. That our base was located rather centrally near Dallas helped. We spent the summer of 2019 traveling from coast to coast doing deliverance seminars. Many of my invitations came from smaller Hispanic churches, and small inner-city churches, where nobody visits. It was a joy to minister to these needy people. We got to visit Ruth's family along the way, as well as daughter Becky, husband Jack and their three boys in Michigan. All the family visiting was a real treat. I always enjoy visiting Becky in May for the Holland, Michigan Tulip Festival. Karen was able to get a week off and fly to Grand Rapids to join us, so I had my three girls altogether again.

We did a seminar in Bakersfield, California, and saw daughter Karen in Pasadena. We spent a week in Claremont teaching for Wagner University and ministering at a church there. We were able to visit the Los Angeles County Fair, and that was a huge treat for me. I didn't get food poisoning this time like I did in 1955!

On another junket we went to a conference in Alabama where I ministered to individuals for four days. Then we proceeded on to North Carolina, spent a week there with a Glory of Zion house church and did a seminar there and ministered to a couple dozen of that group. We then dropped down to Charlotte and visited a student of Peter's who set up a seminar for me there. We had the great privilege of touring the grounds of the Billy Graham "Cove." We were allowed to place two bouquets of flowers on Billy and Ruth's graves and got a private tour of everything there. Then we moved on down to Valdosta, Georgia, to the home of another of Peter's former students for a weeklong seminar and ministering to individuals. From there we headed south to Florida where we had another week seminar near Orlando and then on down to Vero Beach to spend a delightful week with Peter's sister, Margo. We then headed on home.

It was a great year of freedom in travel. Ruth had fixed up the rear section of the 40-foot R.V.as a handicap bedroom for me. She attached a tow-bar to the back and we are able to pull my handicap van behind. This enables us to park the R.V. in a trailer park and travel comfortably in the van to attend meetings. That makes our entire rig just about as long as a semi-truck, but Ruth is able to handle it with no problem. She does not like to back up with the van hooked up, but who can blame her?

Ruth also installed a T.V. so I could continue to watch my fun Hallmark movies and the church services I enjoy: Glory of Zion, Bobby Schuller and Joel Osteen, and my son-in-law from Grand Rapids, Jack Sytsema. She bought a large Craftsman toolbox on wheels, and the front of that with the drawers served to hold all of my fold-up clothes, toiletries and incidentals. Then she built in a fold-down shelf to house my computer and act as a desk, allowing me a good space for my wheelchair and footrest. It worked spectacularly. Ruth hand built a bedside table that had wheels that slide under the bed and the table hangs over the bed where my missing leg would ordinarily be, so I have my C-Pap breathing machine and needed nighttime items within reach. Ruth is very inventive and a genius at that sort of thing. She was able to tie down that furniture, along with my commode to heavy rings on the floor and absolutely nothing moved as we bumped along. Peter and I slept in twin hospital beds shoved together to look like a king size bed for the last ten years of his life, so I even had an extra bed to place back there, and just the right size. I could raise the head and enjoy my television after a long day's work. I could close the door between her quarters in the front and mine in the rear since she loved the heat, but I like to sleep cool, and we can adjust the temperatures accordingly.

Ruth is a mechanic and that has come in handy many times on the road. Often when I am away teaching during the days, she continues to make repairs and upgrades on the elderly R.V. It seems as though something is always in need of repair. At several of our stops, men from the church or conference have pitched in and volunteered to help fix a leaky skylight, a broken drawer or build in more storage space for canned food and boxes. We have had such a delightful time on the road. This past summer she has undertaken the enormous task of buffing and waxing the entire exterior, and had to use scaffolding to complete the job because the vehicle is so tall, about 13 feet.

Then COVID-19 hit in March of 2020. We had 12 seminars and teaching engagements scheduled for the spring, summer and fall of 2020, but had to cancel them all, and call off the trip. I rescheduled a few by Zoom but had to call off the rest. I had purchased a large inventory of books for that summer, since some of the books I recommend are hard to come by. I invested a great deal of cash in stocking up on books, since they sold so very well the summer before. But Zoom conferences do not have a book table, so that set me back financially. I have done a myriad of deliverances by Zoom and they seem to work okay, but I still prefer to do them in person. During the COVID year, I did the local deliverances in my backyard, under my oak trees, in the torrid Texas summer heat using fans and practicing social distancing.

That brings everything up to date. I plan to continue traveling with Ruth and the R.V. when travel restrictions lift and when it is safe for an old lady (I am 89 at this writing) to be out and about. I plan to continue to teach as long as invitations come forth and to do deliverances over tormented people as long as I have life and breath. My plan is, as I told my boss, Chuck Pierce, to "die with my *boots* on."

What did I learn from this period of my life? Mainly I learned that death is an enemy, but God is faithful and saw me through. How I thank God for Chuck Pierce, who has taken over as a son and who is there for me. I am grateful for being able to minister again. I was able to finish Peter's last book and was surprised and blessed that Destiny Image was interested in publishing these memoirs. I am so happy to be back in ministry once again, and happy that I feel well enough to travel the nation to do seminars. I am grateful for Zoom that has permitted me to continue to do personal deliverances here and abroad.

CHAPTER 17

Escapes From Death

I have come so very close to death that I wanted to write down some of my close escapes before they "escape" my memory.

During dangerous or treacherous times, I have often read an extra Psalm in addition to other Bible reading. Those pages in my Bible when closed, are a different dark, used color and sort of stand out in the middle of my Bible. I know folks who delight in getting a new Bible periodically and especially delight in digesting new translations. I differ from them in that I love to review the underlining and the various notes I have taken in the margins explaining what God spoke to me when there was a special need, an answer to prayer or an assignment directly from Him.

I miss hymns. I love to think I am singing a hymn written and sung by my ancestors 500 years ago. I love roots and tradition. I know I am old-fashioned, but I find these hymns comforting. Maybe I love the Psalms because they express the music I chose to give up, they renew the lyrics of songs I sang in Glee Club or All State Choir back when we had just won World War II and were so grateful. Maybe it is just something that comes with nostalgia and old age.

I love to think about Psalm 91, where God tells us He sends angels to watch over and protect us. Also, very special to me is Psalm 68:19-20 which reads "Blessed be the Lord who daily loads us with benefits, the God of our salvation! Selah. Our God is the God of salvation; and to God the Lord belong escapes from death" (NKJV). I have lived in poverty, in primitive surroundings and in comfortable ones, and I have seen God at work many times to save my life and the lives of my family members. The only possible reason I can think of is that He isn't finished with teaching me or using me.

I got pneumonia back in the days when it was a killer and I was just three or four years old. I was violently ill but survived. It was before the days of antibiotics and I lived in a drafty, wood and coal-heated farmhouse in the snow belt of New York State. But back then we managed, and our folks prayed a lot. I survived it along with measles, mumps, chicken pox and with only a smallpox vaccination and diphtheria shot. We prayed hard not to get polio, which was dreaded in my childhood. Mercifully we all escaped that.

Then there was the doozy of a car accident where our car with our entire family rolled over three times. In those days we had no seatbelts and no safety glass, but once again we escaped death and survived, and no one was thrown from the wreckage.

Then there was the time when I was maybe 10 years old and somehow, I got a kite. It was a nice breezy summer morning, and I was looking for some strong twine to use to fly the kite. I can't recall how it happened, but I acquired a very large spool of sturdy copper wire, so I decided to use that. Sure enough, I got the kite up in the air and it was sailing along beautifully. It was early in the morning; I was barefoot on our spacious front lawn and the grass was wet with the dew that had collected overnight. Dad, Mom and my brothers were finishing up the farm chores in the barn after milking and I was alone enjoying my newfound entertainment. What I had not noticed were the high-tension electric wires that went through our property to some farmhouses up the hill behind our land. Then it happened! My copper wire hit the electric line and I heard a strange sound like someone striking a match.

I felt a shock from the wire as it touched the high-tension wire and bounced off. I did have the good sense to let go of my precious kite and the wire, and I never did find it either. They just floated off into the wild blue yonder. I felt God spared me from being electrocuted.

When I was about 16, I used the tractor and for some reason had to go up to visit my dear friends George and Francis Matis. They lived on land adjoining ours, but I had to go on a triangular route along a gravel road, then on to an asphalt road to get to their home. Our little Case SC tractor had a special speed called "highway speed" that was above third gear that could be used when one was on a safe, smooth road and wanted to get somewhere fast. So, I put the thing in highway speed and got to their house. Whatever the business was, I accomplished it and got back on the tractor seat that I had parked in their driveway. I forgot that I had the thing in highway speed, and I let out the hand clutch and took off in a jolt on to the asphalt road that passed in front on their house just as another car came speeding from my right. I had a reflex move which was to hit the foot brake with my left foot. It caused the tractor to do a rapid 360 to the left, narrowly missing the speeding car by what looked like inches. I got my foot off the brake just in time to fall behind that car and go along my merry way right behind it. It was reminiscent of some Abbot and Costello old action movie. I was shaking all the way home and later thought, *What if my reflex had been to hit the right foot brake?* I would have done a 360 to the right and hit that car head-on and probably been thrown to my death. I might have caused injury or death to some of the passengers of the other vehicle. Wow, what a narrow escape!

Then there was the time the brakes went out on our old 1938 Dodge as I was on my way to work as a newlywed. I was going down a fairly steep hill approaching a stop sign, and the brake pedal went right to the floor. I used the hand emergency brake to get the car stopped just short of a very busy road in rush hour. Sometimes it pays to be a farm girl and have a few mechanical "plan Bs" in your mental toolbox in case of emergency.

There was also the food poisoning incident in 1955 after attending the Los Angeles County Fair. I had a horrific fever and was so violently ill, but antibiotics saved by life once again. I never wanted to be that sick again!

When we were new missionaries, Peter almost died in the jungle of eastern Bolivia when he was attacked by a swarm of fire ants and bitten horribly on his legs. His throat was closing off and his ears and lips became horribly swollen and purple. He could not talk, but wrote me a note saying, "I can't breathe through my mouth." I got a jar of Vicks VapoRub and spread it under his nose and on his chest and prayed, and he was soon able to breathe again with the strong fumes of menthol, but he came so close to losing his life.

Our sweet daughter Ruth was born so very prematurely in the jungle with no advantages of modern medicine to help her, but she wanted to live. I had no milk, but God provided the mother's milk from a dear Christian friend who was nursing her own baby at the time. Baby Ruth nearly choked to death the second day of her life, but I just shook her and screamed, "Breathe, Baby, breathe!" And she obligingly did. I am not sure if that was a healing prayer or if it knocked some mucus loose, but she got pink again and kept on breathing. I mentioned before that by the time she should have been born, ten weeks later, she weighed a whopping 7 pounds and 10 ounces! Miraculous!

Peter and I decided to take three-year-old Ruth up to the city of La Paz to get an electroencephalogram to see just how much brain damage she had suffered at birth because we were told she had cerebral palsy and had such trouble trying to walk. We were living in Cocha-bamba at about 8900 ft. of altitude, a delightful city. We were on a bus bound for La Paz and the journey is quite torturous, winding through the mountains of the steep Andes Mountains. It took about 12 hours, most of which was through the mountains, steep hills, narrow sharp curves, no guardrails, and rain forest at times. We frequently would come across spots along the roadside with ten to twenty white wooden crosses, indicating that a truck or bus had gone over the edge and there were multiple fatalities. After ten hours of tough riding, we would hit the Altiplano, a very high, but flat piece of land that stretched for hun-dreds of miles and led to the city of La Paz nestled in a big bowl below. As I recall, the Altiplano was 13,000 feet in elevation and La Paz was about 1,000 feet below.

I recall having been on that bus ride once or twice before. The time came for us to take a supper break and we were traveling along very fast. I noticed that we did not stop at the village and restaurant where the bus usually stopped. Finally, we did come to a halt about a half mile past it. We asked why we were stopped in the middle of nowhere, and the bus driver calmly told us that the air brakes went out and we had totally lost our brakes. We were able to walk back to the restaurant and get supper and wait for help to arrive. But what if that had happened as we were approaching one of those sharp curves we had just driven through safely? Ours might be three white wooden crosses at the bend in the road. Once more, angels held things together until we could arrive at safely. Oh yes, the tests on her brain showed that she was of totally normal intelligence!!

Then there was the incident where I saw an angel push 5-year-old Ruth out of the path of the rapidly oncoming taxi in Cochabamba, Bolivia. She was playing with a friend outside our large church and darted from the sidewalk out into the street directly in front of an oncoming taxi. She was pushed back on to the sidewalk by an invisible angel, so hard and with such force that her hair flew backwards. She had escaped certain death right before my very eyes.

I also recall being caught out on the street walking home from church during our last term in Bolivia, when there was one of our many revolutions in progress. It often involved the university students in our city of Cochabamba. We were about three blocks from home when a group of students came running down the middle of the street, followed by a bevy of policemen standing on a truck bed shooting over their heads to disperse them. I had never come so close to being shot at before, and it was just a case of being in the wrong place at the wrong time, I guess. I decided I did not like the sound of bullets zinging over my head, and I was hoping that those holding the guns were good aims. Peter and I along with another missionary were caught in the gunfire. I don't care to repeat any situation with gunfire ever again.

Then we came back to live in America when Peter accepted a professor assignment at the School of World Mission. Earlier I explained how he felt he was pushed off a 12-foot ladder from a loft in our garage and fell flat on his back on to our concrete garage floor. He recovered with no broken bones, but may have severely bruised a few angels in that one. He easily could have broken his back or become paralyzed. God is so good.

Peter always made it a point to spend special times with our girls during the summer when seminary was out. He frequently taught summer school at the invitation of other colleges and seminaries, and he took the equivalent of a round-trip plane ticket in cash and he would drive us all to wherever he was teaching. One year we decided to take a rafting trip down the Colorado River. Karen was already working in one of her first jobs at a nursing home, so it was just Becky, Ruth, Peter and me. We rafted along, going over rapids and had a great time. We had to bring along sleeping bags and spend one night on the banks of the river. As I recall, we had a bunch of airline stewardesses and a couple of stewards in our group. When it came time to go to bed, we withdrew from that group because they were a little noisy. We set up our little spot and settled down for the night. What we did not realize was that the river was raging at that time of year with snowmelt and was rather swift. We had not noticed it, but we chose a nice level spot—maybe 15 feet from the bank right along a bend in the river. In the middle of the night, we heard a rumbling and crashing sound and the riverbank was giving way and caving into the river. We all scrambled away from the river cave-in but realized that the very spot where we were sleeping was headed downstream toward Arizona. The big casualty was that someone had stepped on Becky's glasses and she had trouble seeing without them. Somebody had grabbed them when we picked up our sleeping bags and rapidly retreated. We somehow got them either replaced or repaired, but the great news is that we were all alive and well.

I recall that on a second rafting trip down the Colorado River, Becky (maybe 12 years old or so, but just as soon as she was able) was wearing contact lenses by then, she was taking them out to go swimming with the group in a calm pool at the river's edge. As she was removing the contacts, the wind caught one of them and it flew off the end of her finger into a very large patch of tall brown grass and had gone to seed. Becky did not have any backup lenses with her and I promised her that if she would go swimming with Ruth and enjoy herself, I would find that lens. It took me about an hour and some "Please, God, help me find this" prayer, but I FOUND IT in the middle of that hayfield. It gave the adage "looking for a needle in a haystack" new meaning. We went on to enjoy our vacation and Becky could see everything just fine.

During the decade of the 1990s, Peter and I traveled overseas a great deal on various prayer assignments, doing seminars and other teaching stints and international meetings and conferences. Peter was teaching in Japan on one occasion when I had to have some pins removed from my toes after some foot reconstruction due to arthritis complications and Charcot Foot. It turned out that I "threw a clot" and got a life-threatening case of pulmonary emboli. Several intercessors rushed to the hospital and Peter wanted to leave his responsibilities in Japan and rush home to be by my side, but I asked him to stay and "not give the devil the satisfaction of pulling him off his assignment." Peter did not come home, and after a lengthy hospital stay, I recovered. But that was a very close one. I recall that my good friend Pastor Jim Marocco, one of Peter's former students who has a number of churches in the Hawaiian Islands and in other parts of the world, happened to be at Fuller Seminary at the time. When he heard I was in danger of losing my life, he grabbed the first Korean student he could find and asked for a ride to the emergency room. I am sure that patients on the fourth floor of the hospital were blessed and healed by his prayers over me on the ground floor of the emergency room, he prayed so loud, but effectively. All things considered; I got better pretty quickly. Still, it was another escape from death, and my doctor even confirmed that.

Then, over the course of the years I have had several life-threatening infections that have settled in my artificial joints, which cannot cleanse themselves. I previously described the one diagnosed as a flesh-eating bacterium that was caused by my scratching a bug bite while teaching a deliverance seminar in Malaysia. Another I remember was at a time when I had to leave a birthday party for Cindy Jacobs, and I barely survived that one. There was another while in Alaska. I am sure there were more I can't even remember.

Probably the most dramatic escape from death took place while in Guatemala. I previously wrote about it a few chapters ago, but will recount it again. Peter and I have a great friend, Harold Caballeros there in Guatemala City. There were some spectacular things going on and we wanted to see them firsthand. Almolonga is a city where the Christian indigenous folks have been so blessed and the land there yields crops and flowers that are extraordinary. Anyway, we were on our way to visit that area. We were in a small private six-passenger plane and were landing in the village of Quetzaltenango. A strange thing happened. The landing gear would not come down and we landed straight on the belly of the plane. It was a dirt landing strip, mercifully. The body split open enough to form a plowshare and it picked up bushels of dirt all along the strip and dumped it on us passengers. Our eyeglasses were so covered with dirt that we could not see anything. I was sitting closest to the door and Peter yelled to me, "Open the door, open the door!" probably fearing an explosion, which, mercifully did not happen. We were all able to scramble out, unharmed, but very dirty. The plane was a torn-open bunch of wreckage, the wings were torn and the propellors were all bent every which way. We needed a very long bus ride back to Guatemala City through the beautiful mountains. We celebrated being alive by eating tortillas and *chicharrons* (crispy fried pork belly or pigskin). It is not a huge number of passengers that walk away from a plane crash. God was not through with us yet.

I so vividly recall the carbon monoxide poisoning that happened to daughter Becky, her husband Jack and baby Nick in Colorado Springs. I previously wrote about that, but it does belong in this litany of the escapes from death. There were TWO carbon monoxide spills, each from a different furnace two weeks apart in our lovely new home that we built there. My evaluation of that is the devil was downright mad at the progress made leading up to the beautiful Ephesus celebration in October of 1999. He tried hard to take us out, but once again, "to our God belong escapes from death." I am so glad I am one of His kids.

After I wrote the above in September of 2020, I had another brush with death. In 2018 I was diagnosed with a condition called "watermelon stomach," a situation where the walls of the stomach become thin and the blood vessels seep blood. The only way an individual can find out that they have this is when the hemoglobin levels drop significantly. During 2018 and 2019, I had my stomach cauterized two times to correct this condition when my hemoglobin dropped below seven. But then in September 2020, I began vomiting some black matter that looked like digesting blood to me. My hemoglobin dropped to 5.8, and I was told to be rushed to the emergency room. It turns out that I had been bleeding quite a bit and was actually bleeding to death. The doctors were able to cauterize my stomach one more time but felt that my condition was exacerbated by a very large hiatal hernia that had entrapped my stomach and part of my spleen, so I needed surgery to correct that situation. Since there is no pain associated with this condition, I had no idea that I was bleeding to death until daughter Ruth measured my hemoglobin and found out that it had dropped to that 5.8 level. A reading pf 7 is considered critically low. When she called the doctor, he instructed her to rush me to the emergency room where they put me in the hospital immediately and soon gave me a blood transfusion of two units of blood. My blood is difficult to match because along the way I have needed a number of blood transfusions and have picked up some antibodies that make finding a match for a transfusion difficult. I had to wait for two days as the hospital franticly searched for a match and finally found the two units they deemed necessary. I was able to get surgery a couple of days later. This saved my life yet one more time.

I am forgetting a bunch more, I am sure. What I want to find out when I get to heaven is how many close calls did I, Peter or my girls have that I never knew about? Word got to me that I would be kidnapped in Nepal when I was on my way to Mount Everest. How many times were there dangerous snakes that cowered back and out of my way at night when I had to be out and about? How many other plane crashes were averted, bullets diverted, or other calamities truncated by the hand of God? How many other times did I eat tainted food or drink poisonous water? I suspect many.

What have I learned over the years of ministry? I learned that I was a poor missionary in my younger days. I did my best, but had such inadequate preparation. Hopefully, Peter and I were able to be led in the right direction and correct the need for readiness in the lives of our students so they were more productive.

I learned that God, by His grace, never put me in a situation He did not give me the ability to handle. I never felt defeated, just battling some things. Peter was so often misunderstood by peers and some colleagues. Although maddening to some, his humility, I am sure, was pleasing to God. He never let jealousy or jabs by those who considered themselves to be more theologically astute or learned than he, drag him down. He was persecuted for his charismatic leanings in a non-charismatic institution of higher learning, but he always stayed true to God's revelation.

I admired him for his courage. I always felt he was at least ten years ahead of the pack in his field of teaching. He said that he wanted to be remembered "as one who accurately heard what the Spirit was saying to the churches and then faithfully communicated that to the Body of Christ." Those are his very words. He lived and died doing his best at that assignment.

I was brought up in humble surroundings and often felt a little inferior to others during my elementary and middle school years. But when I realized how much I had learned by my upbringing and how privileged I was, that melted away. I was so grateful to have a biblical foundation that belief was easy and welcome in my life. I thank God for such a wonderful mom and dad, brothers and sister and home life, that I was loved, cared for so well, and taught the Bible and its commandments. I felt safe and secure in the midst of raging World War II.

I learned, most of all, that the safest place to be in the whole wide world is in the center of God's will. I saw how God blessed and kept me and my family safe in hostile surroundings through many life-threatening situations and illnesses. I learned to "cast all my cares on Him, because He cares for me." Many times, because God had treated me with such loving care and compassion, I wanted to wear the t-shirt that says, "God loves you, but I am His favorite."

God showed me, when I was in profound grief over Peter's passing, a way to get some joy back in my life. I was to find someone worse off than I and help out as I was able. Since I have always enjoyed stocking the food pantries of places like the Salvation Army, I do that as I am able. I hate the thought of hungry people. I don't know where they are, but the Salvation Army does. Ruth and I joined forces to help prepare and serve Thanksgiving dinner to the poor here in Denton, Texas. We have become very adept at peeling potatoes, stripping meat from the turkey bones, and setting tables. The church where we volunteer rents the kitchen and cafeteria of a local school. They have a volunteer chef who oversees the menu and cooking. They served well over 2,000 lovely, homemade dinners at the cafeteria, and Ruth delivers meals along with a free Bible in English or Spanish to shut-ins. I usually greeted the folks at the door, and because there are so many Spanish speaking guests, I am able to converse with them and give instructions needed. Meanwhile, we got a wonderful turkey dinner in the bargain.

For many days in the past couple of years before COVID hit, we rang bells for the Salvation Army and collected cash in the red kettles outside local Walmart and Sam's Club stores. We collected the most in our kettle of anyone in the area. We always had to bring a chopstick along to push down the cash overflowing in our bucket. Ruth would set up her Christmas music, give all kids a tootsie-pop bought with her own money, and on those days I left my prosthetic leg at home. People see that even though I am severely handicapped I can still make a contribution, and it has inspired a few folks to mention that along the way. So, there is always something we can find to do that will bless the less fortunate along the way.

I love the fact that at my advanced age, God has kept my mind pretty sharp, and He can still use me to teach seminars on deliverance and to minister freedom to those bound by Satan's chains. I'm glad I have been able to write a book and edit another one that helped many find freedom.

I love my church and especially need to thank Chuck Pierce and Brian Kooiman and Brandon Larson for their wonderful help transitioning from Colorado to Texas and into widowhood with all that took place. It was the toughest time in my life, and you three have helped me through to peace and happiness on the other side of the valley of death.

I am so thankful for my three girls who put up with a lot because their mom and dad were very busy, but we did so enjoy each one of them. Each is unique, but so very precious to us. We keep in close touch, and we all love one another. I pray diligently for the extended family every day, as is my duty as the matriarch.

I thank God for allowing me to be a helper to my precious Peter for 66 years and 6 days. He was always a loving, wonderful husband and father and tried to serve and please God wholeheartedly. I loved all those traits about him. My girls once complained to me that they couldn't find anybody for a husband who began to resemble their wonderful dad. I just joked with them and said, "Did you look under a cow?"

APPENDIX

Wagner Family Favorite Recipes

BREAKFAST

BIRCHER MUESLI

I first ate this when Peter and I were driving through Switzerland. A friend of ours loaned us his little mountain chalet for a week's break when we were at the height of our busyness with the prayer movement and the Lausanne Committee for World Evangelization. It often necessitated trips to Europe for leaders' meetings. Switzerland is the only place I have been where the photos do not capture its beauty. Peter and I loved listening to the bells around each cow's neck as she grazed on the mountainside all night long. We found this at every breakfast buffet in Switzerland.

1 cup old fashioned rolled oats

½ cup unflavored Greek yogurt

½ cup milk or non-dairy milk

2 medium apples grated on coarse side of a box grater

¼ cup sunflower kernels

¼ cup sliced almonds

½ cup chopped pecans

1/3 cup toasted wheat germ

2 T. oat bran

1/3 cup chopped dates

2 T. tahini (optional)

2 T. raisins

2 T. dried cherries

Optional: 2 tablespoons or more of pepitas (Pumpkin seeds)

6-8 chopped dried apricots

1/3 cup coconut flakes or shredded coconut

Some recipes toasted the rolled oats, seeds and nuts in a 350 oven for 12 minutes, and I would do that. Stir all ingredients together and store in an airtight container. Cover and refrigerate for one hour up to four days. If not using apples, it may be stored for up to a month in the refrigerator. Before serving, add a bit of milk if it has gotten too thick. Top individual servings with additional fresh or dried fruit, nuts and maple syrup or a drizzle of honey.

TURKEY PILE-ON

We were welcomed home from our second term in Bolivia by our precious friends at Bell Friends Church for a party for the whole church. It was hosted by Glen and Irene Main, our closest friends there. Irene worked at a bakery department in a large grocery store and saw to it that we were kept in baked goods during our time there in Huntington Park, California. While we were missionaries, Irene handled all of the hand addressing and mailing of our prayer letters, as there were no label printing machines yet invented. She treated us like her own kids. We were there introduced to Turkey Pile-On, and I have served it at large parties ever since. It is, by far, my most requested recipe. I believe it was invented to use up leftover Thanksgiving turkey and possibly gravy. It was requested at a granddaughter's wedding! And she got it.

I have had equal success using already cooked rotisserie chicken purchased at Sam's Club or your favorite other store. I use dry packaged turkey gravy (I use Pioneer brand packaged gravy, and lots of it) to produce the extra gravy as needed. Ruth figured out that one Sam's chicken (they are far larger than those found in other grocery stores, serves 10 people and she uses 2 packages of Pioneer Turkey gravy powder per chicken). Of course, all turkey scraps and gravy are the original choice, but I adore the chicken. Skin, debone, and cut all meat into small pieces of about a half inch square or smaller. (We then use the bones to make bone broth so nothing was wasted.) The joyous part is this can be prepared a day or two ahead and refrigerated. I suggest making the gravy and adding the meat the day of the event, so it doesn't scorch in the reheat. I like to serve my meat and gravy out of a slow cooker kept on a low heat, so it is piping hot. If meat from a whole leftover bird is used, the bones and roasted skin can be boiled for bone broth or stock or as a base for soup. Be sure there is plenty of gravy with the meat. Toast the coconut (and be sure to use SWEETENED coconut) and the almonds the day before. Likewise, the celery can be chopped, as can the scallions and tomatoes. The ingredients sound like a weird combination, but, trust me, they taste wonderful. If there are allergies or dislikes, simply skip that ingredient. Place the following ingredients, each in a separate bowl in the order listed, and add them to your plate, piling each on top of the last one. This is always served buffet style with people in a line. If using disposable plates, be sure to get the heavy-duty ones, cheap ones can't handle the weight. Warn guests to start small or it will weigh 4 pounds!

TURKEY PILE-ON

Canned or bagged Chinese noodles

Hot, cooked fluffy rice (if you have a rice cooker, this is ideal for keeping it warm)

Turkey or chicken in gravy

Grated cheddar cheese

Chopped celery

Chopped scallion (green onion with tops)

Chopped firm red Roma tomatoes

Canned crushed pineapple

Toasted sweetened coconut

Toasted slivered almonds

STUFFED CABBAGE LEAVES

One of my very favorites growing up. Get the largest head of cabbage you can find, or two smaller ones if a large one is unavailable. Remove the core carefully with a sharp knife. Place cabbage, core hole up, in a large soup kettle. Pour boiling water down the core hole to penetrate leaves. Let the leaves wilt. Remove them one by one and place removed leaves on a cookie sheet to cool. If the center ones are still crisp, bring the water to a boil again until they all wilt. I have used Savoy cabbage with good success also. Remove the top of the thick center spine from the leaf to make it easier to roll, but do not make a hole in the leaf.

If cabbage is huge, brown 1 ½ lbs. ground beef, if smaller use 1 lb.

Add 1 chopped onion

1 small green pepper, chopped

3 cloves of garlic chopped

2 to 3 cups cooked white rice

Salt and pepper to taste

I like to line my baking dish with leftover cabbage cut in bite-sized pieces, so none goes to waste. Place a generous spoonful of filling (about ½ cup or more) on each leaf. Roll up and tuck under all sides. Place in a deep 9 by 13 baking dish, open side down.

Pour over a large can of tomato sauce, or more if a large batch. If the dish is deep and there are cabbage leaves beneath everything, a medium-sized can of V-8 is a nice, juicy addition. Cover with foil and bake at 350 degrees for an hour or until cabbage is very soft.

We served this with breadcrumbs (or bread cut into very small cubes) that had been browned in a stick of butter poured over the top. Or for variety, we browned and crumbled a half pound of bacon and poured the bacon crumbles and oil over the top. I always preferred the brown butter. Both are delicious.

GERMAN GREEN BEANS

This is a constant request from grandkids.

2 lbs. fresh green beans (frozen are fine also) cut in 1-inch pieces

4 medium red or white potatoes, the firm kind, NOT russets, peeled, cut into 1" cubes

Boil until crisp done. Drain, reserve water

Cut about ¾ lb. bacon into one-half inch pieces and brown; remove bacon bits, reserve fat.

In a deep frying pan, make a roux out of the bacon fat and keep adding flour to achieve roux consistency. Carefully add reserved bean water to make a medium thick gravy. Pour over the cooked beans and potatoes. Add crisped bacon bits and a healthy amount of chopped fresh dill—at least two little plastic boxes or more if you can afford it. If it is too stiff, add more water or bean water to make a gravy to hold things together but not runny. Sort of the consistency of a southern green bean casserole. I find dry dill weed is NO SUBSTITUTE for fresh dill.

GERMAN SPINACH can be made in the same way. Cook chopped fresh, frozen or even canned spinach with a few small waxy potatoes chopped, rather small in this case. If using canned spinach, cook the chopped potatoes alone first in salted water until done, reserve the water and juice from canned spinach for gravy. Fry bacon, reserving crisp bits, and make a roux from the oil with regular flour. To make gravy, use water or the liquid from canned spinach with the water. Pour the gravy, along with the bacon, over the spinach and potatoes. This needs to be served in small bowls because it will be a loose mixture. It is one of my favorites.

GERMAN TURNIPS were always a winner for me growing up. You will need a couple of yellow turnips the size of your fist, peeled and chopped in one-inch cubes. Add an equal amount of potatoes, russets are fine here. Boil in salted water until done and mash them together. Save the water they were boiled in. Use about a 1/2 to ¾ pound of sliced bacon, cut into half inch pieces and browned. Pull out bacon pieces and make a roux and gravy out of the fat and cooking water. Add more water if needed. Mix together mashed turnips and potatoes, crispy bacon pieces and gravy. This is very German, and we used the root veggies in the winter in this manner.

PIERROGI

2 cups flour

2 eggs

1 tsp. salt

½ cup water

Mix all together well with hands to form a dough then roll out like a pie crust, but a little thinner. Cut in 3-inch rounds; use a drinking glass if you don't have a cutter. Fill with a filling, pinch edges shut tightly. Drop in boiling, salted water. Boil for 15-20 minutes. Drain, serve with brown butter over the top.

Cheese filling: 1 lb. cottage cheese, 2 eggs, 2 tablespoons sugar, mix well.

Plum filling: Cut 1 Italian prune-plum in half, discard the pit; fill hole with a teaspoon of sugar, encase with the dough, and pinch edges very well. Boil 15-20 minutes and serve with browned butter.

Sauerkraut filling: Use leftover sauerkraut and spare rib meat or smoked pork hock meat, free from bones, mixed together. Drain well, fill pockets, pinch well and boil.

Many Polish people fill them with a mixture of cheese and mashed potatoes, but we never did. We made our own cottage cheese, had grandma's plum tree, and made our own sauerkraut and smoked pig's feet or spareribs.

KLUSKI (GNOCCHI)

My favorite ones were made of potatoes but can also be made without.

2 cups grated, leftover boiled potatoes, or mashed potatoes

1 ½ cups flour

½ tsp. salt

1-2 eggs

Enough milk to make a stiff dough

Form a long skinny one-inch ropes out of the dough and cut in 3/4-inch chunks. Boil in salted water for 10 minutes. Serve with brown butter. Italians serve with a marinara sauce and parmesan cheese.

SIMPLER KLUSKI

2 cups flour

1 egg

1 tsp. baking powder

About ¾ cup milk to make a drop batter

2 medium large red or white waxy potatoes, peeled and cut into ¾ inch cubes

Drop potatoes into boiling, salted water. Let boil for 5 minutes. Drop the kluski batter by heaping teaspoons into the boiling water with the potatoes and boil an additional 10 minutes or until done. Serve with brown butter.

SOUR SALAT (BUTTERMILK SOUP)
Very Cooling After Coming In From A Hot Field Of Harvesting

1 head red leaf lettuce, thoroughly washed, cut in thin strips sprinkled with salt and set aside

½ lb. bacon, cut in small pieces, fried crisp, drained, set aside, and discard oil

1-3 large scallions cut finely

3-4 hard cooked eggs, chopped coarsely

3 quarts buttermilk, ice cold

Squeeze water from lettuce, add to other ingredients in large bowl, serve ice cold. Mama served it with leftover boiled potatoes fried; may add to them onion, bacon, chopped fresh dill, and parsley.

POTATO PANCAKES (LATKES)
This is my very favorite comfort food. I often make them when I am alone.

6 medium russet baking potatoes peeled and shredded rather finely. Place the shredded potatoes in a thin tea towel and twist until all the juice is squeezed out, or press until very well drained through a sturdy wire sieve. Transfer to a medium-sized bowl, then add:

2 eggs

1 large onion, shredded, or very finely chopped

1/3 cup flour

1 tsp. salt

Make a batter of the above ingredients and drop by large table-spoonfuls into hot cooking oil. Flatten and brown on both sides and serve with applesauce.

ROULADEN (BEEF ROLLUPS—VERY GERMAN COMFORT FOOD)

I discovered that here in Texas it is easy to fine large pieces of very thinly sliced beef which the Hispanic folks use for Milanese, and it is readily available. You will need kitchen string cut in 6 – 7 inch long pieces and will need either 2 or 3 per roll.

Meat pieces should measure about 4 x 6 inches, even 5 x 7 to make larger ones.

Lay out a piece of meat on a cutting board and place on one end the fillings

Spread thinly with Dijon mustard (optional)

¼ slice bacon

a piece of dark rye bread,1 inch by three inches

a sprig of fresh parsley

a sprig of fresh dill

a small half-moon piece of sweet onion

a small spear of a dill pickle

a few added caraway seeds

sprinkle with a bit of salt and pepper

Carefully roll up and tie each roll in two or three places.

Brown very well on all sides in a large frying pan. Carefully transfer to a pressure cooker and cover with water that has been used to clean up all the fond from the frying pan, then cook at full pressure for about twenty minutes. Remove from heat. Let stand for five minutes, then cool pot under cold running water to bring pressure down. (This can also be cooked in a slow cooker until the meat is very soft and cooked through.) There should be lots of liquid left after removing the rolls with which to make gravy with flour or corn starch slurry. Serve with mashed potatoes.

BEEF SUKIYAKI

This is a very favorite of the kids and grandkids. Everyone cooks his own in electric frying pans at the table. I prepare the vegetables and meat and pile them in large wooden platters I brought home from Bolivia. I add a few veggies not traditional, but that my family loves.

Prepare white rice. Cook with butter and salt and serve in small bowls to each person.

4 oz. beef suet to lubricate hot frying pans, oil may be substituted

2 lbs. tenderloin or other beef steak of choice, cut into strips about 2 inches by 1 inch by ¼ inch thick and served from a separate bowl

2 bunches scallions, cut in two-inch lengths

1 small or ½ large Chinese cabbage, cut in two-inch lengths

1 bag fresh washed spinach, or three bunches, washed and cut in 2-inch lengths

1 package mung bean threads, softened in water according to directions, drained and in a separate bowl

1 lb. sliced mushrooms

1 lb. firm tofu cut in 1-inch squares, served in separate bowl

1 can bamboo shoots (or more if large crowd)

These last three ingredients are not legitimate, my kids just happened to like them and asked me to add them.

2 cans sliced water chestnuts

1 lb. snow peas

1 lb. bean sprouts

Sauce: Mix in a small pitcher and set aside

1 cup soy sauce

½ cup sake (cheap stuff is just fine)

2/3 cup sugar

Each guest has a small bowl and chopsticks. Some people like to dip their cooked food in a beaten raw egg, beaten with their chopsticks right in their little bowls. Peter loved his sukiyaki served like this.

Heat to max, then grease frying pans with the suet. Figure on three or four rounds of cooking the ingredients, so plan accordingly. Add ¼ of the meat, cook it and shove it to one side.

Add the other ingredients, about a quarter at a time, leaving them in separate piles. Pour over all 1/3 of the soy sauce mixture. Cover and cook until just crisp done. Serve with tongs or very large spoon. Everyone is on their own. Serve with a small bowl of hot cooked rice.

GUMBO, THREE INGREDIENTS

I once tore my shoulder stirring a pot of gumbo on a high stove from my wheelchair, and it necessitated a total reverse shoulder replacement done by the Los Angeles Lakers orthopedic surgeon in Vail, Colorado. My surgeon in Colorado Springs rushed to get his camera when he told me to see how far above my body, I could stretch my arm. When I shot it straight up in the air perpendicular to my body, he said "You can't do that!" He was also an orthopedic surgeon to all the Olympic kids in training in Colorado Springs. I said, "God is good," as he stared in amazement. On to the gumbo:

1 ½ lbs. chicken thigh chunks, cut in bite sized pieces

4 lbs. large shrimp. I search for the raw, easy-peel ones. Peel and reserve shells in 6-quart saucepan. Add 4 quarts of water and boil the shells for 10 minutes. Drain, toss shells, reserve shrimp water. If shrimp are peeled, skip this step.

1 lb. andouille sausage, cut in bite-sized pieces

1 cup Tony Chachere's Instant Roux Mix

3 large onions, cut in small chunks

2 large green peppers, cut in chunks

10 ribs of celery, cut in bite-sized pieces

6 large cloves minced garlic

1 large can diced tomatoes

4 bay leaves

½ tsp. ground thyme

2 lbs. frozen, cut okra (or fresh if available)

4 quarts of water shrimp shells were cooked in for 10 minutes. If shrimp are peeled, remove tail shells before adding shrimp to the pot. Substitute chicken broth for shrimp water.

Salt and pepper to taste

1 cup chopped scallions for garnish

Chopped parsley for garnish

File gumbo powder and hot sauce for serving

Toss chicken chunks in seasoned flour and sauté in hot oil till brown and cooked through, Remove and set aside. Sauté chunked veggies; add chicken, andouille sausage and shrimp water. Cook 10 minutes. Season, and add roux powder. Stir till smooth. If it looks too thin, add more roux powder by tablespoon until achieving the proper consistency. Add tomatoes and shrimp. Cook for 5 minutes. Do not overcook shrimp. Serve immediately over cooked rice. Garnish with scallions, pass file gumbo powder shaker and hot sauce for each guest to add as desired.

KOREAN SHORT RIBS

Many meat markets will now have short ribs cut across the rib bones. Look for these. If they cannot be found, regular short ribs can be used in a pinch. They usually come in 9 to 12-inch slabs. If using regular short ribs, lay the ribs with the bone flat and butterfly them open, so the meat is less than ½ inch thick. Remove excess fat, or there will be flareups on barbeque coals.

Marinade them in the following sauce overnight, turning a couple of times before barbecuing over hot coals to desired doneness

½ cup soy sauce

½ cup water

3-4 chopped scallions, chopped, tops included

3 T. toasted, crushed sesame seeds

2 T. sugar

3-4 cloves fresh garlic, finely chopped

1 ½ tsp. black pepper

2 tsp. sesame oil

I serve these with cooked white rice and Chop Chae

CHOP CHAE

Sauté each vegetable in hot oil with a little salt until crisp done and keep warm.

1 sweet onion, sliced the long way, not across grain, pieces separated

½ lb. fresh mushrooms, sliced

2 carrots sliced in matchsticks

2 stalks celery, cut diagonally in ¼-inch pieces

1 green pepper, cut in 1/4-inch slices

6 scallions, cut in 2-inch pieces

A bunch of spinach or a package of washed salad spinach

2 small bundles of mung bean threads or a large bunch of Korean sweet
   potato noodles

This dish can be changed into a main dish by adding ¾ lb. of thinly
   sliced small pieces of browned beef, such as chuck (optional).

Drain excess oil from vegetables and discard oil.

Mix all together with the following sauce:

2-3 tsp. slightly crushed toasted sesame seeds

2 T. sesame oil

2-3 T. soy sauce

1 T. sugar

Black pepper to taste

Serve hot with ribs and rice

BOK CHOY ORIENTAL SALAD

This recipe is from our chef at my church. We have large conferences, and this is my favorite salad she prepares. She uses napa cabbage instead of bok Choy for the conferences since it tends to keep crispy longer.

1 large head napa cabbage or 2 bok choy bunches, sliced thinly

5 green onions

8 oz slivered almonds

½ cup toasted sesame seeds

½ cup butter

2 packages ramen noodles, crushed into small pieces (do not use seasoning packets)

Dressing

¾ cup sugar

1 cup vegetable oi

½ cup apple cider vinegar

2 T. soy sauce

In a skillet, melt butter, add crushed noodles, almonds and sesame seeds; cook until lightly browned, stirring frequently. Drain on paper towels and set aside to cool.

Mix napa cabbage or bok choy and green onions. Just before serving mix all ingredients together, pour over the dressing, and mix well.

BEEF BARLEY SOUP

My mother made this for us when I was growing up. Except for the celery and green pepper, the vegetables came from our root cellar in the winter, and the bones from our freezer.

Meaty soup bones (hard to find lately), beef shanks, and/or beef ribs with bones. If you have the luxury of an extra half hour of time, brown the bones in large, heavy-bottom stockpot. If not, in a large stockpot, place meat and bones, 1 large chopped onion, 2 crushed garlic cloves, 2 bay leaves, 3 tablespoons salt and cover with water. When it has been boiling about a half hour, add 2/3 cup pearled barley. Boil until the meat is well done, probably another hour; remove edible meat and chop in small pieces. If a lot of fat has collected, turn off heat, blot up excess fat with paper towel pieces and discard.

Meanwhile prepare vegetables:

3-4 stalks celery, chopped

3-4 large carrots, chopped

1 medium green pepper, chopped

½ medium head of cabbage, chopped

1 medium can diced tomatoes with juice

Optional to add protein: 1/2 pound of cut green beans

1 can garbanzo beans, well rinsed and/or

1 can kidney beans, white or red, rinsed

Add all chopped vegetables and chopped meat back to pot, add tomatoes and beans (if desired) at the end. Remove bay leaves. Garnish with 1 cup frozen peas, and fresh chopped Italian parsley and finely chopped scallions, if desired. The soup gets better with age and will keep in the refrigerator up to a week.

BEAN SOUP

One of my favorites. I discovered that there is a 15-bean mix ready for purchase and that may be used. One should aim for 2 pounds of dry beans.

In an 8-quart pot add a handful of each of the following beans until you get 2 lbs.: northern, pinto, large limas, blackeye peas, garbanzos, navy beans, baby limas, kidney beans, white kidney beans, pink, red, black. Pick over to assure there are no stones; wash beans and drain. Measure separately but don't add yet the following grains: handful green split peas, pearl barley, lentils, brown rice, yellow split peas, whole wheatberries. Don't worry if you do not have everything, just use what you have.

Cover beans (not grains) with cold water and bring to a boil. Cover tightly and let stand 45 minutes. Drain. Cover them again with hot water and bring to a boil again. Cover for 45 minutes and drain again. Add grains, stir well, add 5 quarts hot water, and a ham bone and rind or smoked pork hocks. (One could add leftover ham pieces or a Hillshire smoked sausage, but these must be added at the last five minutes or so or else they will dry out.) Brown and add: 3 onions, chopped; 5 cloves garlic, smashed and chopped; 2 stalks celery, chopped. Throw in 2 bay leaves. Boil about an hour on medium-low heat. Test beans to be sure they are cooked and very soft. If not, cook until they are.

(Optional) Add vegetables: 3-4 potatoes, cubed small

4 carrots, cubed small

½ small head of cabbage, cut in one-inch pies

1 medium can diced tomatoes

Now is the time to add chopped ham bits or a Hillshire smoked sausage cut up. Check for salt. Serve garnished with chopped parsley. A warm baguette on the side is a nice accompaniment, especially if slathered with butter.

FRENCH ONION SOUP

A real winner at our house. The result is well worth the effort (serves 6 to 8). Peter found some miniature cast iron cauldrons during one of his trips and we used them for this soup.

4 T. butter

2 T. vegetable oil

2 lbs. onions, thinly sliced on a mandolin (about 7 cups)

1 tsp. salt

3 T. flour

2 quarts of beef stock, fresh or canned

(Or beef and chicken stock combined, in a pinch)

Croutes

12 to 16 one-inch slices of French bread

2 tsp. olive oil

1 large clove garlic, cut the long way

1 cup grated Swiss cheese, or Swiss and freshly grated Parmesan cheese

(I have used provolone in a pinch, and it was o.k.)

In a heavy 5 or 6-quart soup kettle or Dutch Oven, melt the butter and oil over moderate heat. Stir in the onions and the salt; cook uncovered over low heat, stirring occasionally, for 20-30 minutes until the onions are a rich, golden brown. Sprinkle flour over the onions and cook, stirring for 3 minutes. Remove the pan from the heat. In a separate saucepan, bring the stock to a simmer and stir the hot stock into the onions. Return the soup to a low heat and simmer, partially covered for another 40 minutes, skimming off the fat. Taste for seasoning and add salt and pepper as desired.

While the soup simmers, make the croutes. Preheat the oven to 325. Spread slices of bread in one layer on a cookie sheet and bake for 15 minutes. With a pastry brush, lightly coat both sides of the bread with olive oil. Turn the slices over and bake for another 15 minutes, or until the bread is completely dry and lightly browned. Rub each slice with the garlic and set aside.

To serve, preheat the oven to 375. Ladle the soup into individual oven-proof bowls top with a croute, and spread a generous topping of grated cheese on top. Bake for 10 to 20 minutes or until the cheese has melted. Then slide the bowls under the broiler briefly to brown the top.

BEEF KIDNEYS IN SOUR CREAM

Slice as much useable meat from 2 to 3 beef kidneys into pieces about 1 inch by 1/3-inch-thick. Do not use any fat or gristle. Rinse, drain well, set aside.

Fry 1 large, chopped onion.

I like to add a stalk of chopped celery and a half of a green pepper, chopped, fried with the onion. I also like to add a half pound of chopped or sliced mushrooms. Canned, drained sliced mushrooms can be used in a pinch. Add the chopped kidney and fry until just cooked through. Add enough sour cream to form a nice sauce; it will be a good 2 cups or maybe even more. Add salt to taste.

Serve over hot cooked medium- or small-width cooked noodles.

NOODLES AND HAM

Dice up 3 -4 cups leftover ham.

Cook what will be 4-5 servings medium-width noodles.

Cut up finely a small bunch of fresh chives.

Mix with a few cups of sour cream or make a sauce of 3 cans of evaporated milk with 2 tablespoons of vinegar to sour it, add enough of milk or cream mixture to make a nice moist mixture. Adjust salt and pepper seasonings. Place in casserole dish, top with cracker crumbs and bake till golden on top, about a half hour at 375 degrees.

BARLEY MILK SOUP

½ cup fine pearled barley

Boil in 3 cups of water until dry.

Add 1 quart of milk and cook until the barley is soft. Salt to taste.

HOT GERMAN POTATO SALAD

8 medium red or white waxy potatoes (NOT russets or Yukon golds)

8 slices bacon

¾ cup chopped onion

2 T. flour

1 T. sugar

1 ½ tsp. salt

½ tsp. celery seed

1 T. or more to taste of fresh chopped parsley

¾ cup water

1/3 cup apple cider vinegar

Boil potatoes with skins on. If large, cut in half first. Cool until able to handle, peel, slice thinly. Keep warm. Fry bacon until crisp, drain on paper towel, crumble. Sautee onion till translucent, not well done. Blend in flour, sugar, salt, celery seed and cook over low heat till smooth and bubbly. Stir in water and vinegar; bring to boil stirring constantly. Carefully add to potatoes, crumbled bacon and parsley. Mix carefully. Serve warm.

SWEDISH POTATO SALAD

This was brought to a potluck at my house and I adored it. I asked for the recipe and quantities were not given, so I will guess.

6-8 red or white potatoes, boiled, peeled and cubed

2 medium leeks, washed and finely sliced, white and light green parts
   only (don't overdo)

1 T. fresh chopped tarragon

A half jar capers, drained; 1 T. mustard seed; salt to taste

Equal parts mayonnaise and sour cream

Combine ingredients and chill.

PREPARE-AHEAD GREEN SALAD

In a tall, large glass bowl layer the following:

2 large carrots, coarsely grated

1 head shredded iceberg lettuce

3-4 stalks thinly sliced celery

1 package frozen peas

1 green or red pepper

Cucumber slices

Hard-boiled egg slices

Bacon bits

Cover with 1/4 to 1/2-inch mayonnaise.

Top with a layer of grated yellow cheese.

Refrigerate overnight.

FIVE BEAN SALAD

I got this recipe from Mary McGavran, our boss's wife, when Peter took the job of assistant professor at Fuller School of World Mission.

1 can green beans, drained

1 can yellow wax beans, drained

1 can garbanzo beans drained and rinsed

1 can kidney beans, drained and rinsed

1 large handful bean sprouts

1 sweet onion, finely chopped

1 green pepper, finely chopped'

2 stalks celery, finely chopped

In a small pot heat together:

½ cup salad oil

¾ cup vinegar

¾ cup sugar

1 ½ tsp. salt

½ tsp. pepper

Cracked coriander seeds to taste (optional)

Heat until sugar is melted. Cool slightly, Pour over bean mixture. Refrigerate overnight.

FLAMING SPINACH SALAD

One of Wagner absolute favorites

1 lb. baby spinach leaves, washed and dried (available in a bag)

1 bunch watercress, well washed, roughly chopped if large

1 small red onion, thinly sliced and separated into rings

6 slices bacon diced

¼ cup vinegar

1 tsp. sugar

½ tsp. salt

¼ cup brandy

Mix in a large bowl the spinach, watercress and sliced onion. Place diced bacon in a large frying pan or a chafing dish. Cook until crisp. Add vinegar and sugar and bring to a boil. Add greens and toss until slightly wilted. Do not overcook. Lift greens to a warm bowl or platter. Add brandy to the drippings; heat, ignite and pour liquid over the salad when the flames have died down.

ISRAELI SALAD

This is a staple on Israeli tables, wonderful for the summertime especially.

2 cucumbers or 6 Israeli cucumbers, chopped small

4 Roma tomatoes, chopped small

1 cup fresh parsley, chopped

1/2 cup fresh mint leaves, chopped

½ sweet onion, chopped fine (optional)

6-8 radishes chopped (optional)

½ cup extra virgin olive oil

Salt and freshly ground pepper to taste

Combine all ingredients and enjoy.

SOUTHERN SHRIMP BOIL

I was alone sitting alongside a couple of other gals having breakfast in a hotel in Alabama once and could not help but overhear one of the ladies, with a distinct northern accent talking with her friend and laughing about an error she had made. She was invited to a "Shrimp Ball," so, thinking it was a dance, got all dressed up and turned up in her heels and fancy attire, only to find out that the party was in the backyard under the trees on picnic tables covered with newspapers. She had misinterpreted the southern accent for "Boil." Ever since then, our family has lovingly called this meal a Shrimp Ball. We love it for a crowd, especially since it is so informal and needs few utensils. A gallon of ice cream or a pecan pie (or both) rounds out the festivities.

Set long tables with throw-away plastic tablecloths and generously cover the center of the tablecloths with thick, clean newspapers. Napkins and a plastic fork are nice, but the meal is eaten cave-man style using hands as utensils. Some folks like to stand rolls of paper towels here and there for folks to tear off to use as napkins. It is usually boiled over a high-flamed camping burner in a very large pot preferably with a basket.

SHRIMP

At least 4 quarts of water or more, depending on the size of the crowd

1 can of beer for every 4 quarts of water

½ cup Old Bay Seasoning

2 T. salt

8 red potatoes, quartered, or three small whole red or white boiling potatoes per person

1 lb. boiling onions, peeled, left whole, or three onions cut into wedges

2 lbs. lean smoked sausage, 1 pound may be andouille, if desired, cut in 1-inch slices

8 ears fresh sweet corn, cobs broken in half

1 carrot per person, cut into quarters

½ lb. large, raw, shell-on shrimp per person, the easy-peel kind is nice, if desired.

2 fresh lemons quartered and squeezed into the water, throw the rinds in the pot to boil

Good dash of cayenne pepper

Season water with your choice of 4-6 cloves, 5 cloves garlic, peeled and crushed, 4 bay leaves, black pepper, a few good dashes tabasco sauce.

2 crabs per person (optional), hard to come by in Texas

Boil the water in a very large kettle with a basket on the stove or a large outside cooker. Season the water with the beer, the juice of two lemons, or 2 tablespoons vinegar. Add the potatoes and cook for 8 minutes. Add carrots, sausage and onions. Bring back to a boil. Add the shrimp. Cook a few minutes, just until the shrimp turn pink in color, about 4 minutes only. DO NOT OVERCOOK. Stir to mix up the contents, lift out the basket and shake a little to drain well. Pour the food the length of the table onto the newspapers. You could use large platters, but my gang likes it dumped onto the table. Everyone can have a plastic fork to aid in spearing vegetables. People grab what they want, peel and dunk in desired sauce and make a neat pile of shells and cobs. When finished, save leftovers and roll up the refuse and toss.

Serve with cocktail sauce, Dijon mustard, and/or melted butter. Pass tabasco sauce to season melted butter if desired.

BEEF TONGUE

Our daughter Ruth says that if she has her choice between a magnificent filet mignon and beef tongue, she will choose beef tongue every time, hands down! It is so pricey because it is so highly prized by the Hispanic folks for use in tacos that it is a rare treat now and then.

Wash a whole beef tongue well and place it in a large stock pot. Cover it with water a couple of inches of water above the tongue. Chop a large onion and several cloves of garlic and add them to the water along with several teaspoons of salt. Add four tablespoons of pickling spice and a bay leaf to a piece of cheesecloth and tie it in a bundle so the spices will not escape; add it to the water. Boil for about an hour and when a fork can pierce the meat it is cooked, depending on the size of the tongue. Remove the tongue from the water and cool slightly but remove the skin over the meat while it is warm. Slice across the grain and serve. My favorite piece is the tip of the tongue. A whole, boiled tongue reminds me of the shape of a foot in a soft shoe after it is cooked.

PANCAKES WITH CREAM GRAVY

Daughter Karen asked to include this. She is an intensive care nurse and has been for over 40 years. Occasionally when she arrives home after a hard day, her comfort food is a stack of pancakes, just made from a box mix. The top pancake has a fried egg over-easy so the yolk is runny. Make a bechamel sauce to act like a gravy: 6 T. flour, 6 T. butter, a pinch of salt and lots of freshly ground pepper, and about 2 ½ cups milk, to make a thick gravy. Add more milk if too thick. Pour over pancakes, layer by layer as consumed.

SPANISH RICE

1 ½ pounds ground beef

3 stalks chopped celery

1 large onion, chopped

1 green pepper, chopped

Salt and pepper

3 cloves garlic, chopped and reserved to add with the rice

A generous sprinkle of Lawry's seasoned salt

1 large can of diced tomatoes

1 medium-sized can of tomato sauce

2 cups of medium grain, or other, rice

Enough hot water to finish cooking and adjust to the desired consistency

Crumble and brown the beef. Drain excess fat. Place the beef in a 6-quart Dutch oven. In the same frying pan, place a little oil and cook until limp but not brown the celery, onions, and green pepper. Add these to the pot. Add the rice to the frying pan with just a little oil. Stir-fry until opaque with a few brown grains. Add to the pot. Then add about 2 cups of water to the frying pan and clean out all of the pan really well, scraping the bottom and sides. Add the water to the pot. Add the tomatoes, tomato sauce, and chopped garlic along with the seasonings. Stir and cover tightly. Cook over low heat. Check after 10 to 15 minutes and add a little hot water, if it is needed. If it looks anemic add another 8-ounce can of tomato sauce. The rice needs to be cooked through but not mush. I served this with a tossed green salad and crusty bread and butter. This was daughter Becky's request to be included in the cookbook portion. I always used the above method, but have recently discovered a rice cooker and that may be used, following directions to sear meat and veggies first.

TAMALE PIE

Prepare cornmeal mush by boiling 2 ½ cups of water, 3 tablespoons of butter, and 1 teaspoon of salt. Mix 1 ¼ cups of yellow cornmeal with one cup of cold water and add the mixture slowly to the boiling water, stirring constantly. Cook over low heat about five minutes, stirring constantly. Pour into a 9 x 13 greased casserole dish, pulling some of the mush up the sides of the casserole dish if possible.

Grate 12 ounces to 1-pound yellow cheese and set it aside for the topping.

Sauté in 1 tablespoon of oil, 1 chopped onion and 1 chopped green pepper. Add in and sauté 1 ½ pounds of ground beef, crumbled. Cook for 10 minutes. Then add:

1 16-oz. can of tomato sauce

1 12-oz. can of corn, drained

1 can of black pitted olives drained

2 cloves of minced garlic

1 T. of sugar

1 tsp. of salt

2 T. of chili powder (optional)

Place the mixture into the mush-lined casserole, top with grated cheese. Bake in 375° oven for 35 minutes until bubbly and the cheese is melted and slightly brown. Serve with a green salad and crusty bread.

OXTAILS

This used to be an inexpensive cut of meat, but it now seems a bit expensive. It is probably because the refugees from other countries highly prize them, would be my guess. I love these.

1 package oxtails, cut into joints

4 T. oil

1 large onion, chopped

1 green pepper, chopped

4 cloves garlic, sliced

1 stalk celery, chopped

1 tsp. powdered thyme

1 tsp. marjoram

1 tsp. dried parsley

Salt and pepper to taste

1 15-oz. can tomato sauce

2 cups of water

Brown tail pieces in oil on all sides. Add onion and brown slightly. Add everything to pressure cooker. Seal and pressure-cook on high for 40 minutes. Cool down pot by running cold water over top of the cooker, until pressure has been released.

LAMB SHANKS

1 lamb shank per person

4 cloves garlic

1 onion, chopped

1 tsp. thyme

1 tsp. marjoram

1 tsp. Italian seasoning

2 cups water

Brown shanks on all sides. Add onions, brown slightly. Rinse frying pan out well with the water and add all to pressure cooker. Seal and cook for 30 minutes at full pressure, for medium-sized shanks, 5 – 10 minutes more for large shanks.

GOULASH

Becky also requested this simple goulash recipe that we often had as a quick supper with a green salad and baguette:

Brown a pound of beef, crumbled in a Dutch oven

Add, chopped:

1 onion

2 stalks celery

1 green pepper

Cook until the vegetables are soft, not brown.

Add several cloves of garlic minced.

Add a large can of tomato sauce, or a can of cream of tomato soup and a small can of sauce.

Add a half box to one full pound of macaroni or shells, cooked and drained.

If dry, add additional tomato sauce to taste.

Serve with Parmesan cheese on the side for those who like it.

SWEDISH MEATBALLS

Another Becky request:

Mix together:

1 ½ to 2 pounds of ground beef

1 package of onion soup mix

2 slices of bread, crumbled or cubed

2 eggs

¼ cup water

1/3 cup ketchup

Pepper to taste

Form into balls of desired size, between a ping-pong sized ball and a golf ball. Brown well on all sides in a high-sided skillet. Drain off excess fat. They may also be baked in a 375-degree oven on a cookie tin until nicely browned, probably about a half hour. If baked, place them in a three or four quart pot and proceed with the rest below.

Add:

1 can of cream of mushroom soup

1 can of cream of celery soup

1 12-oz. can of mushrooms, sliced, or use stems and pieces

Scrape the bottom of pan well to release brown goodness. If too thick, can be thinned with the water from the mushrooms or hot water or milk to make a sauce. Simmer over low heat for 10 minutes Serve hot over rice or cooked medium egg noodles. The soups are quite salty, so check seasoning before adding more salt.

BEEF RIBS, BOLIVIAN-STYLE

Look for a meaty slab of beef ribs. Trim off all the excess fat and remove the silver skin from the inside, if possible. The Bolivians would rub the meat all over with vinegar. Then they would make a rub of the salt, pepper, and very generous amounts of cumin, some finely chopped onion, and minced garlic. Rub both sides of the meat generously. Let this marinade for a good half hour or up to overnight in the refrigerator, and grill over hot coals or under the broiler to the desired temperature.

RATATOUILLE

In a Dutch oven, place

3 T. oil. Sauté briefly in the oil:

1 large sweet onion, cut in eighths

1 red, green or yellow or orange pepper, cut in bite-sized pieces

Add:

1 medium can diced tomatoes

3 cloves minced garlic

2 zucchinis cut in bite-sized pieces

1 small eggplant or two or three Japanese eggplants, cut in bite-sized pieces

1 bay leaf

1 package beef smoked sausage, such as Hillshire Farms

Simmer until the vegetables are just cooked crisp done, and serve immediately.

BEEF FONDUE

Cut up into bite-sized pieces a chuck roast, discarding fat. Can also cube sirloin steak or any other steak available.

Heat oil in fondue pot.

Have each person spear and cook meat to desired doneness.
Serve with dips:

1. Karen's Sauce (recipe follows)

2. Dad's Sauce (recipe follows)

3. Creamed horseradish sauce (can buy prepared)

4. Hot mustard sauce (can buy prepared)

5. Cream cheese softened with milk, add plenty of chopped chives

6. Guacamole

Karen's Sauce:

Stir in small skillet until caramelized: 2 T. of sugar

Add:

2 T. butter

2 T. finely chopped onion

2 T. catsup

6 T. mayo

Dad's Sauce:

½ cup catsup

2 T. vinegar

12 drops tabasco sauce

4 tsp. prepared horseradish

1 T. grated onion

¼ cup finely chopped celery

1 tsp. Worcestershire sauce

¼ tsp. salt

2 T. minced parsley

1 clove minced garlic

Combine all ingredients and serve with fondue meat.

CUBAN ARROZ CON POLLO (CHICKEN WITH RICE)

I got this recipe from a Cuban pastor's wife while we were living in Princeton, N.J., on our first furlough in 1961. It is the very dry sherry that gives this dish its distinctive, nutty flavor.

1 chicken, cut in pieces, fried in oil and removed

Then fry:

1 chopped green pepper

1 large onion, chopped

2 canned pimentos, chopped (or one small jar chopped pimentos)

5 cloves garlic, minced

Add 1 large can tomato sauce and add chicken pieces.

Season with:

½ tsp. Mexican oregano

½ tsp. pepper

1 ½ tsp. cumin

3 bay leaves

1 cup very dry sherry

1 ½ tsp. salt

Simmer 10 minutes. Add 2 cups rice plus six cups water. Simmer until rice is done, but not overcooked. Just before serving add 1/2 of a small package frozen peas, or 1 can peas. Garnish with pimento strips, the other half of the peas and purple onion rings, sliced very thin (sweet onion rings will do also, or scallions in a pinch).

BRAZILIAN BLACK BEANS

Our first term of missionary service was in eastern lowland jungle of Bolivia, a couple hundred miles from the Brazilian border. We frequently took the train to Corumba, Brazil, where we did grocery shopping. Some of our food was influenced by the Brazilians. Black beans and rice is a Brazilian staple. It is frequently served with collard greens and cheese bread.

1 package smoked ham hocks

2 bay leaves

1 lb. dry black beans

For the sofrito (spices and sauce to pour over toward end of cooking):

1 large minced onion

3-5 cloves garlic, minced

¾ bunch parsley, finely chopped (no stems)

Salt and pepper to taste

2 T. olive oil

1 small can diced tomatoes

1 tsp. cumin, optional

Soak the beans overnight. Discard soaking water.

In a pressure cooker, combine soaked beans, ham hocks and bay leaves. Add enough water to cover beans by 3 inches, about 6 cups. Bring to a boil. Cover and lock the lid. Cook for 45 minutes. Shut off the heat and let pressure drop on its own. Meanwhile in large frying pan, sauté the onion, garlic, parsley and salt and pepper until the onion is translucent. Add tomatoes. Add the onion mixture to the beans and cook, uncovered until the beans have a thick consistency.

Note: Most Brazilians add several more kinds of meat to their beans, including browned cubes of pork shoulder, smoked sausage, fresh hot Italian sausage, and/or dried beef or cubes of corned beef. Some add quartered pigs' feet and ears. Add raw meats with smoked hocks. Add cooked meats with the sofrito to guard flavor and consistency.

Serve with boiled white rice and collard greens

BRAZILIAN COLLARD GREENS WITH BACON

Most Southerners in the U.S. boil their collard greens for about an hour. The Brazilians cut theirs fine and just wilt them, so they remain bright green and crunchy. I love this method. It is a common accompaniment to black beans and rice.

1 bunch collard greens, thick stem removed, then folded and shredded to the thickness of fine egg noodles, about ¼ inch wide

Several thick slices of bacon, minced

½ onion minced

2 cloves garlic, minced

1 T. olive oil

Salt and pepper to taste

Heat the olive oil in a medium skillet over medium heat. Add the bacon and cook until brown, 3-4 minutes. Add onions and cook until transparent, about 2 minutes. Add garlic and cook until fragrant, about a minute. Turn off the heat. Add the collard greens and toss gently until the greens wilt. Serve immediately.

BRAZILIAN CHEESE BREAD

This rounds out the Brazilian meal. I have never met anyone who does not adore this delicacy. The only special item you need is mini-muffin tins.

1 large egg (at room temperature or placed in warm water for a few minutes)

1/3 cup extra virgin olive oil

2/3 cup milk

1 ½ cups tapioca flour (find this among Bob's Red Mill flours)

½ cup grated white cheese, such as feta or fresh farmer's cheese or firm Mexican white cheese

1 tsp. or more salt

Preheat oven to 400 degrees. Spread each muffin cup with olive oil. Blend all ingredients in a blender. Pour batter into muffin tins, not quite to the top. Bake 15-20 minutes, or until puffed and golden brown. Serve warm.

BARLEY AND MUSHROOM CASSEROLE

This is one of my very favorite dishes to be used as a starch. Barley is very widely used in German cooking.

1 cup pearled barley

1 large onion

8 oz. fresh mushrooms, chopped, or more if desired. I use up to a pound

5 T. butter

2 cups chicken broth (Can use bouillon cubes in a pinch)

Chop onion add mushrooms and salt and sauté in the butter in a frying pan with high sides.

Add the barley and toast to brown barley lightly. Taste for seasoning. Pour into buttered 2-quart casserole dish, pour over the chicken broth, and bake in 350-degree oven for 30 minutes or more, until barley is soft. I also have cooked this on the stovetop, over very low heat, checking that it does not boil dry. More broth may be needed.

RICE, ALMOND, AND MUSHROOM CASSEROLE

Another favorite starch. We had this frequently before we became diabetics.

¼ cup butter

1 cup rice

½ cup slivered almonds

2 T. chopped green onion or green pepper

½ lb. sliced fresh mushrooms

3 cups chicken broth (bouillon cubes and boiling water is okay)

Put all, except liquid, in heavy frying pan and stir till rice is yellow and some of the nuts are slightly brown. Put in 2-quart casserole and bake in 325-degree oven for one hour. Is okay if it stands for a while.

SAUERKRAUT AND SMOKED PORK SHANK

We butchered our own hogs and smoked sausages, ham and bacon. This was a very favorite meal of mine. Barley is a prized German grain. Other smoked meat may be substituted, such as smoked pork neck-bones, a meaty ham bone, or smoked sausages. If using sausage, add it the last 10 minutes of cooking time so it does not dry out. We made and canned our own delicious sauerkraut and grew our own potatoes. We did buy the barley, however.

1 package meaty, smoked pork shanks

1 jar sauerkraut, about a quart

¾ cup pearled barley

Put everything together in a heavy pot, like a Dutch oven. Add a little water if needed and cook, covered, until the meat falls off the bone and the skin is soft and the barley is very soft, about an hour. Everything soft is edible, including the skin and soft connective tissue.

Serve this with fluffy mashed potatoes and a pan gravy smothering everything. To make the pan gravy, I toast about a cup of flour in a dry frying pan with high sides. When the color of a brown paper bag (a little on the light side), I add about a half cup peanut or other flavorless oil, then enough water to make a thick gravy. I fish out a piece of meat, place a layer of mashed potatoes in a pasta serving dish, ladle over the sauerkraut and barley mixture and top the whole thing with the pan gravy. It is one of my most comforting, happy childhood memory dishes.

BOLIVIAN PEANUT SOUP

I adore this simple soup. Use good Mexican oregano for great flavor.

4-6 pounds meaty soup bones, or beef shank bones, or meaty beef ribs

1 chopped onion

1 large carrot, washed and chopped

2 stalks celery, chopped

2 quarts cold water

¼ lb. raw peanuts

2 T. peas

2 yellow peppers, ground, or other spicey peppers of your choice such as jalapeno (optional)

6 large waxy potatoes, peeled and cut into 8 wedges each

¼ cup rice

1 large chopped onion

½ cup chopped parsley

2 chopped tomatoes

½ tsp. good oregano, crushed

2 T. lard or oil

¼ tsp. each black pepper and ground cumin

Salt to taste

Put beef bones, onion, carrot, celery and salt into a stockpot and boil for 2 ½ hours. Remove meat from bones, cut up small, and set aside. Strain and place cooked broth into same or another kettle. Add the peas and ground (or blended) peanuts. Bring back to soft boil, being careful as it tends to want to boil over. Lower heat and simmer for 15 minutes. Add the potatoes, reserved meat and rice. While this is simmering, prepare the following sauce: brown the chopped onion, tomato and parsley in oil or lard. Add the yellow peppers, simmer for 5 minutes. Add oregano, pepper and cumin. Add the sauce to the soup. Pass additional oregano if desired. Serves 6.

TUSCAN SAUSAGE SOUP

I adore hot Italian Sausage. This is similar to Olive Garden's Sausage soup.

1 lb. hot Italian sausage, crumbled

½ lb. chopped bacon slices

1 qt. water

2 cans or a box chicken broth

2 garlic cloves, peeled and chopped

3-4 potatoes, peeled and diced

1 medium onion, peeled and chopped

1 bunch kale or swiss chard, shredded rather fine

1 cup heavy whipping cream

Salt and pepper to taste

Brown sausage, drain, and set aside.

Brown bacon, not too crispy, drain, set aside.

Pour water, broth, garlic, potatoes, and onion in a pot. Simmer over medium heat until the potatoes are tender. Add sausage and bacon and simmer for 10 minutes. Add kale or chard and cream to pot. Season with salt and pepper. Heat thoroughly.

KAREN POTTER'S CHICKEN TORTILLA SOUP

3-4 bouillon cubes

1 whole chicken or 4-6 breast halves

4-5 carrots, cut in ¼ inch slices

3-4 celery stalks, cut same size

½ tsp. ground cumin

2-3 T. chopped cilantro, plus more for garnish at end

12 whole allspice

1 bell pepper

Puree in blender:

1 4-oz.can Ortega chiles

2 medium onions

1 15-oz. can diced tomatoes

7 cloves garlic

½ tsp. ground pepper

Prepare and set aside for serving:

1 dozen corn tortillas cut in strips 1/3 inch by 3 inches browned in oil, drained on paper towels.

1 lb. shredded jack cheese mixed with 1 1/2 lb. cheddar cheese

1 large, firm avocado cut in thick slices

Chopped cilantro

In large stockpot place 5 quarts of liquid, bouillon cubes and a teaspoon salt, the chicken or breast meat, bell pepper and allspice. Cook 30 minutes to an hour until the chicken is well done. Strain. Remove meat from bones and chop as desired. Set aside. Add to the chicken stock celery, carrots, pureed sauce, cumin, cilantro, pepper and garlic. Simmer for at least one hour

Add more bouillon cubes if needed for added flavor. Check for salt and add more if needed. Return reserved chicken meat and stir well.

To serve: Place a small handful of tortilla strips and a few tablespoons of grated cheese in the bottom of a soup bowl. Ladle soup on top. Garnish with two slices of avocado and lots of cilantro.

WAGNER'S LOBSTER BISQUE

It is a joke to have leftover lobster meat, but I sometimes throw an extra little one in the pot to make this delicious bisque the next day.

Combine and set aside:

1-2 cups chopped lobster meat, cut fine

½ cup dry or very dry sherry

Sauté in 1 stick of butter:

3 medium carrots, shredded

3 stalks celery, cut fine

½ large onion or 1 medium onion, chopped fine

2 large cloves minced garlic

When the onion is translucent, add:

3 cups chicken broth, may be made with bouillon cubes

1 cup white wine of your choice

Puree with a blending wand and set aside.

Add a dash of cayenne pepper.

Add 5 drops red food color and 3 drops yellow food color.

Add lobster meat and set aside.

Make a roux of:

½ cup butter

½ cup flour

4 cups half and half

Add lobster meat to the roux and the other ingredients. Garnish with a few leaves of fresh thyme and serve immediately. Some folks like to add a shot of dry sherry for that nutty flavor.

I do.

VICHYSSOISE

A very favorite soup served for Christmas dinner made the day before and chilled in refrigerator. This is especially a favorite of grandson Chris Potter. Somebody gave it the nickname "Viscous Soise" and, yes, the final "s" is pronounced, I have been informed by those in the know.

6 large leeks

1 large onion

6 T. butter

8 medium-sized russet potatoes, chopped small

8 cups chicken broth

2 ½ to 3 cups half and half

salt and white pepper

chives finely chopped for garnish

Thoroughly wash the white and light green parts of the leeks and chop the onion. Sauté leeks and onions in butter, only until translucent. Cook potatoes and leeks in the chicken broth and simmer until tender, about 15 minutes. Cool slightly. Place in a blender and blend until very smooth, add half-and-half, salt and pepper. Chill overnight. Mix well. Taste for salt and pepper. Serve in bowls or mugs garnished with chives. It is to be served very cold.

Our Christmas dinner was this soup, a standing rib roast beef, served with horseradish sauce, baked potatoes, creamed spinach, Yorkshire pudding and Mrs. Reagan's persimmon pudding for dessert. Since many people have their own way of roasting beef to their desired doneness, I will simply say that we usually used a 5-rib standing rib roast, and cooked it using the very quick method of an extremely hot oven and then removing it for several hours, then returning it to the hot oven until it reached the desired temperature when measured with a meat thermometer. My husband Peter always liked his beef very rare, and I liked mine medium rare so there was always something to suit everyone's taste. The roast rested while we prayed and enjoyed the vichyssoise. I will, however, give the recipe for the horseradish sauce, because it is such a winner. We got this recipe from the folks at Lawry's Prime Rib of Beverly Hills, California. They actually handed out pamphlets with their famous recipes upon request, at the time.

LAWRY'S HORSERADISH SAUCE

Whip 1 cup of whipping cream until it holds firm peaks. Add ½ teaspoon Lawry seasoned salt. Add 2-4 tablespoons or more of peeled, fresh, finely grated horseradish root, according to taste. I liked it with about a half cup of freshly grated horseradish. Add a dash of Tabasco sauce if desired, and fold in all ingredients together well, and serve with freshly carved prime rib. It does not keep well; it turns dark and unappetizing, and seems to lose its zip, so make it fresh for each meal.

BAKED RUSSET POTATOES

I always preferred baking my potatoes directly on the oven rack without wrapping them in aluminum foil. I prefer a charred, crispy skin on mine, which I devour with butter. I used very large premium russet potatoes, readily available at holiday time, prick them several times on each side with a fork, rub them with a little butter or olive oil, roll them in coarse salt and bake in a 400-degree oven about 45 minutes or more, until a fork easily pierces them. I serve them split and squeezed open and pass the garnishes of butter, grated cheddar cheese, bacon bits, sour cream, and chopped green onions, or chives, if they were available. If there are leftovers, reheat in the microwave for another round of yumminess. Additional garnishes may be needed.

YORKSHIRE PUDDING

¾ cup of flour

½ tsp. salt

3 eggs

¾ cup milk

½ cup of drippings from the roast prime rib of beef

Preheat the oven to 450°. Place the muffin tins or skillet with a couple of tablespoons of beef drippings into the oven to get them screaming hot. Meanwhile make the batter. Stir together the flour and salt in a bowl. Beat together the eggs in the milk until light and frothy. Stir in the dry ingredients just until incorporated. Pour the drippings into a medium-sized cast iron skillet or Yorkshire pudding large cupcake holders; put the pan in the oven and get the drippings (about 1 – 2 tablespoons per muffin tin) smoking hot before pouring in the batter till the muffin tins are about two thirds full. Return to the oven and bake until golden brown and puffed and dry 15 to 20 minutes

Makes 6 large muffins

CREAMED SPINACH (ALSO GIVEN TO US BY LAWRY'S PRIME RIB)

1 10-oz. package frozen chopped spinach

2 slices bacon cut fine

½ cup finely chopped onion

2 T. flour

1 tsp. Lawry's seasoned salt

1 large clove minced garlic

1 cup milk

Cook the spinach according to the package directions. Drain well. Fry bacon and onions together until the onions are tender, about 10 minutes. Remove from heat. Add flour, seasoned salt and minced garlic. Blend thoroughly. Slowly add milk. Return to heat and stir until thickened. Add spinach and mix thoroughly. Makes 4 servings.

CHEESE FONDUE

Peter and I often had this on Sunday evenings instead of a supper. We loved it!

½ lb. freshly grated Swiss cheese

½ lb. grated Muenster or Gruyere cheese

1 1/2 T. corn starch

2 cups of dry, white wine, I prefer Sauvignon Blanc or Chablis

1 1/2 tsp. salt

Dash of ground pepper

4 T. kirsch (cherry liqueur)

1 tsp. lemon juice

A few grates of fresh nutmeg

Italian bread cut in 1-inch cubes

1-2 apples cut in 1-inch cubes

Use 1-2 small loaves of very crusty Italian or French bread cut in 1-inch cubes. Hard, crusty rolls, such as ciabatta may also be used. When the bread was gone, I loved to finish up with an apple cut in one-inch cubes, dipped in the hot, melted cheese.

Toss together the shredded cheese with the cornstarch. Rub fondue pot with halved pieces of the garlic, discard garlic pieces. Add wine to the pot and cook over a medium flame on the stove until heated and bubbly. Slowly add the cheese and stir in a figure 8 motion until all is melted and the mixture is creamy and smooth. Stir in seasonings and add kirsch and move the pot to fondue cooking equipment on table. Keep cheese warm and bubbly over low heat under fondue pot. Each person spears a cube of bread and stirs the cheese with it before eating it. As the meal progresses, the fondue may thicken, if so, stir in a few ounces of warm wine. If the liquid in the mixture should separate from the fat, add 1 tablespoon of cornstarch diluted with a half cup white wine. Do not drink anything cold while eating this meal. Often a brown crust forms on the bottom of the pot and this is considered a delicacy. The hostess removes it and cuts a piece for each guest.

ANTICUCHOS (BEEF HEART ON SKEWERS)

Whenever we are able to find a beef heart, we rejoice. Lamb heart or veal heart work well also.

I have never tried to prepare these with pork heart. Cut the beef heart in strips, after removing all visible fat and the strings on the inside of the heart. The strips should be about two or three inches long and 1/3 inch thick. In Bolivia and Peru these delicacies are served at soccer games. They are threaded on cleaned bicycle spokes or other proper skewers, grilled over hot coals and dipped in the delicious peanut sauce; recipe follows. If we are in a rush, the strips may be quickly sautéed in a frying pan with a little oil. They are served with small boiled potatoes that are also dunked in the peanut sauce. I prepare extra sauce and freeze the leftovers for another feast.

Peanut Sauce made with Texas ingredients

Blend in a blender:

2 cans Rotel (a blend of tomatoes and green chiles, choose desired heat)

1 small can tomato sauce

Sautéed mixture of 1 onion, chopped fine, 1 chopped green pepper
    2 large celery stalks, chopped fine

Salt to taste

1 tsp. powdered cumin

2 tsp. garlic powder or 3 cloves fresh garlic, minced

Place blended mixture in a deep-sided frying pan.

Add:

1 1/2 cups chunky peanut butter

¼ tsp cayenne pepper or a good squeeze of Sriracha chile sauce to taste

Cook gently until all is blended well. Serve hot with grilled heart and potatoes. Freeze leftovers in airtight freezer bags.

GREEN CORN TAMALES

This is a Bolivian recipe Karen has perfected over the years. We adore these.

16 ears mature sweet corn

1 cup powdered milk

2-pound packages Queso Fresco or Ranchero cheese, broken in pieces

¼ cup vegetable or peanut oil

2 tsp. salt

6 T. cornstarch

Cut off the cob at the very bottom of the ear of corn and gently peel off the husks, Save the large husks. Cut corn off the cobs and place in a food processor, Add remaining ingredients and process until smooth. Fill the husks with a few tablespoons of the batter and fold into triangles. Place on a cookie sheet with the open side down. If not using the husks, mixture may be placed in casserole dishes, about an inch thick. Bake at 375-degree oven until brown. Cut into 3-inch squares and serve hot with butter.

PETER'S FROG LEGS

When Peter was a little boy, he would catch frogs and keep them in a rain barrel until there were enough for a meal. Now we buy them in stores that carry them. They are usually available in Asian grocery stores, frozen and skinned and are much larger and meatier than the stream-caught ones of Peter's childhood. Peter always prepared these for our dinner.

16-20 oz. frog legs, usually 8 medium-sized saddles

Enough milk to marinate then in a bowl

1 tsp. garlic salt

Pepper

Flour to dust them in a food bag

6 T. butter

6 T. cooking oil

3 tsp. crushed garlic

1/3 cup very dry sherry

2 tsp. or more chopped parsley

Soak the frog legs in milk for two hours (if you don't do this it still works). This softens the flavor.

Dry them with a paper towel. Season with garlic salt and pepper. Put flour in plastic bag and dust saddles; shake off excess flour. Heat a deep serving platter or shallow bowl in the oven until it is warm. Place the butter and oil in a frying pan and brown the saddles carefully, turning only once carefully with tongs, the meat is very soft and delicate. Remove the saddles to the heated serving dish.

SAUCE

Turn the heat down to medium under same frying pan. Add the crushed garlic and stir for 30 seconds. Add the sherry and bring it to a boil. Ignite sauce to flambe. When fire goes out, pour the sauce over the frog legs and garnish with chopped parsley. This serves two hungry frog-leg lovers.

NEW ENGLAND BOILED DINNER

This is a big winner in the Wagner household. Corned beef is usually on sale in March for St. Patrick's Day; I buy a few and freeze those not used if I get a bargain but is worth the extra price any time of year! I prefer the flat cut, Ruth likes the point cut. They all taste the same.

I get the biggest piece of corned beef I can find, 5 lbs. or more, it seems to shrink a lot during cooking.

2 large garlic cloves

1 bay leaf

An extra tablespoon pickling spice to add to the packet that comes with the meat

About 4 ½ hours before serving, place the meat in an 8-quart stock pot along with the spices. Cover with water an inch above the meat and bring to a boil. Cook over low heat for 3 to 3 ½ hours until the meat is fork tender. Remove the meat, cover and keep warm. Add the following vegetables to the water in the pot:

1 medium rutabaga, cut in 8ths or 10ths

10 medium carrots

10 small red potatoes, scrubbed

10 small boiling onions, peeled

4 stalks of celery, cut in 2-inch lengths

2 large sweet potatoes or yams cut into 10 pieces

1 medium cabbage, cut into 10 wedges, keeping the core to hold wedges together

Parsley to garnish platter

Slice the corned beef and arrange on a large platter. Add vegetables to the platter. Pass butter for vegetables and mustards of your choice for the meat. This is well worth the invested time.

THE BEST BAKED BEANS EVER

I got this recipe from a dear neighbor across the street from us in Altadena, California. It has been a picnic favorite ever since.

Brown and drain:

1 lb. hamburger

1 large chopped onion

1 lb. bacon, cut in one-inch pieces

Add with juice:

1 21-oz. can pork and beans

1 15-oz. can lima beans with ham sauce

1 27-oz. can kidney beans

½ cup catsup

1 tsp. dry mustard

1 tsp. vinegar

2 T. molasses

Place mixture in a casserole or 9 x 13 baking dish. Bake covered at 350 degrees for 1 hour.

ARMENIAN KEBAB PACKETS

These are wonderful for a crowd for a picnic and are a bit different from plain old hamburgers.

I served these to a crowd of 50 and got rave reviews.

Allow ¼ lb. ground beef per person (or ground lamb to be authentic, or a mixture of half beef and lamb)

Also allow one nine-inch pita bread per person. Warm these in the oven on low and keep them wrapped in a towel to keep them pliable. Cut about 1/3 off the top of each so as to open a hold for the meat and fixings. Some folks like to use the pita bread as is and put fillings in the middle, leaving pita closed. Serve each one in a couple thickness of paper towels since they can be pretty messy to eat. Have extra napkins available at the place settings.

To each pound of ground meat add:

2 T. flour

2 T. water

Sprinkle of salt

½ tsp. allspice (optional, but suggested if using lamb)

½ tsp. ground cinnamon (also optional)

Mix together and shape into 5-inch sausages, using ¼ pound of meat each. These may be grilled or may be skewered the long way if the crowd is small. Brown well over the coals. If using a skewer, add to the tip a few slices of green pepper and mild onion pieces that have been brushed with olive oil. A larger quantity may be prepared cooking slightly in a frying pan.

Prepare and mix well a sauce of:

1 cup plain Greek yogurt

3 chopped scallions, using white and green parts

2 tsp. mustard of your choice

To serve, open the pita, or keep it whole and fill, then fold over. Either way, it will be messy.

Fill with a meat roll; add alongside green peppers and onion pieces, thin wedges of tomato, cucumber slices, and radish slices. Douse sauce over all. Enjoy with salads of your choice and fresh fruit for dessert.

CHICKEN CHOP SUEY

(May be made with 2 lbs. shrimp, all shells removed; DO NOT OVER-COOK. Do not soak in sherry.)

2 lbs. boneless, skinless chicken thighs, cut in ½-inch cubes

Enough very dry sherry to cover pieces in a small bowl. Stir to loosen chicken pieces. Marinate for a couple of hours. Meanwhile prepare vegetables:

2 stalks celery, cut on the diagonal

1 small sweet onion, cut in 1/3-inch slices, the long way

A good handful Chinese peas, ends and strings removed, cut in half

1 red pepper, cut in chunks, or a green or yellow pepper if desired

1 small napa cabbage, sliced

1 can sliced water chestnuts, drained

1 can bamboo shoots, drained

1 medium carrot, cut into matchstick shapes

2 cups chicken broth (may use bouillon cubes)

Cornstarch slurry, made of ¼ cup cornstarch and ½ cup cold water

In a plastic bag, place about a half cup cornstarch. Shake the chicken pieces to coat and brown well in a screaming hot wok with a few tablespoons of peanut oil or other oil. Remove and set aside. Stir-fry the remaining ingredients in the wok until crisp-done. Add chicken stock. Thicken with corn starch slurry, a little at a time until arriving at the desired consistency. Serve over fried Chinese noodles with small bowls of cooked white rice on the side.

DESSERTS

THE BEST PUMPKIN PIE

This was always made every Thanksgiving. Peter liked his served with a slice of cheddar cheese. I liked mine smothered with whipped cream.

1 unbaked 9-inch pie shell

1 ½ tsp. salt

1 ½ tsp. cinnamon

½ tsp. nutmeg

½ tsp. ginger

½ tsp. allspice

½ tsp. cloves

1 1/2 cups canned pumpkin

1 large can evaporated milk

2 eggs

Combine all ingredients except pie shell and beat well. Pour into unbaked pie shell.

Bake in a hot oven at 425 degrees for 15 minutes. Lower oven to moderate temperature of 350 degrees. Continue baking about 40 minutes, until the custard is firm.

NANCY REAGAN'S PERSIMMON PUDDING

Served every Christmas at the Wagner home.

½ cup melted butter

1 cup flour, sifted

¼ tsp. salt

1 tsp. cinnamon

½ tsp. nutmeg

½ tsp. allspice

½ tsp. cloves

1 cup puréed persimmon pulp

2 tsp. baking soda

2 tsp. warm water

3 T. brandy and an additional ¼ cup is set aside for flaming

1 tsp. vanilla

2 lightly beaten eggs

1 cup seedless raisins

1½ cups chopped walnuts

Brandy whipped cream sauce (recipe follows)

Stir together sugar and butter. Sift flour with salt and spices. Add to sugar mixture. Add pulp mix, soda, and water to mixture. Add 3 tablespoons of brandy, vanilla, eggs, raisins and nuts. Turn into a 5 to 6 cup metal ring mold that has been buttered or sprayed. Cover with aluminum foil, tie down with string. Place on a rack in a Dutch oven. Add warm water halfway up the mold. Cover and steam slowly for 2 ½ hours. Let stand five minutes. Unmold onto a serving platter. When ready to serve, warm 1/4 cup brandy and pour over the pudding. Ignite immediately. Serve with Brandy Whipped Cream recipe that follows:

BRANDY WHIPPED CREAM SAUCE

1 egg

1/3 cup melted butter

1 cup sifted powdered sugar sifted

Salt

1 T. of brandy or Rum flavoring

1 cup whipping cream

Beat the egg until light and fluffy. Beat in sugar, butter, salt, and flavoring. In a separate bowl whip cream until stiff. Gently fold in the egg mixture. Cover and chill until ready to serve.

TZARISENAHOSEN (TORN PANTS) (BOW TIES)

Beat together in electric mixer until lemon colored:

1 cup of egg yolks, 1 whole egg, ½ cup water

Add 2 tablespoons of cream.

Mix with enough flour to make a thin dough, add 1 tablespoon of sugar, and a pinch of salt. Mix well, roll out thin on a floured board. Cut in strips 1 ½ inches by 6 inches, smaller if desired. Cut a slit in the center of each strip about 1 1/3-inch-long and loop one end through the hole, to look like a bow tie. Fry in hot oil, drain on paper towels. Dust with powdered sugar. They are very delicate!

GRANDMA'S ANISE CHRISTMAS COOKIES

This looks like 4 times a recipe to me......it can be halved very easily, but I suggest writing down the new measurements so as to keep the proportions accurate.

Mix in a very large bowl:

7 cups sugar

1lb. softened butter

1 lb. Crisco

12 beaten eggs

1 16-oz. canned evaporated milk

1 orange, grated rind and juice

5 T. honey

3 T. brandy or wine

1 tsp. vanilla

1/2 cup crushed anise seed (or more or less)

1 tsp. salt

4 heaping tsp. baking powder

1 tsp. baking soda

½ tsp. cream of tartar

About 28 cups flour

Rolls best when chilled

Roll out thin, less than ¼ inch thick; cut with Christmas cookie cutters decorate with colored sugar or sprinkles.

Bake at 375 till lightly brown, 12 minutes or so. Cool thoroughly on racks and store in airtight containers. The flavor improves with age. My mama and I always used to bake these shortly after Thanksgiving. There were so many that they could last into the New Year.

SPRITZ COOKIES

Granddaughter Jenny remembered doing this at our home and asked me to include it. You will need a cookie press for this recipe.

Mix together

1 cup room-temperature butter

2/3 cup sugar

3 egg yoks

1 tsp. almond flavoring

Work in with hands: 2 ½ cups sifted flour

Force the dough through a cookie press on to an ungreased cookie sheet into the desired shapes. Bake at 400° for seven to 10 minutes until cookies are set but not brown.

LAURA BUSH'S COWBOY COOKIES

This recipe came from the Bush/Gore presidential campaign in 2000. These cookies won a contest between Laura Bush and Tipper Gore, who submitted a recipe for ginger snaps. I love these, but be warned, this is a big batch. However, I have kept them in closed plastic jars for two months! They are a bit of a pain to make, but the results are scrumptious. The cookies will be large.

3 cups all-purpose flour

1 T. of baking powder

1 T. baking soda

1 T. ground cinnamon

1 tsp. salt

Three sticks of butter at room temperature

1 ½ cups of granulated sugar

1 ½ cups of packed light brown sugar

3 eggs

1 T. vanilla

3 cups semi-sweet chocolate chips

3 cups old-fashioned rolled oats

2 cups unsweetened flaked coconut

2 cups (8 ounces) chopped pecans

Heat oven to 350 degrees. Mix flour, baking powder, baking soda, cinnamon and salt in a bowl. In a very large bowl, beat butter with a hand mixer until creamy. Gradually beat in sugars and combine thoroughly. Add eggs one at a time, beating after each. Add vanilla and beat. Stir in flour mixture until just combined. Stir in chocolate chips, oats, coconut and pecans. For each cookie drop a scant ¼ cup dough onto an ungreased cookie sheet, spacing 3 inches apart. Bake for 15 to 17 minutes, until the edges are brown; rotate the cookie sheets halfway through baking. Remove cookies to a rack to cool. Store in an airtight container.

GRISWOLD PECAN PIE

1 9-inch pie shell, baked and cooled

6 ounces semi-sweet chocolate chips

1 ½ cups pecan halves

¼ cup butter

½ cup dark maple syrup

½ cup coconut sugar

2 large eggs, beaten

Heat the oven to 325 degrees. In pie shell, evenly spread chocolate chips over the bottom, then spread pecan halves evenly over the top of the chocolate chips. Set aside. In a 1-quart saucepan, melt the butter over medium heat. Remove and let cool for two minutes. Stir in the maple syrup, coconut sugar, and eggs. Pour mixture over pecans and chocolate chips in the pie shell, making sure pecans are completely covered. Bake for 45 minutes or until firm. If the crimped pie shell is getting too brown, cover the shell edges with strips of aluminum foil. Serve warm (with whipped cream, for a decadent treat).

CARAMEL POPCORN BALLS

2 quarts popped corn, salted

28 Kraft Caramels, paper peeled off

2 T. water

1 cup roasted peanuts

Melt caramels and water over very low heat or in a covered double boiler. Stir until the sauce is smooth. Pour over the popcorn and nuts and toss until all is well coated. With hands moistened with cold water, form 8 balls. May wrap in Saran wrap if desired and tie with a piece of thin, colored ribbon. This will keep them clean, and they will not stick together in a big wooden bowl.

Index

About The Author

Doris M. Wagner
Widow of the late Dr. C. Peter Wagner

Doris was born in 1932 in St. Johnsville, New York, and raised on a dairy farm. She married C. Peter Wagner in 1950, attended Biola University in Los Angeles from 1952-1955, and served as a missionary to Bolivia from 1956-1971. Along with her husband, Doris was involved in evangelism, church planting, teaching in a Bible school and seminary, and mission administration. Doris also ran a Bible correspondence school with hundreds of students throughout Bolivia.

When Peter was invited to become an assistant professor—and later a full professor—at the Fuller Seminary School of World Mission in Pasadena, California, Doris served as Peter's assistant and office manager during his tenure as Professor of Church Growth from 1971-1991. She also served as mission project director for the Charles E. Fuller Institute for Evangelism and Church Growth and was a research librarian for the Fuller School of World Mission. She and Peter were good friends of John Wimber, founder of the Vineyard group of churches, who introduced them to praying for the sick and demonized during the the 1980s. Doris began doing personal deliverance in the '80s and has ministered to hundreds, if not thousands of individuals.

In 1991, she and Peter founded Global Harvest Ministries while Peter continued teaching at the School of World Mission. The focus of this ministry was to connect worldwide prayer networks to pray for the unreached people groups in the 10/40 window, run under the leadership of Luis Bush and the AD2000 Organization. Doris served as executive director of the AD2000 United Prayer Track from 1992-2000. There were 1739 unreached people groups in 1992, and due to the communication of the need and prayer, many have been reached and now have a viable church in their midst. Today, there are only about 500 unreached people groups in the most restricted of areas in the world.

Doris has two published books: *How to Cast Out Demons: A Beginner's Guide* and *How to Minister Freedom* (out of print).

She has completed her Doctor of Practical Ministry from Wagner University and is an ordained minister, serving under Chuck D. Pierce and Global Spheres and Glory of Zion. She continues to specialize in equipping the Body of Christ in the fields of deliverance and spiritual warfare through conferences, seminars, and teaching at Wagner University. She resides in Texas with her daughter, Ruth Irons, who assists her with her disabilities since she lost a leg recently. Doris has three adult children, ten grandchildren, and seven great-grandchildren.